Puppet Cookbook
Third Edition

Jump-start your Puppet deployment using engaging and practical recipes

Thomas Uphill

John Arundel

[PACKT] open source*
PUBLISHING   community experience distilled

BIRMINGHAM - MUMBAI

Puppet Cookbook
Third Edition

First published: October 2011

Second edition: August 2013

Third edition: February 2015

Production reference: 1170215

Published by Packt Publishing Ltd.
Livery Place
35 Livery Street
Birmingham B3 2PB, UK.

ISBN 978-1-78439-488-2

www.packtpub.com

Credits

About the Authors

Thomas Uphill is an RHCA who has been using Puppet since 0.24. He has worked as a system administrator for almost 20 years, most recently with RHEL systems. He recently wrote *Mastering Puppet, Packt Publishing* a book for managing Puppet in large deployments. He has given tutorials on Puppet at LISA and LOPSA-East. When not at the Puppet User Group of Seattle (PUGS), he can be found at http://ramblings.narrabilis.com.

Thank you to John Arundel for the previous editions of this book, I had a great foundation for this rewrite. I would like to thank my wife Priya Fernandes for her support and encouragement while I was updating this book. Thanks to my fellow PUGS Andy and Justin for their suggestions. Thanks to my reviewers, Jeroen Hooyberghs, James Fryman, and Dhruv Ahuja for taking the time to find all the errors they did.

John Arundel has worked in the IT industry for most of his life, and during that time has done wrong (or seen others do wrong) almost everything that you can do wrong with computers. That comprehensive knowledge of what not to do, he feels, is one of his greatest assets as a consultant. He is still adding to it.

He spent much of his career working in very large corporations and, as a result, now likes to work with very small corporations. They like working with him too, not only because he can tell them about things that should not be done, but also because he can confidently inform them that big companies don't know what they're doing either.

Off the clock, he enjoys gardening, competitive rifle shooting, and other gentle hobbies. You can follow him on Twitter @bitfield. If your company is small enough, you can hire him there too.

About the Reviewers

Dhruv Ahuja is a senior DevOps engineer at a leading financial data vendor. He specializes in software delivery optimization and infrastructure automation. He also holds a master's degree in advanced software engineering from King's College London, and won the Red Hat UK Channel Consultant of the Year award in 2012 for delivering progressive solutions. A long history in software development and systems administration equip him with aptness in both areas. In this era of infrastructure as code, he believes that declarative abstraction and accurate interfaces are key to a scalable business software lifecycle process.

James Fryman is an information technologist who builds, designs, curates, and evangelizes automation in all layers of the IT stack. Over the last decade, James has held roles in information technology that includes the domains of information security, service delivery, IT operations, IT development, and IT management. He has learned through these experiences the importance of automation in all facets of information technology to accelerate delivery, and reduce human errors throughout an application lifecycle. He is also a frequent speaker on the topic of automation at conferences throughout the world.

Now a senior DevOps engineer at StackStorm, James most recently worked at GitHub assisting in the development and curation of systems scaling within the Operations group.

> My wife Melanie is awesome and deserves much more than just the words printed here.

Jeroen Hooyberghs is an open source and Linux consultant, working for Open-Future in Belgium. In this position, as well as when he was involved in Linux system administration, he has built up technical expertise in a lot of open source solutions, such as Puppet. In 2014, he became a Puppet Certified Professional and official Puppet trainer. As a reviewer, he also contributed to *Mastering Puppet, Thomas Uphill, Packt Publishing*.

Pedro Morgado holds a master's degree in informatics and computing engineering at FEUP (Faculdade de Engenharia da Universidade do Porto) and did his master's thesis on object-oriented patterns and service-oriented patterns.

Since 2009, he has been working with several different programming languages, frameworks, and technologies, which includes the main object-oriented programming languages such as PHP, Python, C/C++, Java, and JavaScript, as well as web languages such as HTML, JSON, and XML. He has worked with different database technologies such as MySQL, PostgreSQL, Oracle SQL, and SQL Server, and also with different caching systems and search engines.

He has worked as an IT consultant in the banking field for a year, and has built a recommendation system (data mining and text mining) as a research assistant at INESC (Technology and Science-Associated Laboratory) where he worked for a period of 1 year. Finally, he focused on web projects as a technical lead at Rocket Internet AG, for which he built scalable systems for FoodPanda, CupoNation, Camudi, and Lamudi. Due to his experience, he has specialized in project management and product development based in an e-commerce area. For more information, take a look at his LinkedIn account (`https://www.linkedin.com/in/pedrombmorgado`).

www.PacktPub.com

Support files, eBooks, discount offers, and more

For support files and downloads related to your book, please visit www.PacktPub.com.

Did you know that Packt offers eBook versions of every book published, with PDF and ePub files available? You can upgrade to the eBook version at www.PacktPub.com and as a print book customer, you are entitled to a discount on the eBook copy. Get in touch with us at service@packtpub.com for more details.

At www.PacktPub.com, you can also read a collection of free technical articles, sign up for a range of free newsletters and receive exclusive discounts and offers on Packt books and eBooks.

https://www2.packtpub.com/books/subscription/packtlib

Do you need instant solutions to your IT questions? PacktLib is Packt's online digital book library. Here, you can search, access, and read Packt's entire library of books.

Why Subscribe?

- ▶ Fully searchable across every book published by Packt
- ▶ Copy and paste, print, and bookmark content
- ▶ On demand and accessible via a web browser

Free Access for Packt account holders

If you have an account with Packt at www.PacktPub.com, you can use this to access PacktLib today and view 9 entirely free books. Simply use your login credentials for immediate access.

Table of Contents

Preface

Configuration management has become a requirement for system administrators. Knowing how to use configuration management tools, such as Puppet, enables administrators to take full advantage of automated provisioning systems and cloud resources. There is a natural progression from performing a task, scripting a task to creating a module in Puppet, or Puppetizing a task.

This book takes you beyond the basics and explores the full power of Puppet, showing you in detail how to tackle a variety of real-world problems and applications. At every step, it shows you exactly what commands you need to type and includes complete code samples for every recipe. It takes you from a rudimentary knowledge of Puppet to a more complete and expert understanding of Puppet's latest and most advanced features, community best practices, scaling, and performance. This edition of the book includes recipes for configuring and using Hiera, puppetdb and operating a centralized puppetmaster configuration.

This book also includes real examples from production systems and techniques that are in use in some of the world's largest Puppet installations. It will show you different ways to do things using Puppet, and point out some of the pros and cons of these approaches.

The book is structured so that you can dip in at any point and try out a recipe without having to work your way through from cover to cover. Whatever your level of Puppet experience, there's something for you—from simple workflow tips to advanced, high-performance Puppet architectures.

Puppet is an ever-changing ecosystem of tools. I've tried to include all the tools that I feel are important today, such as r10k. The #puppet IRC channel, puppetlabs blog (`http://puppetlabs.com/blog`), and the Forge (`http://forge.puppetlabs.com`) are great resources to stay up to date with the changes being made to Puppet.

What this book covers

Chapter 1, *Puppet Language and Style*, introduces the Puppet language and shows how to write manifests. The Puppet linting tool, puppet-lint, is introduced and we review best practices to write Puppet code. Metaparameters are shown with examples. We also preview proposed changes to the Puppet language by using the future parser.

Chapter 2, *Puppet Infrastructure*, is all about how to deploy Puppet in your environment. We cover the two main methods of installation, centralized and decentralized (masterless). We show you how to use Git to centrally manage your code. We also configure puppetdb and Hiera.

Chapter 3, *Writing Better Manifests*, deals with organizing your Puppet manifests. Manifests are used to build modules; we introduce the concept of roles and profiles to abstract how modules are applied to machines. Parameterized classes are introduced. We also show you how to efficiently define resources with arrays of resources and resource defaults.

Chapter 4, *Working with Files and Packages*, shows you how to manage files using snippets (fragments). We introduce the power of templating with both Ruby (ERB) and Puppet (EPP) templates. We also explore ways to secure information stored in your Puppet manifests.

Chapter 5, *Users and Virtual Resources*, deals with the advanced topic of virtual and exported resources. Virtual resources are a way of defining resources but not applying them by default. Exported resources are similar but are used to have resources from one machine, applied to one or more other machines.

Chapter 6, *Managing Resources and Files*, is about dealing with directories and purging resources not controlled by Puppet. We show you how to have file resources applied differently on different machines. Methods for managing host entries in /etc/hosts are shown with exported resources examples.

Chapter 7, *Managing Applications*, shows you how to use Puppet to manage your deployed applications. Using public Forge modules, we configure Apache, nginx, and MySQL.

Chapter 8, *Internode Coordination*, explores exported resources. We use exported resources to configure NFS, haproxy, and iptables.

Chapter 9, *External Tools and the Puppet Ecosystem*, shows you how to extend Puppet with your own types and providers, how to make your own facts, as well as some of the more advanced tools such as Puppet-librarian and r10k.

Chapter 10, *Monitoring, Reporting, and Troubleshooting*, is the final chapter where we show you how to leverage Puppet to see where the problems are in your infrastructure. Some of the more common problems are shown with solutions.

What you need for this book

You will need a computer capable of running Linux Virtual Machines. The examples in the book use Debian and Enterprise Linux-based distributions. You will also need an Internet connection to utilize the repositories provided by puppetlabs.

Who this book is for

This book assumes a familiarity with Linux administration. The examples require some experience with command-line usage and basic text file editing. Although beneficial, previous coding experience is not required.

Conventions

In this book, you will find a number of styles of text that distinguish between different kinds of information. Here are some examples of these styles, and an explanation of their meaning.

Code words in text, database table names, folder names, filenames, file extensions, pathnames, dummy URLs, user input, and Twitter handles are shown as follows: "You can concatenate arrays with the + operator or append them with the << operator."

A block of code is set as follows:

```
slice ($firewall_rules,2) |$ip, $port| {
  firewall {"$port from $ip":
    dport  => $port,
    source => "$ip",
    action => 'accept',
  }
}
```

Any command-line input or output is written as follows:

```
Notice: 1
Notice: 2
Notice: 3
Notice: 4
Notice: 5
# cp /usr/src/asterisk-addons/configs/cdr_mysql.conf.sample
    /etc/asterisk/cdr_mysql.conf
```

New terms and **important words** are shown in bold. Words that you see on the screen, in menus or dialog boxes for example, appear in the text like this: "In this graph it is easy to see that **Package['ntp']** is the first resource to apply, then **File['/etc/ntp.conf']** and finally **Service['ntp']**."

Warnings or important notes appear in a box like this.

Tips and tricks appear like this.

Reader feedback

Feedback from our readers is always welcome. Let us know what you think about this book—what you liked or may have disliked. Reader feedback is important for us to develop titles that you really get the most out of.

To send us general feedback, simply send an e-mail to feedback@packtpub.com, and mention the book title via the subject of your message.

If there is a topic that you have expertise in and you are interested in either writing or contributing to a book, see our author guide on www.packtpub.com/authors.

Customer support

Now that you are the proud owner of a Packt book, we have a number of things to help you to get the most from your purchase.

Downloading the example code

You can download the example code files for all Packt books you have purchased from your account at http://www.packtpub.com. If you purchased this book elsewhere, you can visit http://www.packtpub.com/support and register to have the files e-mailed directly to you.

Errata

Although we have taken every care to ensure the accuracy of our content, mistakes do happen. If you find a mistake in one of our books—maybe a mistake in the text or the code—we would be grateful if you could report this to us. By doing so, you can save other readers from frustration and help us improve subsequent versions of this book. If you find any errata, please report them by visiting http://www.packtpub.com/submit-errata, selecting your book, clicking on the **Errata Submission Form** link, and entering the details of your errata. Once your errata are verified, your submission will be accepted and the errata will be uploaded to our website or added to any list of existing errata under the Errata section of that title.

To view the previously submitted errata, go to https://www.packtpub.com/books/content/support and enter the name of the book in the search field. The required information will appear under the **Errata** section.

Piracy

Piracy of copyright material on the Internet is an ongoing problem across all media. At Packt, we take the protection of our copyright and licenses very seriously. If you come across any illegal copies of our works, in any form, on the Internet, please provide us with the location address or website name immediately so that we can pursue a remedy.

Please contact us at copyright@packtpub.com with a link to the suspected pirated material.

We appreciate your help in protecting our authors, and our ability to bring you valuable content.

Questions

You can contact us at questions@packtpub.com if you are having a problem with any aspect of the book, and we will do our best to address it.

1
Puppet Language and Style

"Computer language design is just like a stroll in the park. Jurassic Park, that is."

— *Larry Wall*

In this chapter, we will cover the following recipes:

- ▸ Adding a resource to a node
- ▸ Using **Facter** to describe a node
- ▸ Installing a package before starting a service
- ▸ Installing, configuring, and starting a service
- ▸ Using community **Puppet** style
- ▸ Creating a manifest
- ▸ Checking your manifests with Puppet-lint
- ▸ Using modules
- ▸ Using standard naming conventions
- ▸ Using inline templates
- ▸ Iterating over multiple items
- ▸ Writing powerful conditional statements
- ▸ Using regular expressions in if statements
- ▸ Using selectors and case statements
- ▸ Using the in operator
- ▸ Using regular expression substitutions
- ▸ Using the future parser

Introduction

In this chapter, we'll start with the basics of Puppet syntax and show you how some of the syntactic sugar in Puppet is used. We'll then move on to how Puppet deals with dependencies and how to make Puppet do the work for you.

We'll look at how to organize and structure your code into modules following community conventions, so that other people will find it easy to read and maintain your code. I'll also show you some powerful features of Puppet language, which will let you write concise, yet expressive manifests.

Adding a resource to a node

This recipe will introduce the language and show you the basics of writing Puppet code. A beginner may wish to reference *Puppet 3: Beginner's Guide, John Arundel, Packt Publishing* in addition to this section. Puppet code files are called manifests; manifests declare resources. A resource in Puppet may be a type, class, or node. A type is something like a file or package or anything that has a type declared in the language. The current list of standard types is available on puppetlabs website at `https://docs.puppetlabs.com/references/latest/type.html`. I find myself referencing this site very often. You may define your own types, either using a mechanism, similar to a subroutine, named **defined types**, or you can extend the language using a custom type. Types are the heart of the language; they describe the things that make up a node (node is the word Puppet uses for client computers/devices). Puppet uses resources to describe the state of a node; for example, we will declare the following package resource for a node using a site manifest (`site.pp`).

How to do it...

Create a `site.pp` file and place the following code in it:

```
node default {
  package { 'httpd':
    ensure => 'installed'
  }
}
```

Downloading the example code

You can download the example code files for all Packt books you have purchased from your account at `http://www.packtpub.com`. If you purchased this book elsewhere, you can visit `http://www.packtpub.com/support` and register to have the files e-mailed directly to you.

How it works...

This manifest will ensure that any node, on which this manifest is applied, will install a package called 'httpd'. The default keyword is a wildcard to Puppet; it applies anything within the node default definition to any node. When Puppet applies the manifest to a node, it uses a **Resource Abstraction Layer** (**RAL**) to translate the package type into the package management system of the target node. What this means is that we can use the same manifest to install the httpd package on any system for which Puppet has a **Provider** for the package type. Providers are the pieces of code that do the real work of applying a manifest. When the previous code is applied to a node running on a YUM-based distribution, the YUM provider will be used to install the httpd RPM packages. When the same code is applied to a node running on an **APT**-based distribution, the APT provider will be used to install the httpd DEB package (which may not exist, most debian-based systems call this package apache2; we'll deal with this sort of naming problem later).

Using Facter to describe a node

Facter is a separate utility upon which Puppet depends. It is the system used by Puppet to gather information about the target system (node); facter calls the nuggets of information facts. You may run facter from the command line to obtain real-time information from the system.

How to do it...

1. Use facter to find the current uptime of the system, the uptime fact:

    ```
    t@cookbook ~$ facter uptime
    0:12 hours
    ```

2. Compare this with the output of the Linux uptime command:

    ```
    t@cookbook ~$ uptime
     01:18:52 up 12 min,  1 user,  load average: 0.00, 0.00, 0.00
    ```

How it works...

When facter is installed (as a dependency for puppet), several fact definitions are installed by default. You can reference each of these facts by name from the command line.

There's more...

Running facter without any arguments causes facter to print all the facts known about the system. We will see in later chapters that facter can be extended with your own custom facts. All facts are available for you to use as variables; variables are discussed in the next section.

Variables

Variables in Puppet are marked with a dollar sign ($) character. When using variables within a manifest, it is preferred to enclose the variable within braces "${myvariable}" instead of "$myvariable". All of the facts from `facter` can be referenced as top scope variables (we will discuss scope in the next section). For example, the **fully qualified domain name (FQDN)** of the node may be referenced by "${::fqdn}". Variables can only contain alphabetic characters, numerals, and the underscore character (_). As a matter of style, variables should start with an alphabetic character. Never use dashes in variable names.

Scope

In the variable example explained in the *There's more...* section, the fully qualified domain name was referred to as ${::fqdn} rather than ${fqdn}; the double colons are how Puppet differentiates scope. The highest level scope, top scope or global, is referred to by two colons (::) at the beginning of a variable identifier. To reduce namespace collisions, always use fully scoped variable identifiers in your manifests. For a Unix user, think of top scope variables as the / (root) level. You can refer to variables using the double colon syntax similar to how you would refer to a directory by its full path. For the developer, you can think of top scope variables as global variables; however, unlike global variables, you must always refer to them with the double colon notation to guarantee that a local variable isn't obscuring the top scope variable.

Installing a package before starting a service

To show how ordering works, we'll create a manifest that installs `httpd` and then ensures the `httpd` package service is running.

How to do it...

1. We start by creating a manifest that defines the service:

```
service {'httpd':
  ensure  => running,
  require => Package['httpd'],
}
```

2. The service definition references a package resource named `httpd`; we now need to define that resource:

```
package {'httpd':
  ensure => 'installed',
}
```

How it works...

In this example, the package will be installed before the service is started. Using `require` within the definition of the `httpd` service ensures that the package is installed first, regardless of the order within the manifest file.

Capitalization

Capitalization is important in Puppet. In our previous example, we created a package named `httpd`. If we wanted to refer to this package later, we would capitalize its type (`package`) as follows:

```
Package['httpd']
```

To refer to a class, for example, the `something::somewhere` class, which has already been included/defined in your manifest, you can reference it with the full path as follows:

```
Class['something::somewhere']
```

When you have a defined type, for example the following defined type:

```
example::thing {'one':}
```

The preceding resource may be referenced later as follows:

```
Example::Thing['one']
```

Knowing how to reference previously defined resources is necessary for the next section on metaparameters and ordering.

Learning metaparameters and ordering

All the manifests that will be used to define a node are compiled into a catalog. A catalog is the code that will be applied to configure a node. It is important to remember that manifests are not applied to nodes sequentially. There is no inherent order to the application of manifests. With this in mind, in the previous `httpd` example, what if we wanted to ensure that the `httpd` process started after the `httpd` package was installed?

We couldn't rely on the `httpd` service coming after the `httpd` package in the manifests. What we have to do is use metaparameters to tell Puppet the order in which we want resources applied to the node. Metaparameters are parameters that can be applied to any resource and are not specific to any one resource type. They are used for catalog compilation and as hints to Puppet but not to define anything about the resource to which they are attached. When dealing with ordering, there are four metaparameters used:

- `before`
- `require`
- `notify`
- `subscribe`

The before and require metaparameters specify a direct ordering; notify implies before and subscribe implies require. The notify metaparameter is only applicable to services; what notify does is tell a service to restart after the notifying resource has been applied to the node (this is most often a package or file resource). In the case of files, once the file is created on the node, a notify parameter will restart any services mentioned. The subscribe metaparameter has the same effect but is defined on the service; the service will subscribe to the file.

Trifecta

The relationship between package and service previously mentioned is an important and powerful paradigm of Puppet. Adding one more resource-type file into the fold, creates what puppeteers refer to as the **trifecta**. Almost all system administration tasks revolve around these three resource types. As a system administrator, you install a package, configure the package with files, and then start the service.

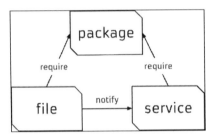

Diagram of Trifecta (Files require package for directory, service requires files and package)

Idempotency

A key concept of Puppet is that the state of the system when a catalog is applied to a node cannot affect the outcome of Puppet run. In other words, at the end of Puppet run (if the run was successful), the system will be in a known state and any further application of the catalog will result in a system that is in the same state. This property of Puppet is known as idempotency. **Idempotency** is the property that no matter how many times you do something, it remains in the same state as the first time you did it. For instance, if you had a light switch and you gave the instruction to turn it on, the light would turn on. If you gave the instruction again, the light would remain on.

Installing, configuring, and starting a service

There are many examples of this pattern online. In our simple example, we will create an Apache configuration file under /etc/httpd/conf.d/cookbook.conf. The /etc/httpd/conf.d directory will not exist until the httpd package is installed. After this file is created, we would want httpd to restart to notice the change; we can achieve this with a notify parameter.

How to do it...

We will need the same definitions as our last example; we need the package and service installed. We now need two more things. We need the configuration file and index page (index.html) created. For this, we follow these steps:

1. As in the previous example, we ensure the service is running and specify that the service requires the httpd package:

```
service {'httpd':
  ensure => running,
  require => Package['httpd'],
}
```

2. We then define the package as follows:

```
package {'httpd':
  ensure => installed,
}
```

3. Now, we create the /etc/httpd/conf.d/cookbook.conf configuration file; the /etc/httpd/conf.d directory will not exist until the httpd package is installed. The require metaparameter tells Puppet that this file requires the httpd package to be installed before it is created:

```
file {'/etc/httpd/conf.d/cookbook.conf':
  content => "<VirtualHost *:80>\nServername
    cookbook\nDocumentRoot
    /var/www/cookbook\n</VirtualHost>\n",
  require => Package['httpd'],
  notify => Service['httpd'],
}
```

4. We then go on to create an index.html file for our virtual host in /var/www/cookbook. This directory won't exist yet, so we need to create this as well, using the following code:

```
file {'/var/www/cookbook':
  ensure => directory,
}
file {'/var/www/cookbook/index.html':
  content => "<html><h1>Hello World!</h1></html>\n",
  require => File['/var/www/cookbook'],
}
```

How it works...

The `require` attribute to the file resources tell Puppet that we need the `/var/www/cookbook` directory created before we can create the `index.html` file. The important concept to remember is that we cannot assume anything about the target system (node). We need to define everything on which the target depends. Anytime you create a file in a manifest, you have to ensure that the directory containing that file exists. Anytime you specify that a service should be running, you have to ensure that the package providing that service is installed.

In this example, using metaparameters, we can be confident that no matter what state the node is in before running Puppet, after Puppet runs, the following will be true:

- ▸ `httpd` will be running
- ▸ The `VirtualHost` configuration file will exist
- ▸ `httpd` will restart and be aware of the `VirtualHost` file
- ▸ The `DocumentRoot` directory will exist
- ▸ An `index.html` file will exist in the `DocumentRoot` directory

Using community Puppet style

If other people need to read or maintain your manifests, or if you want to share code with the community, it's a good idea to follow the existing style conventions as closely as possible. These govern such aspects of your code as layout, spacing, quoting, alignment, and variable references, and the official puppetlabs recommendations on style are available at `http://docs.puppetlabs.com/guides/style_guide.html`.

How to do it...

In this section, I'll show you a few of the more important examples and how to make sure that your code is style compliant.

Indentation

Indent your manifests using two spaces (not tabs), as follows:

```
service {'httpd':
  ensure  => running,
}
```

Quoting

Always quote your resource names, as follows:

```
package { 'exim4':
```

We cannot do this as follows though:

```
package { exim4:
```

Use single quotes for all strings, except when:

- The string contains variable references such as "${::fqdn}"
- The string contains character escape sequences such as "\n"

Consider the following code:

```
file { '/etc/motd':
  content => "Welcome to ${::fqdn}\n"
}
```

Puppet doesn't process variable references or escape sequences unless they're inside double quotes.

Always quote parameter values that are not reserved words in Puppet. For example, the following values are not reserved words:

```
name => 'Nucky Thompson',
mode => '0700',
owner => 'deploy',
```

However, these values are reserved words and therefore not quoted:

```
ensure => installed,
enable => true,
ensure => running,
```

False

There is only one thing in Puppet that is false, that is, the word `false` without any quotes. The string `"false"` evaluates to `true` and the string `"true"` also evaluates to true. Actually, everything besides the literal false evaluates to true (when treated as a Boolean):

```
if "false" {
  notify { 'True': }
}
if 'false' {
  notify { 'Also true': }
}
```

```
if false {
  notify { 'Not true': }
}
```

When this code is run through `puppet apply`, the first two notifies are triggered. The final notify is not triggered; it is the only one that evaluates to `false`.

Variables

Always include curly braces ({ }) around variable names when referring to them in strings, for example, as follows:

```
source => "puppet:///modules/webserver/${brand}.conf",
```

Otherwise, Puppet's parser has to guess which characters should be a part of the variable name and which belong to the surrounding string. Curly braces make it explicit.

Parameters

Always end lines that declare parameters with a comma, even if it is the last parameter:

```
service { 'memcached':
  ensure => running,
  enable => true,
}
```

This is allowed by Puppet, and makes it easier if you want to add parameters later, or reorder the existing parameters.

When declaring a resource with a single parameter, make the declaration all on one line and with no trailing comma, as shown in the following snippet:

```
package { 'puppet': ensure => installed }
```

Where there is more than one parameter, give each parameter its own line:

```
package { 'rake':
  ensure   => installed,
  provider => gem,
  require  => Package['rubygems'],
}
```

To make the code easier to read, line up the parameter arrows in line with the longest parameter, as follows:

```
file { "/var/www/${app}/shared/config/rvmrc":
  owner   => 'deploy',
  group   => 'deploy',
```

```
    content => template('rails/rvmrc.erb'),
    require => File["/var/www/${app}/shared/config"],
}
```

The arrows should be aligned per resource, but not across the whole file, otherwise it can make it difficult for you to cut and paste code from one file to another.

Symlinks

When declaring file resources which are symlinks, use `ensure => link` and set the target attribute, as follows:

```
file { '/etc/php5/cli/php.ini':
    ensure => link,
    target => '/etc/php.ini',
}
```

Creating a manifest

If you already have some Puppet code (known as a Puppet manifest), you can skip this section and go on to the next. If not, we'll see how to create and apply a simple manifest.

How to do it...

To create and apply a simple manifest, follow these steps:

1. First, install Puppet locally on your machine or create a virtual machine and install Puppet on that machine. For YUM-based systems, use `https://yum.puppetlabs.com/` and for APT-based systems, use `https://apt.puppetlabs.com/`. You may also use gem to install Puppet. For our examples, we'll install Puppet using gem on a Debian Wheezy system (hostname: `cookbook`). To use gem, we need the `rubygems` package as follows:

   ```
   t@cookbook:~$ sudo apt-get install rubygems
   Reading package lists... Done
   Building dependency tree
   Reading state information... Done
   The following NEW packages will be installed:
     rubygems
   0 upgraded, 1 newly installed, 0 to remove and 0 not upgraded.
   Need to get 0 B/597 kB of archives.
   After this operation, 3,844 kB of additional disk space will be used.
   ```

```
Selecting previously unselected package rubygems.
(Reading database ... 30390 files and directories currently
installed.)
Unpacking rubygems (from .../rubygems_1.8.24-1_all.deb) ...
Processing triggers for man-db ...
Setting up rubygems (1.8.24-1) ...
```

2. Now, use `gem` to install Puppet:

    ```
    t@cookbook $ sudo gem install puppet
    Successfully installed hiera-1.3.4
    Fetching: facter-2.3.0.gem (100%)
    Successfully installed facter-2.3.0
    Fetching: puppet-3.7.3.gem (100%)
    Successfully installed puppet-3.7.3
    Installing ri documentation for hiera-1.3.4
    Installing ri documentation for facter-2.3.0
    Installing ri documentation for puppet-3.7.3
    Done installing documentation for hiera, facter, puppet after 239
    seconds
    ```

3. Three gems are installed. Now, with Puppet installed, we can create a directory to contain our Puppet code:

    ```
    t@cookbook:~$ mkdir -p .puppet/manifests
    t@cookbook:~$ cd .puppet/manifests
    t@cookbook:~/.puppet/manifests$
    ```

4. Within your `manifests` directory, create the `site.pp` file with the following content:

    ```
    node default {
      file { '/tmp/hello':
        content => "Hello, world!\n",
      }
    }
    ```

5. Test your manifest with the `puppet apply` command. This will tell Puppet to read the manifest, compare it to the state of the machine, and make any necessary changes to that state:

    ```
    t@cookbook:~/.puppet/manifests$ puppet apply site.pp
    Notice: Compiled catalog for cookbook in environment production in
    0.14 seconds
    Notice: /Stage[main]/Main/Node[default]/File[/tmp/hello]/ensure:
    defined content as '{md5}746308829575e17c3331bbcb00c0898b'
    Notice: Finished catalog run in 0.04 seconds
    ```

6. To see if Puppet did what we expected (create the `/tmp/hello` file with the `Hello, world!` content), run the following command:

```
t@cookbook:~/puppet/manifests$ cat /tmp/hello
Hello, world!
 t@cookbook:~/puppet/manifests$
```

 Note that creating the file in `/tmp` did not require special permissions. We did not run Puppet via `sudo`. Puppet need not be run through `sudo`; there are cases where running via an unprivileged user can be useful.

There's more...

When several people are working on a code base, it's easy for style inconsistencies to creep in. Fortunately, there's a tool available which can automatically check your code for compliance with the style guide: `puppet-lint`. We'll see how to use this in the next section.

Checking your manifests with Puppet-lint

The puppetlabs official style guide outlines a number of style conventions for Puppet code, some of which we've touched on in the preceding section. For example, according to the style guide, manifests:

- Must use two-space soft tabs
- Must not use literal tab characters
- Must not contain trailing white space
- Should not exceed an 80 character line width
- Should align parameter arrows (`=>`) within blocks

Following the style guide will make sure that your Puppet code is easy to read and maintain, and if you're planning to release your code to the public, style compliance is essential.

The `puppet-lint` tool will automatically check your code against the style guide. The next section explains how to use it.

Getting ready

Here's what you need to do to install Puppet-lint:

1. We'll install Puppet-lint using the gem provider because the gem version is much more up to date than the APT or RPM packages available. Create a `puppet-lint.pp` manifest as shown in the following code snippet:

```
package {'puppet-lint':
  ensure => 'installed',
  provider => 'gem',
}
```

2. Run `puppet apply` on the `puppet-lint.pp` manifest, as shown in the following command:

```
t@cookbook ~$ puppet apply puppet-lint.pp Notice: Compiled catalog
for node1.example.com in environment production in 0.42 seconds

Notice: /Stage[main]/Main/Package[puppet-lint]/ensure: created

Notice: Finished catalog run in 2.96 seconds

t@cookbook ~$ gem list puppet-lint *** LOCAL GEMS *** puppet-lint
(1.0.1)
```

How to do it...

Follow these steps to use Puppet-lint:

1. Choose a Puppet manifest file that you want to check with Puppet-lint, and run the following command:

```
t@cookbook ~$ puppet-lint puppet-lint.pp

WARNING: indentation of => is not properly aligned on line 2

ERROR: trailing whitespace found on line 4
```

2. As you can see, Puppet-lint found a number of problems with the manifest file. Correct the errors, save the file, and rerun Puppet-lint to check that all is well. If successful, you'll see no output:

```
t@cookbook ~$ puppet-lint puppet-lint.pp

t@cookbook ~$
```

There's more...

You can find out more about Puppet-lint at `https://github.com/rodjek/puppet-lint`.

Should you follow Puppet style guide and, by extension, keep your code lint-clean? It's up to you, but here are a couple of things to think about:

▸ It makes sense to use some style conventions, especially when you're working collaboratively on code. Unless you and your colleagues can agree on standards for whitespace, tabs, quoting, alignment, and so on, your code will be messy and difficult to read or maintain.

▸ If you're choosing a set of style conventions to follow, the logical choice would be that issued by puppetlabs and adopted by the community for use in public modules.

Having said that, it's possible to tell Puppet-lint to ignore certain checks if you've chosen not to adopt them in your codebase. For example, if you don't want Puppet-lint to warn you about code lines exceeding 80 characters, you can run Puppet-lint with the following option:

```
t@cookbook ~$ puppet-lint --no-80chars-check
```

Run `puppet-lint --help` to see the complete list of check configuration commands.

See also

▸ The *Automatic syntax checking with Git hooks* recipe in *Chapter 2, Puppet Infrastructure*

▸ The *Testing your Puppet manifests with rspec-puppet* recipe in *Chapter 9, External Tools and the Puppet Ecosystem*

Using modules

One of the most important things you can do to make your Puppet manifests clearer and more maintainable is to organize them into modules.

Modules are self-contained bundles of Puppet code that include all the files necessary to implement a thing. Modules may contain flat files, templates, Puppet manifests, custom fact declarations, augeas lenses, and custom Puppet types and providers.

Separating things into modules makes it easier to reuse and share code; it's also the most logical way to organize your manifests. In this example, we'll create a module to manage memcached, a memory caching system commonly used with web applications.

How to do it...

Following are the steps to create an example module:

1. We will use Puppet's module subcommand to create the directory structure for our new module:

```
t@cookbook:~$ mkdir -p .puppet/modules
t@cookbook:~$ cd .puppet/modules
t@cookbook:~/.puppet/modules$ puppet module generate thomas-memcached
We need to create a metadata.json file for this module.  Please
answer the following questions; if the question is not applicable
to this module, feel free to leave it blank. Puppet uses Semantic
Versioning (semver.org) to version modules.What version is this
module?  [0.1.0]
--> Who wrote this module?   [thomas]
--> What license does this module code fall under?   [Apache 2.0]
--> How would you describe this module in a single sentence?
--> A module to install memcached Where is this module's source
code repository?
--> Where can others go to learn more about this module?
--> Where can others go to file issues about this module?
-->
----------------------------------------
{
  "name": "thomas-memcached",
  "version": "0.1.0",
  "author": "thomas",
  "summary": "A module to install memcached",
  "license": "Apache 2.0",
  "source": "",
  "issues_url": null,
  "project_page": null,
  "dependencies": [
    {
      "version_range": ">= 1.0.0",
      "name": "puppetlabs-stdlib"
    }
  ]
}
```

```
------------------------------------------
About to generate this metadata; continue? [n/Y]
--> y
Notice: Generating module at /home/thomas/.puppet/modules/thomas-
memcached...
Notice: Populating ERB templates...
Finished; module generated in thomas-memcached.
thomas-memcached/manifests
thomas-memcached/manifests/init.pp
thomas-memcached/spec
thomas-memcached/spec/classes
thomas-memcached/spec/classes/init_spec.rb
thomas-memcached/spec/spec_helper.rb
thomas-memcached/README.md
thomas-memcached/metadata.json
thomas-memcached/Rakefile
thomas-memcached/tests
thomas-memcached/tests/init.pp
```

This command creates the module directory and creates some empty files as starting points. To use the module, we'll create a symlink to the module name (memcached).

```
t@cookbook:~/.puppet/modules$ ln -s thomas-memcached memcached
```

2. Now, edit memcached/manifests/init.pp and change the class definition at the end of the file to the following. Note that puppet module generate created many lines of comments; in a production module you would want to edit those default comments:

```
class memcached {
  package { 'memcached':
    ensure => installed,
  }

  file { '/etc/memcached.conf':
    source  => 'puppet:///modules/memcached/memcached.conf',
    owner   => 'root',
    group   => 'root',
    mode    => '0644',
    require => Package['memcached'],
  }
```

```
    service { 'memcached':
      ensure  => running,
      enable  => true,
      require => [Package['memcached'],
                  File['/etc/memcached.conf']],
    }
  }
```

3. Create the `modules/thomas-memcached/files` directory and then create a file named `memcached.conf` with the following contents:

```
-m 64
-p 11211
-u nobody
-1 127.0.0.1
```

4. Change your `site.pp` file to the following:

```
node default {
    include memcached
}
```

5. We would like this module to install memcached. We'll need to run Puppet with root privileges, and we'll use sudo for that. We'll need Puppet to be able to find the module in our home directory; we can specify this on the command line when we run Puppet as shown in the following code snippet:

```
t@cookbook:~$ sudo puppet apply --modulepath=/home/thomas/.puppet/
modules /home/thomas/.puppet/manifests/site.pp
Notice: Compiled catalog for cookbook.example.com in environment
production in 0.33 seconds
Notice: /Stage[main]/Memcached/File[/etc/memcached.conf]/content:
content changed '{md5}a977521922a151c959ac953712840803' to '{md5}9
429eff3e3354c0be232a020bcf78f75'
Notice: Finished catalog run in 0.11 seconds
```

6. Check whether the new service is running:

```
t@cookbook:~$ sudo service memcached status
[ ok ] memcached is running.
```

How it works...

When we created the module using Puppet's module generate command, we used the name `thomas-memcached`. The name before the hyphen is your username or your username on Puppet forge (an online repository of modules). Since we want Puppet to be able to find the module by the name `memcached`, we make a symbolic link between `thomas-memcached` and `memcached`.

Modules have a specific directory structure. Not all of these directories need to be present, but if they are, this is how they should be organized:

```
modules/
   └MODULE_NAME/              never use a dash (-) in a module name
      └examples/              example usage of the module
      └files/                 flat files used by the module
      └lib/
         └facter/             define new facts for facter
         └puppet/
            └parser/
               └functions/    define a new puppet function, like
sort()
            └provider/    define a provider for a new or existing type
            └util/        define helper functions (in ruby)
            └type/        define a new type in puppet
      └manifests/
         └init.pp       class MODULE_NAME { }
      └spec/ rSpec       tests
      └templates/        erb template files used by the module
```

All manifest files (those containing Puppet code) live in the manifests directory. In our example, the memcached class is defined in the manifests/init.pp file, which will be imported automatically.

Inside the memcached class, we refer to the memcached.conf file:

```
file { '/etc/memcached.conf':
  source => 'puppet:///modules/memcached/memcached.conf',
}
```

The preceding source parameter tells Puppet to look for the file in:

```
MODULEPATH/      (/home/thomas/.puppet/modules)
   └memcached/
      └files/
         └memcached.conf
```

There's more...

Learn to love modules because they'll make your Puppet life a lot easier. They're not complicated, however, practice and experience will help you judge when things should be grouped into modules, and how best to arrange your module structure. Modules can hold more than manifests and files as we'll see in the next two sections.

Templates

If you need to use a template as a part of the module, place it in the module's templates directory and refer to it as follows:

```
file { '/etc/memcached.conf':
  content => template('memcached/memcached.conf.erb'),
}
```

Puppet will look for the file in:

```
MODULEPATH/memcached/templates/memcached.conf.erb
```

Facts, functions, types, and providers

Modules can also contain custom facts, custom functions, custom types, and providers.

For more information about these, refer to *Chapter 9, External Tools and the Puppet Ecosystem*.

Third-party modules

You can download modules provided by other people and use them in your own manifests just like the modules you create. For more on this, see Using Public Modules recipe in *Chapter 7, Managing Applications*.

Module organization

For more details on how to organize your modules, see puppetlabs website:

```
http://docs.puppetlabs.com/puppet/3/reference/modules_fundamentals.
html
```

See also

- The *Creating custom facts* recipe in *Chapter 9, External Tools and the Puppet Ecosystem*
- The *Using public modules* recipe in *Chapter 7, Managing Applications*
- The *Creating your own resource types* recipe in *Chapter 9, External Tools and the Puppet Ecosystem*
- The *Creating your own providers* recipe in *Chapter 9, External Tools and the Puppet Ecosystem*

Using standard naming conventions

Choosing appropriate and informative names for your modules and classes will be a big help when it comes to maintaining your code. This is even truer if other people need to read and work on your manifests.

How to do it...

Here are some tips on how to name things in your manifests:

1. Name modules after the software or service they manage, for example, `apache` or `haproxy`.

2. Name classes within modules (subclasses) after the function or service they provide to the module, for example, `apache::vhosts` or `rails::dependencies`.

3. If a class within a module disables the service provided by that module, name it `disabled`. For example, a class that disables Apache should be named `apache::disabled`.

4. Create a roles and profiles hierarchy of modules. Each node should have a single role consisting of one or more profiles. Each profile module should configure a single service.

5. The module that manages users should be named `user`.

6. Within the user module, declare your virtual users within the class `user::virtual` (for more on virtual users and other resources, see the *Using virtual resources* recipe in *Chapter 5, Users and Virtual Resources*).

7. Within the user module, subclasses for particular groups of users should be named after the group, for example, `user::sysadmins` or `user::contractors`.

8. When using Puppet to deploy the config files for different services, name the file after the service, but with a suffix indicating what kind of file it is, for example:

    ❑   Apache init script: `apache.init`

    ❑   Logrotate config snippet for Rails: `rails.logrotate`

    ❑   Nginx vhost file for mywizzoapp: `mywizzoapp.vhost.nginx`

    ❑   MySQL config for standalone server: `standalone.mysql`

9. If you need to deploy a different version of a file depending on the operating system release, for example, you can use a naming convention like the following:

    ```
    memcached.lucid.conf
    memcached.precise.conf
    ```

10. You can have Puppet automatically select the appropriate version as follows:

    ```
    source = > "puppet:///modules/memcached
       /memcached.${::lsbdistrelease}.conf",
    ```

11. If you need to manage, for example, different Ruby versions, name the class after the version it is responsible for, for example, `ruby192` or `ruby186`.

There's more...

Puppet community maintains a set of best practice guidelines for your Puppet infrastructure, which includes some hints on naming conventions:

```
http://docs.puppetlabs.com/guides/best_practices.html
```

Some people prefer to include multiple classes on a node by using a comma-separated list, rather than separate `include` statements, for example:

```
node 'server014' inherits 'server' {
    include mail::server, repo::gem, repo::apt, zabbix
}
```

This is a matter of style, but I prefer to use separate `include` statements, one on a line, because it makes it easier to copy and move around class inclusions between nodes without having to tidy up the commas and indentation every time.

I mentioned inheritance in a couple of the preceding examples; if you're not sure what this is, don't worry, I'll explain this in detail in the next chapter.

Using inline templates

Templates are a powerful way of using **Embedded Ruby** (**ERB**) to help build config files dynamically. You can also use ERB syntax directly without having to use a separate file by calling the `inline_template` function. ERB allows you to use conditional logic, iterate over arrays, and include variables.

How to do it...

Here's an example of how to use `inline_template`:

Pass your Ruby code to `inline_template` within Puppet manifest, as follows:

```
cron { 'chkrootkit':
  command => '/usr/sbin/chkrootkit >
    /var/log/chkrootkit.log 2>&1',
  hour    => inline_template('<%= @hostname.sum % 24 %>'),
  minute  => '00',
}
```

How it works...

Anything inside the string passed to `inline_template` is executed as if it were an ERB template. That is, anything inside the `<%=` and `%>` delimiters will be executed as Ruby code, and the rest will be treated as a string.

In this example, we use `inline_template` to compute a different hour for this cron resource (a scheduled job) for each machine, so that the same job does not run at the same time on all machines. For more on this technique, see the *Distributing cron jobs efficiently* recipe in *Chapter 6, Managing Resources and Files*.

There's more...

In ERB code, whether inside a template file or an `inline_template` string, you can access your Puppet variables directly by name using an @ prefix, if they are in the current scope or the top scope (facts):

```
<%= @fqdn %>
```

To reference variables in another scope, use `scope.lookupvar`, as follows:

```
<%= "The value of something from otherclass is " +
    scope.lookupvar('otherclass::something') %>
```

You should use inline templates sparingly. If you really need to use some complicated logic in your manifest, consider using a custom function instead (see the *Creating custom functions* recipe in *Chapter 9, External Tools and the Puppet Ecosystem*).

See also

- ▶ The *Using ERB templates* recipe in *Chapter 4, Working with Files and Packages*
- ▶ The *Using array iteration in templates* recipe in *Chapter 4, Working with Files and Packages*

Iterating over multiple items

Arrays are a powerful feature in Puppet; wherever you want to perform the same operation on a list of things, an array may be able to help. You can create an array just by putting its content in square brackets:

```
$lunch = [ 'franks', 'beans', 'mustard' ]
```

How to do it...

Here's a common example of how arrays are used:

1. Add the following code to your manifest:

```
$packages = [ 'ruby1.8-dev',
    'ruby1.8',
    'ri1.8',
    'rdoc1.8',
    'irb1.8',
    'libreadline-ruby1.8',
    'libruby1.8',
    'libopenssl-ruby' ]

package { $packages: ensure => installed }
```

2. Run Puppet and note that each package should now be installed.

How it works...

Where Puppet encounters an array as the name of a resource, it creates a resource for each element in the array. In the example, a new package resource is created for each of the packages in the `$packages` array, with the same parameters (`ensure => installed`). This is a very compact way to instantiate many similar resources.

There's more...

Although arrays will take you a long way with Puppet, it's also useful to know about an even more flexible data structure: the hash.

Using hashes

A hash is like an array, but each of the elements can be stored and looked up by name (referred to as the key), for example (`hash.pp`):

```
$interface = {
    'name' => 'eth0',
    'ip'   => '192.168.0.1',
    'mac'  => '52:54:00:4a:60:07'
}
notify { "(${interface['ip']}) at ${interface['mac']} on
    ${interface['name']}": }
```

When we run Puppet on this, we see the following notify in the output:

```
t@cookbook:~/.puppet/manifests$ puppet apply hash.pp
Notice: (192.168.0.1) at 52:54:00:4a:60:07 on etho
```

Hash values can be anything that you can assign to variables, strings, function calls, expressions, and even other hashes or arrays. Hashes are useful to store a bunch of information about a particular thing because by accessing each element of the hash using a key, we can quickly find the information for which we are looking.

Creating arrays with the split function

You can declare literal arrays using square brackets, as follows:

```
define lunchprint() {
  notify { "Lunch included ${name}":}":: }
}

$lunch = ['egg', 'beans', 'chips']
lunchprint { $lunch: }
```

Now, when we run Puppet on the preceding code, we see the following notice messages in the output:

```
t@mylaptop ~ $ puppet apply lunchprint.pp
...
Notice: Lunch included chips
Notice: Lunch included beans
Notice: Lunch included egg
```

However, Puppet can also create arrays for you from strings, using the `split` function, as follows:

```
$menu = 'egg beans chips'
$items = split($menu, ' ')
lunchprint { $items: }
```

Running `puppet apply` against this new manifest, we see the same messages in the output:

```
t@mylaptop ~ $ puppet apply lunchprint2.pp
...
Notice: Lunch included chips
Notice: Lunch included beans
Notice: Lunch included egg.
```

Note that `split` takes two arguments: the first argument is the string to be split. The second argument is the character to split on; in this example, a single space. As Puppet works its way through the string, when it encounters a space, it will interpret it as the end of one item and the beginning of the next. So, given the string `'egg beans chips'`, this will be split into three items.

The character to split on can be any character or string:

```
$menu = 'egg and beans and chips'
$items = split($menu, ' and ')
```

The character can also be a regular expression, for example, a set of alternatives separated by a | (pipe) character:

```
$lunch = 'egg:beans,chips'
$items = split($lunch, ':|,')
```

Writing powerful conditional statements

Puppet's `if` statement allows you to change the manifest behavior based on the value of a variable or an expression. With it, you can apply different resources or parameter values depending on certain facts about the node, for example, the operating system, or the memory size.

You can also set variables within the manifest, which can change the behavior of included classes. For example, nodes in data center A might need to use different DNS servers than nodes in data center B, or you might need to include one set of classes for an Ubuntu system, and a different set for other systems.

How to do it...

Here's an example of a useful conditional statement. Add the following code to your manifest:

```
if $::timezone == 'UTC' {
  notify { 'Universal Time Coordinated':}
} else {
  notify { "$::timezone is not UTC": }
}
```

How it works...

Puppet treats whatever follows an `if` keyword as an expression and evaluates it. If the expression evaluates to true, Puppet will execute the code within the curly braces.

Optionally, you can add an else branch, which will be executed if the expression evaluates to false.

There's more...

Here are some more tips on using `if` statements.

Elsif branches

You can add further tests using the `elsif` keyword, as follows:

```
if $::timezone == 'UTC' {
  notify { 'Universal Time Coordinated': }
} elsif $::timezone == 'GMT' {
  notify { 'Greenwich Mean Time': }
} else {
  notify { "$::timezone is not UTC": }
}
```

Comparisons

You can check whether two values are equal using the `==` syntax, as in our example:

```
if $::timezone == 'UTC' {

}
```

Alternatively, you can check whether they are not equal using `!=`:

```
if $::timezone != 'UTC' {
  ...
}
```

You can also compare numeric values using `<` and `>`:

```
if $::uptime_days > 365 {
  notify { 'Time to upgrade your kernel!': }
}
```

To test whether a value is greater (or less) than or equal to another value, use `<=` or `>=`:

```
if $::mtu_eth0 <= 1500 {
  notify {"Not Jumbo Frames": }
}
```

Combining expressions

You can put together the kind of simple expressions described previously into more complex logical expressions, using and, or, and not:

```
if ($::uptime_days > 365) and ($::kernel == 'Linux') {
  …
}

if ($role == 'webserver') and ( ($datacenter == 'A') or ($datacenter
== 'B') ) {
  …
}
```

See also

▶ The *Using the in operator* recipe in this chapter

▶ The *Using selectors and case statements* recipe in this chapter

Using regular expressions in if statements

Another kind of expression you can test in if statements and other conditionals is the regular expression. A regular expression is a powerful way to compare strings using pattern matching.

How to do it...

This is one example of using a regular expression in a conditional statement. Add the following to your manifest:

```
if $::architecture =~ /64/ {
  notify { '64Bit OS Installed': }
} else {
  notify { 'Upgrade to 64Bit': }
  fail('Not 64 Bit')
}
```

How it works...

Puppet treats the text supplied between the forward slashes as a regular expression, specifying the text to be matched. If the match succeeds, the `if` expression will be true and so the code between the first set of curly braces will be executed. In this example, we used a regular expression because different distributions have different ideas on what to call `64bit`; some use `amd64`, while others use `x86_64`. The only thing we can count on is the presence of the number 64 within the fact. Some facts that have version numbers in them are treated as strings to Puppet. For instance, `$::facterversion`. On my test system, this is `2.0.1`, but when I try to compare that with `2`, Puppet fails to make the comparison:

```
Error: comparison of String with 2 failed at /home/thomas/.puppet/
manifests/version.pp:1 on node cookbook.example.com
```

If you wanted instead to do something if the text does not match, use `!~` rather than `=~`:

```
if $::kernel !~ /Linux/ {
    notify { 'Not Linux, could be Windows, MacOS X, AIX, or ?': }
}
```

There's more...

Regular expressions are very powerful, but can be difficult to understand and debug. If you find yourself using a regular expression so complex that you can't see at a glance what it does, think about simplifying your design to make it easier. However, one particularly useful feature of regular expressions is the ability to capture patterns.

Capturing patterns

You can not only match text using a regular expression, but also capture the matched text and store it in a variable:

```
$input = 'Puppet is better than manual configuration'
if $input =~ /(.*) is better than (.*)/ {
    notify { "You said '${0}'. Looks like you're comparing ${1}
        to ${2}!": }
}
```

The preceding code produces this output:

You said 'Puppet is better than manual configuration'. Looks like you're comparing Puppet to manual configuration!

The variable `$0` stores the whole matched text (assuming the overall match succeeded). If you put brackets around any part of the regular expression, it creates a group, and any matched groups will also be stored in variables. The first matched group will be `$1`, the second `$2`, and so on, as shown in the preceding example.

Regular expression syntax

Puppet's regular expression syntax is the same as Ruby's, so resources that explain Ruby's regular expression syntax will also help you with Puppet. You can find a good introduction to Ruby's regular expression syntax at this website:

```
http://www.tutorialspoint.com/ruby/ruby_regular_expressions.htm.
```

See also

▶ Refer to the *Using regular expression substitutions* recipe in this chapter

Using selectors and case statements

Although you could write any conditional statement using `if`, Puppet provides a couple of extra forms to help you express conditionals more easily: the selector and the `case` statement.

How to do it...

Here are some examples of selector and `case` statements:

1. Add the following code to your manifest:

    ```
    $systemtype = $::operatingsystem ? {
      'Ubuntu' => 'debianlike',
      'Debian' => 'debianlike',
      'RedHat' => 'redhatlike',
      'Fedora' => 'redhatlike',
      'CentOS' => 'redhatlike',
      default  => 'unknown',
    }

    notify { "You have a ${systemtype} system": }
    ```

2. Add the following code to your manifest:

    ```
    class debianlike {
      notify { 'Special manifest for Debian-like systems': }
    }

    class redhatlike {
      notify { 'Special manifest for RedHat-like systems': }
    }

    case $::operatingsystem {
      'Ubuntu',
    ```

```
'Debian': {
  include debianlike
}
'RedHat',
'Fedora',
'CentOS',
'Springdale': {
  include redhatlike
}
default: {
  notify { "I don't know what kind of system you have!":
  }
}
}
}
```

How it works...

Our example demonstrates both the selector and the `case` statement, so let's see in detail how each of them works.

Selector

In the first example, we used a selector (the `?` operator) to choose a value for the `$systemtype` variable depending on the value of `$::operatingsystem`. This is similar to the ternary operator in C or Ruby, but instead of choosing between two possible values, you can have as many values as you like.

Puppet will compare the value of `$::operatingsystem` to each of the possible values we have supplied in Ubuntu, Debian, and so on. These values could be regular expressions (for example, for a partial string match, or to use wildcards), but in our case, we have just used literal strings.

As soon as it finds a match, the selector expression returns whatever value is associated with the matching string. If the value of `$::operatingsystem` is Fedora, for example, the selector expression will return the `redhatlike` string and this will be assigned to the variable `$systemtype`.

Case statement

Unlike selectors, the `case` statement does not return a value. `case` statements come in handy when you want to execute different code depending on the value of some expression. In our second example, we used the `case` statement to include either the `debianlike` or `redhatlike` class, depending on the value of `$::operatingsystem`.

Again, Puppet compares the value of `$::operatingsystem` to a list of potential matches. These could be regular expressions or strings, or as in our example, comma-separated lists of strings. When it finds a match, the associated code between curly braces is executed. So, if the value of `$::operatingsystem` is Ubuntu, then the code including `debianlike` will be executed.

There's more...

Once you've got a grip of the basic use of selectors and `case` statements, you may find the following tips useful.

Regular expressions

As with `if` statements, you can use regular expressions with selectors and `case` statements, and you can also capture the values of the matched groups and refer to them using $1, $2, and so on:

```
case $::lsbdistdescription {
  /Ubuntu (.+)/: {
    notify { "You have Ubuntu version ${1}": }
  }
  /CentOS (.+)/: {
    notify { "You have CentOS version ${1}": }
  }
  default: {}
}
```

Defaults

Both selectors and `case` statements let you specify a default value, which is chosen if none of the other options match (the style guide suggests you always have a default clause defined):

```
$lunch = 'Filet mignon.'
$lunchtype =  $lunch ? {
  /fries/ => 'unhealthy',
  /salad/ => 'healthy',
  default => 'unknown',
}

notify { "Your lunch was ${lunchtype}": }
```

The output is as follows:

```
t@mylaptop ~ $ puppet apply lunchtype.pp
Notice: Your lunch was unknown
```

Notice: /Stage[main]/Main/Notify[Your lunch was unknown]/message: defined
'message' as 'Your lunch was unknown'

When the default action shouldn't normally occur, use the `fail()` function to halt the
Puppet run.

Using the in operator

The `in` operator tests whether one string contains another string. Here's an example:

```
if 'spring' in 'springfield'
```

The preceding expression is true if the `spring` string is a substring of `springfield`, which it
is. The `in` operator can also test for membership of arrays as follows:

```
if $crewmember in ['Frank', 'Dave', 'HAL' ]
```

When `in` is used with a hash, it tests whether the string is a key of the hash:

```
$ifaces = { 'lo'   => '127.0.0.1',
            'eth0' => '192.168.0.1' }
if 'eth0' in $ifaces {
  notify { "eth0 has address ${ifaces['eth0']}": }
}
```

How to do it...

The following steps will show you how to use the `in` operator:

1. Add the following code to your manifest:

    ```
    if $::operatingsystem in [ 'Ubuntu', 'Debian' ] {
      notify { 'Debian-type operating system detected': }
    } elsif $::operatingsystem in [ 'RedHat', 'Fedora', 'SuSE',
      'CentOS' ] {
      notify { 'RedHat-type operating system detected': }
    } else {
      notify { 'Some other operating system detected': }
    }
    ```

2. Run Puppet:

    ```
    t@cookbook:~/.puppet/manifests$ puppet apply in.pp
    Notice: Compiled catalog for cookbook.example.com in environment
    production in 0.03 seconds
    Notice: Debian-type operating system detected
    ```

```
Notice: /Stage[main]/Main/Notify[Debian-type operating system
detected]/message: defined 'message' as 'Debian-type operating
system detected'

Notice: Finished catalog run in 0.02 seconds
```

There's more...

The value of an `in` expression is Boolean (true or false) so you can assign it to a variable:

```
$debianlike = $::operatingsystem in [ 'Debian', 'Ubuntu' ]

if $debianlike {
  notify { 'You are in a maze of twisty little packages, all alike': }
}
```

Using regular expression substitutions

Puppet's `regsubst` function provides an easy way to manipulate text, search and replace expressions within strings, or extract patterns from strings. We often need to do this with data obtained from a fact, for example, or from external programs.

In this example, we'll see how to use `regsubst` to extract the first three octets of an IPv4 address (the network part, assuming it's a `/24` class C address).

How to do it...

Follow these steps to build the example:

1. Add the following code to your manifest:
    ```
    $class_c = regsubst($::ipaddress, '(.*)\..*', '\1.0')
    notify { "The network part of ${::ipaddress} is ${class_c}": }
    ```

2. Run Puppet:
    ```
    t@cookbook:~/.puppet/manifests$ puppet apply ipaddress.pp

    Notice: Compiled catalog for cookbook.example.com in environment
    production in 0.02 seconds

    Notice: The network part of 192.168.122.148 is

      192.168.122.0

    Notice: /Stage[main]/Main/Notify[The network part of
    192.168.122.148 is

      192.168.122.0]/message: defined 'message' as 'The network part
    of 192.168.122.148 is
    ```

```
192.168.122.0'
```
```
Notice: Finished catalog run in 0.03 seconds
```

How it works...

The `regsubst` function takes at least three parameters: source, pattern, and replacement. In our example, we specified the source string as `$::ipaddress`, which, on this machine, is as follows:

```
192.168.122.148
```

We specify the `pattern` function as follows:

```
(.*)\..*
```

We specify the `replacement` function as follows:

```
\1.0
```

The pattern captures all of the string up to the last period (`\.`) in the `\1` variable. We then match on `.*`, which matches everything to the end of the string, so when we replace the string at the end with `\1.0`, we end up with only the network portion of the IP address, which evaluates to the following:

```
192.168.122.0
```

We could have got the same result in other ways, of course, including the following:

```
$class_c = regsubst($::ipaddress, '\.\d+$', '.0')
```

Here, we only match the last octet and replace it with `.0`, which achieves the same result without capturing.

There's more...

The `pattern` function can be any regular expression, using the same (Ruby) syntax as regular expressions in `if` statements.

See also

- ▶ The *Importing dynamic information* recipe in *Chapter 3, Writing Better Manifests*
- ▶ The *Getting information about the environment* recipe in *Chapter 3, Writing Better Manifests*
- ▶ The *Using regular expressions in if statements* recipe in this chapter

Using the future parser

Puppet language is evolving at the moment; many features that are expected to be included in the next major release (4) are available if you enable the future parser.

Getting ready

▶ Ensure that the `rgen` gem is installed.

▶ Set `parser = future` in the `[main]` section of your `puppet.conf`(`/etc/puppet/puppet.conf` for open source Puppet as `root`, `/etc/puppetlabs/puppet/puppet.conf` for Puppet `Enterprise`, and `~/.puppet/puppet.conf` for a non-root user running puppet).

▶ To temporarily test with the future parser, use `--parser=future` on the command line.

How to do it...

Many of the experimental features deal with how code is evaluated, for example, in an earlier example we compared the value of the `$::facterversion` fact with a number, but the value is treated as a string so the code fails to compile. Using the future parser, the value is converted and no error is reported as shown in the following command line output:

```
t@cookbook:~/.puppet/manifests$ puppet apply --parser=future version.pp
Notice: Compiled catalog for cookbook.example.com in environment
production in 0.36 seconds
Notice: Finished catalog run in 0.03 seconds
```

Appending to and concatenating arrays

You can concatenate arrays with the + operator or append them with the << operator. In the following example, we use the ternary operator to assign a specific package name to the $apache variable. We then append that value to an array using the << operator:

```
$apache = $::osfamily ? {
  'Debian' => 'apache2',
  'RedHat' => 'httpd'
}
$packages = ['memcached'] << $apache
package {$packages: ensure => installed}
```

If we have two arrays, we can use the + operator to concatenate the two arrays. In this example, we define an array of system administrators ($sysadmins) and another array of application owners ($appowners). We can then concatenate the array and use it as an argument to our allowed users:

```
$sysadmins = [ 'thomas','john','josko' ]
$appowners = [ 'mike', 'patty', 'erin' ]
$users = $sysadmins + $appowners
notice ($users)
```

When we apply this manifest, we see that the two arrays have been joined as shown in the following command line output:

```
t@cookbook:~/.puppet/manifests$ puppet apply --parser=future concat.pp
Notice: [thomas, john, josko, mike, patty, erin]
```

```
Notice: Compiled catalog for cookbook.example.com in environment
production in 0.36 seconds
```

```
Notice: Finished catalog run in 0.03 seconds
```

Merging Hashes

If we have two hashes, we can merge them using the same + operator we used for arrays. Consider our $interfaces hash from a previous example; we can add another interface to the hash:

```
$iface = {
  'name' => 'eth0',
  'ip'   => '192.168.0.1',
  'mac'  => '52:54:00:4a:60:07'
}  + {'route' => '192.168.0.254'}
notice ($iface)
```

When we apply this manifest, we see that the route attribute has been merged into the hash (your results may differ, the order in which the hash prints is unpredictable), as follows:

```
t@cookbook:~/.puppet/manifests$ puppet apply --parser=future hash2.pp
Notice: {route => 192.168.0.254, name => eth0, ip => 192.168.0.1, mac =>
52:54:00:4a:60:07}
```

```
Notice: Compiled catalog for cookbook.example.com in environment
production in 0.36 seconds
```

```
Notice: Finished catalog run in 0.03 seconds
```

Lambda functions

Lambda functions are iterators applied to arrays or hashes. You iterate through the array or hash and apply an iterator function such as each, map, filter, reduce, or slice to each element of the array or key of the hash. Some of the lambda functions return a calculated array or value; others such as each only return the input array or hash.

Lambda functions such as map and reduce use temporary variables that are thrown away after the lambda has finished. Use of lambda functions is something best shown by example. In the next few sections, we will show an example usage of each of the lambda functions.

Reduce

Reduce is used to reduce the array to a single value. This can be used to calculate the maximum or minimum of the array, or in this case, the sum of the elements of the array:

```
$count = [1,2,3,4,5]
$sum = reduce($count) | $total, $i | { $total + $i }
notice("Sum is $sum")
```

This preceding code will compute the sum of the $count array and store it in the $sum variable, as follows:

```
t@cookbook:~/.puppet/manifests$ puppet apply --parser future lambda.pp
Notice: Sum is 15
Notice: Compiled catalog for cookbook.example.com in environment
production in 0.36 seconds
Notice: Finished catalog run in 0.03 seconds
```

Filter

Filter is used to filter the array or hash based upon a test within the lambda function. For instance to filter our $count array as follows:

```
$filter = filter ($count) | $i | { $i > 3 }
notice("Filtered array is $filter")
```

When we apply this manifest, we see that only elements 4 and 5 are in the result:

```
Notice: Filtered array is [4, 5]
```

Map

Map is used to apply a function to each element of the array. For instance, if we wanted (for some unknown reason) to compute the square of all the elements of the array, we would use map as follows:

```
$map = map ($count) | $i | { $i * $i }
notice("Square of array is $map")
```

The result of applying this manifest is a new array with every element of the original array squared (multiplied by itself), as shown in the following command line output:

```
Notice: Square of array is [1, 4, 9, 16, 25]
```

Slice

Slice is useful when you have related values stored in the same array in a sequential order. For instance, if we had the destination and port information for a firewall in an array, we could split them up into pairs and perform operations on those pairs:

```
$firewall_rules = ['192.168.0.1','80','192.168.0.10','443']
slice ($firewall_rules,2) |$ip, $port| { notice("Allow $ip on
   $port") }
```

When applied, this manifest will produce the following notices:

Notice: Allow 192.168.0.1 on 80

Notice: Allow 192.168.0.10 on 443

To make this a useful example, create a new firewall resource within the block of the slice instead of notice:

```
slice ($firewall_rules,2) |$ip, $port| {
  firewall {"$port from $ip":
    dport  => $port,
    source => "$ip",
    action => 'accept',
  }
}
```

Each

Each is used to iterate over the elements of the array but lacks the ability to capture the results like the other functions. Each is the simplest case where you simply wish to do something with each element of the array, as shown in the following code snippet:

```
each ($count) |$c| { notice($c) }
```

As expected, this executes the notice for each element of the $count array, as follows:

Notice: 1

Notice: 2

Notice: 3

Notice: 4

Notice: 5

Other features

There are other new features of Puppet language available when using the future parser. Some increase readability or compactness of code. For more information, refer to the documentation on puppetlabs website at http://docs.puppetlabs.com/puppet/latest/reference/experiments_future.html.

2
Puppet Infrastructure

"Computers in the future may have as few as 1,000 vacuum tubes and weigh only 1.5 tons."

— *Popular Mechanics, 1949*

In this chapter, we will cover:

- ▶ Installing Puppet
- ▶ Managing your manifests with Git
- ▶ Creating a decentralized Puppet architecture
- ▶ Writing a papply script
- ▶ Running Puppet from cron
- ▶ Bootstrapping Puppet with bash
- ▶ Creating a centralized Puppet infrastructure
- ▶ Creating certificates with multiple DNS names
- ▶ Running Puppet from passenger
- ▶ Setting up the environment
- ▶ Configuring PuppetDB
- ▶ Configuring Hiera
- ▶ Setting-node specific data with Hiera
- ▶ Storing secret data with hiera-gpg
- ▶ Using MessagePack serialization
- ▶ Automatic syntax checking with Git hooks
- ▶ Pushing code around with Git
- ▶ Managing environments with Git

Introduction

In this chapter, we will cover how to deploy Puppet in a centralized and decentralized manner. With each approach, we'll see a combination of best practices, my personal experience, and community solutions.

We'll configure and use both PuppetDB and Hiera. PuppetDB is used with exported resources, which we will cover in *Chapter 5, Users and Virtual Resources*. Hiera is used to separate variable data from Puppet code.

Finally, I'll introduce Git and see how to use Git to organize our code and our infrastructure.

Because Linux distributions, such as Ubuntu, Red Hat, and CentOS, differ in the specific details of package names, configuration file paths, and many other things, I have decided that for reasons of space and clarity the best approach for this book is to pick one distribution (*Debian 7* named as *Wheezy*) and stick to that. However, Puppet runs on most popular operating systems, so you should have very little trouble adapting the recipes to your own favorite OS and distribution.

At the time of writing, Puppet 3.7.2 is the latest stable version available, this is the version of Puppet used in the book. The syntax of Puppet commands changes often, so be aware that while older versions of Puppet are still perfectly usable, they may not support all of the features and syntax described in this book. As we saw in *Chapter 1, Puppet Language and Style*, the future parser showcases features of the language scheduled to become default in Version 4 of Puppet.

Installing Puppet

In *Chapter 1, Puppet Language and Style*, we installed Puppet as a rubygem using the gem install. When deploying to several nodes, this may not be the best approach. Using the package manager of your chosen distribution is the best way to keep your Puppet versions similar on all of the nodes in your deployment. Puppet labs maintain repositories for APT-based and YUM-based distributions.

Getting ready

If your Linux distribution uses APT for package management, go to `http://apt.puppetlabs.com/` and download the appropriate Puppet labs release package for your distribution. For our wheezy cookbook node, we will use `http://apt.puppetlabs.com/puppetlabs-release-wheezy.deb`.

If you are using a Linux distribution that uses YUM for package management, go to `http://yum.puppetlabs.com/` and download the appropriate Puppet labs release package for your distribution.

How to do it...

1. Once you have found the appropriate Puppet labs release package for your distribution, the steps to install Puppet are the same for either APT or YUM:

   ❑ Install Puppet labs release package

   ❑ Install Puppet package

2. Once you have installed Puppet, verify the version of Puppet as shown in the following example:

   ```
   t@ckbk:~ puppet --version 3.7.2
   ```

Now that we have a method to install Puppet on our nodes, we need to turn our attention to keeping our Puppet manifests organized. In the next section, we will see how to use Git to keep our code organized and consistent.

Managing your manifests with Git

It's a great idea to put your Puppet manifests in a version control system such as Git or Subversion (Git is the de facto standard for Puppet). This gives you several advantages:

- You can undo changes and revert to any previous version of your manifest

- You can experiment with new features using a branch

- If several people need to make changes to the manifests, they can make them independently, in their own working copies, and then merge their changes later

- You can use the `git log` feature to see what was changed, and when (and by whom)

Getting ready

In this section, we'll import your existing manifest files into Git. If you have created a Puppet directory in a previous section use that, otherwise, use your existing manifest directory.

In this example, we'll create a new Git repository on a server accessible from all our nodes. There are several steps we need to take to have our code held in a Git repository:

1. Install Git on a central server.

2. Create a user to run Git and own the repository.

3. Create a repository to hold the code.

4. Create **SSH** keys to allow key-based access to the repository.

5. Install Git on a node and download the latest version from our Git repository.

How to do it...

Follow these steps:

1. First, install Git on your Git server (`git.example.com` in our example). The easiest way to do this is using Puppet. Create the following manifest, call it `git.pp`:

```
package {'git':
  ensure => installed
}
```

2. Apply this manifest using `puppet apply git.pp`, this will install Git.

3. Next, create a Git user that the nodes will use to log in and retrieve the latest code. Again, we'll do this with puppet. We'll also create a directory to hold our repository (`/home/git/repos`) as shown in the following code snippet:

```
group { 'git':
  gid => 1111,
}
user {'git':
  uid => 1111,
  gid => 1111,
  comment => 'Git User',
  home => '/home/git',
  require => Group['git'],
}
file {'/home/git':
  ensure => 'directory',
  owner => 1111,
  group => 1111,
  require => User['git'],
}
file {'/home/git/repos':
  ensure => 'directory',
  owner => 1111,
  group => 1111,
  require => File['/home/git']
}
```

4. After applying that manifest, log in as the Git user and create an empty Git repository using the following command:

```
# sudo -iu git
git@git $ cd repos
git@git $ git init --bare puppet.git
Initialized empty Git repository in /home/git/repos/puppet.git/
```

5. Set a password for the Git user, we'll need to log in remotely after the next step:

```
[root@git ~]# passwd git
Changing password for user git.
New password:
Retype new password:
passwd: all authentication tokens updated successfully.
```

6. Now back on your local machine, create an `ssh` key for our nodes to use to update the repository:

```
t@mylaptop ~ $ cd .ssh
t@mylaptop ~/.ssh $ ssh-keygen -b 4096 -f git_rsa
Generating public/private rsa key pair.
Enter passphrase (empty for no passphrase):
Enter same passphrase again:
Your identification has been saved in git_rsa.
Your public key has been saved in git_rsa.pub.
The key fingerprint is:
87:35:0e:4e:d2:96:5f:e4:ce:64:4a:d5:76:c8:2b:e4 thomas@mylaptop
```

7. Now copy the newly created public key to the `authorized_keys` file. This will allow us to connect to the Git server using this new key:

```
t@mylaptop ~/.ssh $ ssh-copy-id -i git_rsa git@git.example.com
git@git.example.com's password:
Number of key(s) added: 1
```

8. Now try logging into the machine, with: "ssh 'git@git.example.com'" and check to make sure that only the key(s) you wanted were added.

9. Next, configure `ssh` to use your key when accessing the Git server and add the following to your `~/.ssh/config` file:

```
Host git git.example.com
    User git
    IdentityFile /home/thomas/.ssh/git_rsa
```

10. Clone the repo onto your machine into a directory named Puppet (substitute your server name if you didn't use `git.example.com`):

```
t@mylaptop ~$ git clone git@git.example.com:repos/puppet.git
Cloning into 'puppet'...
warning: You appear to have cloned an empty repository.
Checking connectivity... done.
```

We've created a Git repository; before we commit any changes to the repository, it's a good idea to set your name and e-mail in Git. Your name and e-mail will be appended to each commit you make.

11. When you are working in a large team, knowing who made a change is very important; for this, use the following code snippet:

```
t@mylaptop puppet$ git config --global user.email
"thomas@narrabilis.com"
t@mylaptop puppet$ git config --global user.name "Thomas
Uphill"
```

12. You can verify your Git settings using the following snippet:

```
t@mylaptop ~$ git config --global --list
user.name=Thomas Uphill
user.email=thomas@narrabilis.com
core.editor=vim
merge.tool=vimdiff
color.ui=true
push.default=simple
```

13. Now that we have Git configured properly, change directory to your repository directory and create a new site manifest as shown in the following snippet:

```
t@mylaptop ~$ cd puppet
t@mylaptop puppet$ mkdir manifests
t@mylaptop puppet$ vim manifests/site.pp
node default {
   include base
}
```

14. This site manifest will install our base class on every node; we will create the base class using the Puppet module as we did in *Chapter 1, Puppet Language and Style*:

```
t@mylaptop puppet$ mkdir modules
t@mylaptop puppet$ cd modules
t@mylaptop modules$ puppet module generate thomas-base
Notice: Generating module at /home/tuphill/puppet/modules/thomas-
base
thomas-base
thomas-base/Modulefile
thomas-base/README
thomas-base/manifests
thomas-base/manifests/init.pp
thomas-base/spec
thomas-base/spec/spec_helper.rb
```

```
thomas-base/tests
thomas-base/tests/init.pp
t@mylaptop modules$ ln -s thomas-base base
```

15. As a last step, we create a symbolic link between the `thomas-base` directory and `base`. Now to make sure our module does something useful, add the following to the body of the `base` class defined in `thomas-base/manifests/init.pp`:

```
class base {
  file {'/etc/motd':
    content => "${::fqdn}\nManaged by puppet ${::puppetversion}\n"
  }
}
```

16. Now add the new base module and site manifest to Git using `git add` and `git commit` as follows:

```
t@mylaptop modules$ cd ..
t@mylaptop puppet$ git add modules manifests
t@mylaptop puppet$ git status
On branch master
Initial commit
Changes to be committed:
  (use "git rm --cached <file>..." to unstage)
new file:   manifests/site.pp
new file:   modules/base
new file:   modules/thomas-base/Modulefile
new file:   modules/thomas-base/README
new file:   modules/thomas-base/manifests/init.pp
new file:   modules/thomas-base/spec/spec_helper.rb
new file:   modules/thomas-base/tests/init.pp
t@mylaptop puppet$ git commit -m "Initial commit with simple base module"
[master (root-commit) 3e1f837] Initial commit with simple base module
 7 files changed, 102 insertions(+)
 create mode 100644 manifests/site.pp
 create mode 120000 modules/base
 create mode 100644 modules/thomas-base/Modulefile
 create mode 100644 modules/thomas-base/README
```

```
create mode 100644 modules/thomas-base/manifests/init.pp
create mode 100644 modules/thomas-base/spec/spec_helper.rb
create mode 100644 modules/thomas-base/tests/init.pp
```

17. At this point your changes to the Git repository have been committed locally; you now need to push those changes back to `git.example.com` so that other nodes can retrieve the updated files:

```
t@mylaptop puppet$ git push origin master
Counting objects: 15, done.
Delta compression using up to 4 threads.
Compressing objects: 100% (9/9), done.
Writing objects: 100% (15/15), 2.15 KiB | 0 bytes/s, done.
Total 15 (delta 0), reused 0 (delta 0)
To git@git.example.com:repos/puppet.git
 * [new branch]      master -> master
```

How it works...

Git tracks changes to files, and stores a complete history of all changes. The history of the repo is made up of commits. A commit represents the state of the repo at a particular point in time, which you create with the `git commit` command and annotate with a message.

You've now added your Puppet manifest files to the repo and created your first commit. This updates the history of the repo, but only in your local working copy. To synchronize the changes with the `git.example.com` copy, the `git push` command pushes all changes made since the last sync.

There's more...

Now that you have a central Git repository for your Puppet manifests, you can check out multiple copies of it in different places and work on them before committing your changes. For example, if you're working in a team, each member can have their own local copy of the repo and synchronize changes with the others via the central server. You may also choose to use GitHub as your central Git repository server. GitHub offers free Git repository hosting for public repositories, and you can pay for GitHub's premium service if you don't want your Puppet code to be publicly available.

In the next section, we will use our Git repository for both centralized and decentralized Puppet configurations.

Creating a decentralized Puppet architecture

Puppet is a configuration management tool. You can use Puppet to configure and prevent configuration drift in a large number of client computers. If all your client computers are easily reached via a central location, you may choose to have a central Puppet server control all the client computers. In the centralized model, the Puppet server is known as the Puppet master. We will cover how to configure a central Puppet master in a few sections.

If your client computers are widely distributed or you cannot guarantee communication between the client computers and a central location, then a decentralized architecture may be a good fit for your deployment. In the next few sections, we will see how to configure a decentralized Puppet architecture.

As we have seen, we can run the `puppet apply` command directly on a manifest file to have Puppet apply it. The problem with this arrangement is that we need to have the manifests transferred to the client computers.

We can use the Git repository we created in the previous section to transfer our manifests to each new node we create.

Getting ready

Create a new test node, call this new node whatever you wish, I'll use `testnode` for mine. Install Puppet on the machine as we have previously done.

How to do it...

Create a `bootstrap.pp` manifest that will perform the following configuration steps on our new node:

1. Install Git:

    ```
    package {'git':
      ensure => 'installed'
    }
    ```

2. Install the `ssh` key to access `git.example.com` in the Puppet user's home directory (`/var/lib/puppet/.ssh/id_rsa`):

    ```
    File {
      owner => 'puppet',
      group => 'puppet',
    }
    file {'/var/lib/puppet/.ssh':
      ensure => 'directory',
    }
    file {'/var/lib/puppet/.ssh/id_rsa':
    ```

```
  content => "
-----BEGIN RSA PRIVATE KEY-----
  ...
NIjTXmZUlOKefh4MBilqUU3KQG8GBHjzYl2TkFVGLNYGNA0U8VG8SUJq
-----END RSA PRIVATE KEY-----
",
  mode     => 0600,
  require => File['/var/lib/puppet/.ssh']
}
```

3. Download the `ssh` host key from `git.example.com` (`/var/lib/puppet/.ssh/known_hosts`):

```
exec {'download git.example.com host key':
  command => 'sudo -u puppet ssh-keyscan git.example.com >> /var/lib/puppet/.ssh/known_hosts',
  path     => '/usr/bin:/usr/sbin:/bin:/sbin',
  unless  => 'grep git.example.com /var/lib/puppet/.ssh/known_hosts',
  require => File['/var/lib/puppet/.ssh'],
}
```

4. Create a directory to contain the Git repository (`/etc/puppet/cookbook`):

```
file {'/etc/puppet/cookbook':
  ensure => 'directory',
}
```

5. Clone the Puppet repository onto the new machine:

```
exec {'create cookbook':
  command => 'sudo -u puppet git clone git@git.example.com:repos/puppet.git /etc/puppet/cookbook',
  path     => '/usr/bin:/usr/sbin:/bin:/sbin',
  require => [Package['git'],File['/var/lib/puppet/.ssh/id_rsa'],Exec['download git.example.com host key']],
  unless  => 'test -f /etc/puppet/cookbook/.git/config',
}
```

6. Now when we run Puppet apply on the new machine, the `ssh` key will be installed for the Puppet user. The Puppet user will then clone the Git repository into `/etc/puppet/cookbook`:

```
root@testnode /tmp# puppet apply bootstrap.pp
Notice: Compiled catalog for testnode.example.com in environment
production in 0.40 seconds
Notice: /Stage[main]/Main/File[/etc/puppet/cookbook]/ensure:
created
Notice: /Stage[main]/Main/File[/var/lib/puppet/.ssh]/ensure:
created
```

```
Notice: /Stage[main]/Main/Exec[download git.example.com host key]/
returns: executed successfully

Notice: /Stage[main]/Main/File[/var/lib/puppet/.ssh/id_rsa]/
ensure: defined content as '{md5}da61ce6ccc79bc6937bd98c798bc9fd3'

Notice: /Stage[main]/Main/Exec[create cookbook]/returns: executed
successfully

Notice: Finished catalog run in 0.82 seconds
```

> You may have to disable the `tty` requirement of `sudo`. Comment out the line `Defaults requiretty` at `/etc/sudoers` if you have this line. Alternatively, you can set `user => Puppet` within the `'create cookbook'` `exec` type. Beware that using the user attribute will cause any error messages from the command to be lost.

7. Now that your Puppet code is available on the new node, you can apply it using `puppet apply`, specifying that `/etc/puppet/cookbook/modules` will contain the modules:

```
root@testnode ~# puppet apply --modulepath=/etc/puppet/cookbook/
modules /etc/puppet/cookbook/manifests/site.pp
Notice: Compiled catalog for testnode.example.com in environment
production in 0.12 seconds
Notice: /Stage[main]/Base/File[/etc/motd]/content: content changed
'{md5}86d28ff83a8d49d349ba56b5c64b79ee' to '{md5}4c4c3ab7591d94031
8279d78b9c51d4f'
Notice: Finished catalog run in 0.11 seconds
root@testnode /tmp# cat /etc/motd
testnode.example.com
Managed by puppet 3.6.2
```

How it works...

First, our `bootstrap.pp` manifest ensures that Git is installed. The manifest then goes on to ensure that the `ssh` key for the Git user on `git.example.com` is installed into the Puppet user's home directory (`/var/lib/puppet` by default). The manifest then ensures that the host key for `git.example.com` is trusted by the Puppet user. With `ssh` configured, the bootstrap ensures that `/etc/puppet/cookbook` exists and is a directory.

We then use an `exec` to have Git clone the repository into `/etc/puppet/cookbook`. With all the code in place, we then call `puppet apply` a final time to deploy the code from the repository. In a production setting, you would distribute the `bootstrap.pp` manifest to all your nodes, possibly via an internal web server, using a method similar to curl `http://puppet/bootstrap.pp >bootstrap.pp && puppet apply bootstrap.pp`

Writing a papply script

We'd like to make it as quick and easy as possible to apply Puppet on a machine; for this we'll write a little script that wraps the `puppet apply` command with the parameters it needs. We'll deploy the script where it's needed with Puppet itself.

How to do it...

Follow these steps:

1. In your Puppet repo, create the directories needed for a Puppet module:

   ```
   t@mylaptop ~$ cd puppet/modules
   t@mylaptop modules$ mkdir -p puppet/{manifests,files}
   ```

2. Create the `modules/puppet/files/papply.sh` file with the following contents:

   ```
   #!/bin/sh
   sudo puppet apply /etc/puppet/cookbook/manifests/site.pp \
       --modulepath=/etc/puppet/cookbook/modules $*
   ```

3. Create the `modules/puppet/manifests/init.pp` file with the following contents:

   ```
   class puppet {
     file { '/usr/local/bin/papply':
       source => 'puppet:///modules/puppet/papply.sh',
       mode   => '0755',
     }
   }
   ```

4. Modify your `manifests/site.pp` file as follows:

   ```
   node default {
     include base
     include puppet
   }
   ```

5. Add the Puppet module to the Git repository and commit the change as follows:

   ```
   t@mylaptop puppet$ git add manifests/site.pp modules/puppet
   t@mylaptop puppet$ git status
   On branch master
   Your branch is up-to-date with 'origin/master'.
   Changes to be committed:
       (use "git reset HEAD <file>..." to unstage)
   modified:   manifests/site.pp
   ```

```
new file:    modules/puppet/files/papply.sh
new file:    modules/puppet/manifests/init.pp

t@mylaptop puppet$ git commit -m "adding puppet module to include
papply"

[master 7c2e3d5] adding puppet module to include papply
 3 files changed, 11 insertions(+)
 create mode 100644 modules/puppet/files/papply.sh
 create mode 100644 modules/puppet/manifests/init.pp
```

6. Now remember to push the changes to the Git repository on `git.example.com`:

```
t@mylaptop puppet$ git push origin master
Counting objects: 14, done.
Delta compression using up to 4 threads.
Compressing objects: 100% (7/7), done.
Writing objects: 100% (10/10), 894 bytes | 0 bytes/s, done.
Total 10 (delta 0), reused 0 (delta 0)
To git@git.example.com:repos/puppet.git
   23e887c..7c2e3d5  master -> master
```

7. Pull the latest version of the Git repository to your new node (`testnode` for me) as shown in the following command line:

```
root@testnode ~# sudo -iu puppet

puppet@testnode ~$ cd /etc/puppet/cookbook/
puppet@testnode /etc/puppet/cookbook$ git pull origin master
remote: Counting objects: 14, done.
remote: Compressing objects: 100% (7/7), done.
remote: Total 10 (delta 0), reused 0 (delta 0)
Unpacking objects: 100% (10/10), done.
From git.example.com:repos/puppet
 * branch            master      -> FETCH_HEAD
Updating 23e887c..7c2e3d5
Fast-forward
 manifests/site.pp                      |   1 +
 modules/puppet/files/papply.sh         |   4 ++++
 modules/puppet/manifests/init.pp       |   6 ++++++
 3 files changed, 11 insertions(+), 0 deletions(-)
 create mode 100644 modules/puppet/files/papply.sh
 create mode 100644 modules/puppet/manifests/init.pp
```

8. Apply the manifest manually once to install the `papply` script:

```
root@testnode ~# puppet apply /etc/puppet/cookbook/manifests/site.
pp --modulepath /etc/puppet/cookbook/modules

Notice: Compiled catalog for testnode.example.com in environment
production in 0.13 seconds
```

```
Notice: /Stage[main]/Puppet/File[/usr/local/bin/papply]/ensure:
defined content as '{md5}d5c2cdd359306dd6e6441e6fb96e5ef7'

Notice: Finished catalog run in 0.13 seconds
```

9. Finally, test the script:

```
root@testnode ~# papply
Notice: Compiled catalog for testnode.example.com in environment
production in 0.13 seconds

Notice: Finished catalog run in 0.09 seconds
```

Now, whenever you need to run Puppet, you can simply run `papply`. In future, when we apply Puppet changes, I'll ask you to run `papply` instead of the full `puppet apply` command.

How it works...

As you've seen, to run Puppet on a machine and apply a specified manifest file, we use the `puppet apply` command:

puppet apply manifests/site.pp

When you're using modules (such as the Puppet module we just created), you also need to tell Puppet where to search for modules, using the `modulepath` argument:

```
puppet apply manifests/nodes.pp \
   --modulepath=/home/ubuntu/puppet/modules
```

In order to run Puppet with the root privileges it needs, we have to put `sudo` before everything:

```
sudo puppet apply manifests/nodes.pp \
   --modulepath=/home/ubuntu/puppet/modules
```

Finally, any additional arguments passed to `papply` will be passed through to Puppet itself, by adding the `$*` parameter:

```
sudo puppet apply manifests/nodes.pp \
   --modulepath=/home/ubuntu/puppet/modules $*
```

That's a lot of typing, so putting this in a script makes sense. We've added a Puppet file resource that will deploy the script to `/usr/local/bin` and make it executable:

```
file { '/usr/local/bin/papply':
  source => 'puppet:///modules/puppet/papply.sh',
  mode   => '0755',
}
```

Finally, we include the Puppet module in our default node declaration:

```
node default {
```

```
    include base
    include puppet
}
```

You can do the same for any other nodes managed by Puppet.

Running Puppet from cron

You can do a lot with the setup you already have: work on your Puppet manifests as a team, communicate changes via a central Git repository, and manually apply them on a machine using the `papply` script.

However, you still have to log into each machine to update the Git repo and rerun Puppet. It would be helpful to have each machine update itself and apply any changes automatically. Then all you need to do is to push a change to the repo, and it will go out to all your machines within a certain time.

The simplest way to do this is with a **cron** job that pulls updates from the repo at regular intervals and then runs Puppet if anything has changed.

Getting ready

You'll need the Git repo we set up in the *Managing your manifests with Git* and *Creating a decentralized Puppet architecture* recipes, and the `papply` script from the *Writing a papply script* recipe. You'll need to apply the `bootstrap.pp` manifest we created to install `ssh` keys to download the latest repository.

How to do it...

Follow these steps:

1. Copy the `bootstrap.pp` script to any node you wish to enroll. The `bootstrap.pp` manifest includes the private key used to access the Git repository, it should be protected in a production environment.

2. Create the `modules/puppet/files/pull-updates.sh` file with the following contents:

   ```
   #!/bin/sh
   cd /etc/puppet/cookbook
   sudo -u puppet git pull && /usr/local/bin/papply
   ```

3. Modify the `modules/puppet/manifests/init.pp` file and add the following snippet after the `papply` file definition:

   ```
   file { '/usr/local/bin/pull-updates':
     source => 'puppet:///modules/puppet/pull-updates.sh',
   ```

```
    mode    => '0755',
}
cron { 'run-puppet':
  ensure  => 'present',
  user    => 'puppet',
  command => '/usr/local/bin/pull-updates',
  minute  => '*/10',
  hour    => '*',
}
```

4. Commit the changes as before and push to the Git server as shown in the following command line:

```
t@mylaptop puppet$ git add modules/puppet
t@mylaptop puppet$ git commit -m "adding pull-updates"
[master 7e9bac3] adding pull-updates
 2 files changed, 14 insertions(+)
 create mode 100644 modules/puppet/files/pull-updates.sh
t@mylaptop puppet$ git push
Counting objects: 14, done.
Delta compression using up to 4 threads.
Compressing objects: 100% (7/7), done.
Writing objects: 100% (8/8), 839 bytes | 0 bytes/s, done.
Total 8 (delta 0), reused 0 (delta 0)
To git@git.example.com:repos/puppet.git
    7c2e3d5..7e9bac3  master -> master
```

5. Issue a Git pull on the test node:

```
root@testnode ~# cd /etc/puppet/cookbook/

root@testnode /etc/puppet/cookbook# sudo -u puppet git pull

remote: Counting objects: 14, done.

remote: Compressing objects: 100% (7/7), done.

remote: Total 8 (delta 0), reused 0 (delta 0)

Unpacking objects: 100% (8/8), done.

From git.example.com:repos/puppet

    23e887c..7e9bac3  master      -> origin/master

Updating 7c2e3d5..7e9bac3

Fast-forward

 modules/puppet/files/pull-updates.sh |   3 +++

 modules/puppet/manifests/init.pp     |  11 +++++++++++

 2 files changed, 14 insertions(+), 0 deletions(-)

 create mode 100644 modules/puppet/files/pull-updates.sh
```

6. Run Puppet on the test node:

```
root@testnode /etc/puppet/cookbook# papply
Notice: Compiled catalog for testnode.example.com in environment
production in 0.17 seconds
Notice: /Stage[main]/Puppet/Cron[run-puppet]/ensure: created
Notice: /Stage[main]/Puppet/File[/usr/local/bin/pull-updates]/
ensure: defined content as '{md5}04c023feb5d566a417b519ea51586398'
Notice: Finished catalog run in 0.16 seconds
```

7. Check that the `pull-updates` script works properly:

```
root@testnode /etc/puppet/cookbook# pull-updates
Already up-to-date.
Notice: Compiled catalog for testnode.example.com in environment
production in 0.15 seconds
Notice: Finished catalog run in 0.14 seconds
```

8. Verify the `cron` job was created successfully:

```
root@testnode /etc/puppet/cookbook# crontab -l -u puppet
# HEADER: This file was autogenerated at Tue Sep 09 02:31:00 -0400
2014 by puppet.
# HEADER: While it can still be managed manually, it is definitely
not recommended.
# HEADER: Note particularly that the comments starting with
'Puppet Name' should
# HEADER: not be deleted, as doing so could cause duplicate cron
jobs.
# Puppet Name: run-puppet
*/10 * * * * /usr/local/bin/pull-updates
```

How it works...

When we created the `bootstrap.pp` manifest, we made sure that the Puppet user can checkout the Git repository using an `ssh` key. This enables the Puppet user to run the Git pull in the cookbook directory unattended. We've also added the `pull-updates` script, which does this and runs Puppet if any changes are pulled:

```
#!/bin/sh
cd /etc/puppet/cookbook
sudo -u puppet git pull && papply
```

We deploy this script to the node with Puppet:

```
file { '/usr/local/bin/pull-updates':
  source => 'puppet:///modules/puppet/pull-updates.sh',
  mode   => '0755',
}
```

Finally, we've created a `cron` job that runs `pull-updates` at regular intervals (every 10 minutes, but feel free to change this if you need to):

```
cron { 'run-puppet':
  ensure  => 'present',
  command => '/usr/local/bin/pull-updates',
  minute  => '*/10',
  hour    => '*',
}
```

There's more...

Congratulations, you now have a fully-automated Puppet infrastructure! Once you have applied the `bootstrap.pp` manifest, run Puppet on the repository; the machine will be set up to pull any new changes and apply them automatically.

So, for example, if you wanted to add a new user account to all your machines, all you have to do is add the account in your working copy of the manifest, and commit and push the changes to the central Git repository. Within 10 minutes, it will automatically be applied to every machine that's running Puppet.

Bootstrapping Puppet with bash

Previous versions of this book used Rakefiles to bootstrap Puppet. The problem with using Rake to configure a node is that you are running the commands from your laptop; you assume you already have `ssh` access to the machine. Most bootstrap processes work by issuing an easy to remember command from a node once it has been provisioned. In this section, we'll show how to use bash to bootstrap Puppet with a web server and a bootstrap script.

Getting ready

Install httpd on a centrally accessible server and create a password protected area to store the bootstrap script. In my example, I'll use the Git server I set up previously, `git.example.com`. Start by creating a directory in the root of your web server:

```
# cd /var/www/html
# mkdir bootstrap
```

Now perform the following steps:

1. Add the following location definition to your apache configuration:

    ```
    <Location /bootstrap>
    AuthType basic
    AuthName "Bootstrap"
    AuthBasicProvider file
    AuthUserFile /var/www/puppet.passwd
    Require valid-user
    </Location>
    ```

2. Reload your web server to ensure the location configuration is operating. Verify with curl that you cannot download from the bootstrap directory without authentication:

    ```
    [root@bootstrap-test tmp]# curl http://git.example.com/bootstrap/

    <!DOCTYPE HTML PUBLIC "-//IETF//DTD HTML 2.0//EN">

    <html><head>

    <title>401 Authorization Required</title>

    </head><body>

    <h1>Authorization Required</h1>
    ```

3. Create the password file you referenced in the apache configuration (`/var/www/puppet.passwd`):

    ```
    root@git# cd /var/www
    root@git# htpasswd -cb puppet.passwd bootstrap cookbook
    Adding password for user bootstrap
    ```

4. Verify that the username and password permit access to the bootstrap directory as follows:

    ```
    [root@node1 tmp]# curl --user bootstrap:cookbook http://git.example.com/bootstrap/

    <!DOCTYPE HTML PUBLIC "-//W3C//DTD HTML 3.2 Final//EN">

    <html>

     <head>

      <title>Index of /bootstrap</title>
    ```

How to do it...

Now that you have a safe location to store the bootstrap script, create a bootstrap script for each OS you support in the bootstrap directory. In this example, I'll show you how to do this for a Red Hat Enterprise Linux 6-based distribution.

Although the bootstrap location requires a password, there is no encryption since we haven't configured SSL on our server. Without encryption, the location is not very safe.

Create a script named `el6.sh` in the bootstrap directory with the following contents:

```bash
#!/bin/bash

# bootstrap for EL6 distributions
SERVER=git.example.com
LOCATION=/bootstrap
BOOTSTRAP=bootstrap.pp
USER=bootstrap
PASS=cookbook

# install puppet
curl http://yum.puppetlabs.com/RPM-GPG-KEY-puppetlabs >/etc/pki/rpm-
gpg/RPM-GPG-KEY-puppetlabs
rpm --import /etc/pki/rpm-gpg/RPM-GPG-KEY-puppetlabs
yum -y install http://yum.puppetlabs.com/puppetlabs-release-el-6.
noarch.rpm
yum -y install puppet
# download bootstrap
curl --user $USER:$PASS http://$SERVER/$LOCATION/$BOOTSTRAP >/
tmp/$BOOTSTRAP
# apply bootstrap
cd /tmp
puppet apply /tmp/$BOOTSTRAP
# apply puppet
puppet apply --modulepath /etc/puppet/cookbook/modules /etc/puppet/
cookbook/manifests/site.pp
```

How it works...

The apache configuration only permits access to the bootstrap directory with a username and password combination. We supply these with the `--user` argument to curl, thereby getting access to the file. We use a pipe (|) to redirect the output of curl into bash. This causes bash to execute the script. We write our bash script like we would any other bash script. The bash script downloads our `bootstrap.pp` manifest and applies it. Finally, we apply the Puppet manifest from the Git repository and the machine is configured as a member of our decentralized infrastructure.

There's more...

To support another operating system, we only need to create a new bash script. All Linux distributions will support bash scripting, Mac OS X does as well. Since we placed much of our logic into the `bootstrap.pp` manifest, the bootstrap script is quite minimal and easy to port to new operating systems.

Creating a centralized Puppet infrastructure

A configuration management tool such as Puppet is best used when you have many machines to manage. If all the machines can reach a central location, using a centralized Puppet infrastructure might be a good solution. Unfortunately, Puppet doesn't scale well with a large number of nodes. If your deployment has less than 800 servers, a single Puppet master should be able to handle the load, assuming your catalogs are not complex (take less than 10 seconds to compile each catalog). If you have a larger number of nodes, I suggest a load balancing configuration described in *Mastering Puppet, Thomas Uphill, Packt Publishing*.

A Puppet master is a Puppet server that acts as an X509 certificate authority for Puppet and distributes catalogs (compiled manifests) to client nodes. Puppet ships with a built-in web server called **WEBrick,** which can handle a very small number of nodes. In this section, we will see how to use that built-in server to control a very small (less than 10) number of nodes.

Getting ready

The Puppet master process is started by running `puppet master`; most Linux distributions have start and stop scripts for the Puppet master in a separate package. To get started, we'll create a new debian server named `puppet.example.com`.

How to do it...

1. Install Puppet on the new server and then use Puppet to install the Puppet master package:

    ```
    # puppet resource package puppetmaster ensure='installed'
    Notice: /Package[puppetmaster]/ensure: created
    package { 'puppetmaster':
      ensure => '3.7.0-1puppetlabs1',
    }
    ```

2. Now start the Puppet master service and ensure it will start at boot:

    ```
    # puppet resource service puppetmaster ensure=true enable=true
    service { 'puppetmaster':
      ensure => 'running',
      enable => 'true',
    }
    ```

How it works...

The Puppet master package includes the start and stop scripts for the Puppet master service. We use Puppet to install the package and start the service. Once the service is started, we can point another node at the Puppet master (you might need to disable the host-based firewall on your machine).

1. From another node, run `puppet agent` to start a `puppet agent`, which will contact the server and request a new certificate:

   ```
   t@ckbk:~$ sudo puppet agent -t
   Info: Creating a new SSL key for cookbook.example.com
   Info: Caching certificate for ca
   Info: Creating a new SSL certificate request for cookbook.example.
   com
   Info: Certificate Request fingerprint (SHA256): 06:C6:2B:C4:97:5D:
   16:F2:73:82:C4:A9:A7:B1:D0:95:AC:69:7B:27:13:A9:1A:4C:98:20:21:C2:
   50:48:66:A2
   Info: Caching certificate for ca
   Exiting; no certificate found and waitforcert is disabled
   ```

2. Now on the Puppet server, sign the new key:

   ```
   root@puppet:~# puppet cert list
   pu  "cookbook.example.com" (SHA256) 06:C6:2B:C4:97:5D:16:F2:73:82:
   C4:A9:A7:B1:D0:95:AC:69:7B:27:13:A9:1A:4C:98:20:21:C2:50:48:66:A2
   root@puppet:~# puppet cert sign cookbook.example.com
   Notice: Signed certificate request for cookbook.example.com
   Notice: Removing file Puppet::SSL::CertificateRequest
   cookbook.example.com at
   '/var/lib/puppet/ssl/ca/requests/cookbook.example.com.pem'
   ```

3. Return to the cookbook node and run Puppet again:

   ```
   t@ckbk:~$ sudo puppet agent -vt
   Info: Caching certificate for cookbook.example.com
   Info: Caching certificate_revocation_list for ca
   Info: Caching certificate for cookbook.example.comInfo: Retrieving
   pluginfacts
   Info: Retrieving plugin
   Info: Caching catalog for cookbook
   Info: Applying configuration version '1410401823'
   Notice: Finished catalog run in 0.04 seconds
   ```

There's more...

When we ran `puppet agent`, Puppet looked for a host named `puppet.example.com` (since our test node is in the `example.com` domain); if it couldn't find that host, it would then look for a host named Puppet. We can specify the server to contact with the `--server` option to `puppet agent`. When we installed the Puppet master package and started the Puppet master service, Puppet created default SSL certificates based on our hostname. In the next section, we'll see how to create an SSL certificate that has multiple DNS names for our Puppet server.

Creating certificates with multiple DNS names

By default, Puppet will create an SSL certificate for your Puppet master that contains the fully qualified domain name of the server only. Depending on how your network is configured, it can be useful for the server to be known by other names. In this recipe, we'll make a new certificate for our Puppet master that has multiple DNS names.

Getting ready

Install the Puppet master package if you haven't already done so. You will then need to start the Puppet master service at least once to create a **certificate authority (CA)**.

How to do it...

The steps are as follows:

1. Stop the running Puppet master process with the following command:

   ```
   # service puppetmaster stop
   [ ok ] Stopping puppet master.
   ```

2. Delete (`clean`) the current server certificate:

   ```
   # puppet cert clean puppet
   Notice: Revoked certificate with serial 6
   Notice: Removing file Puppet::SSL::Certificate puppet at '/var/lib/puppet/ssl/ca/signed/puppet.pem'
   Notice: Removing file Puppet::SSL::Certificate puppet at '/var/lib/puppet/ssl/certs/puppet.pem'
   Notice: Removing file Puppet::SSL::Key puppet at '/var/lib/puppet/ssl/private_keys/puppet.pem'
   ```

3. Create a new Puppet certificate using Puppet certificate generate with the `--dns-alt-names` option:

```
root@puppet:~# puppet certificate generate puppet --dns-alt-names
puppet.example.com,puppet.example.org,puppet.example.net --ca-
location local
Notice: puppet has a waiting certificate request
true
```

4. Sign the new certificate:

```
root@puppet:~# puppet cert --allow-dns-alt-names sign puppet
Notice: Signed certificate request for puppet
Notice: Removing file Puppet::SSL::CertificateRequest puppet at '/
var/lib/puppet/ssl/ca/requests/puppet.pem'
```

5. Restart the Puppet master process:

```
root@puppet:~# service puppetmaster restart
[ ok ] Restarting puppet master.
```

How it works...

When your puppet agents connect to the Puppet server, they look for a host called `Puppet`, they then look for a host called `Puppet.[your domain]`. If your clients are in different domains, then you need your Puppet master to reply to all the names correctly. By removing the existing certificate and generating a new one, you can have your Puppet master reply to multiple DNS names.

Running Puppet from passenger

The WEBrick server we configured in the previous section is not capable of handling a large number of nodes. To deal with a large number of nodes, a scalable web server is required. Puppet is a ruby process, so we need a way to run a ruby process within a web server. **Passenger** is the solution to this problem. It allows us to run the Puppet master process within a web server (apache by default). Many distributions ship with a puppetmaster-passenger package that configures this for you. In this section, we'll use the package to configure Puppet to run within passenger.

Getting ready

Install the puppetmaster-passenger package:

```
# puppet resource package puppetmaster-passenger ensure=installed
Notice: /Package[puppetmaster-passenger]/ensure: ensure changed 'purged'
```

```
  to 'present'
package { 'puppetmaster-passenger':
  ensure => '3.7.0-1puppetlabs1',
}
```

 Using `puppet resource` to install packages ensures the same command will work on multiple distributions (provided the package names are the same).

How to do it...

The steps are as follows:

1. Ensure the Puppet master site is enabled in your apache configuration. Depending on your distribution this may be at `/etc/httpd/conf.d` or `/etc/apache2/sites-enabled`. The configuration file should be created for you and contain the following information:

    ```
    PassengerHighPerformance on

    PassengerMaxPoolSize 12

    PassengerPoolIdleTime 1500

    # PassengerMaxRequests 1000

    PassengerStatThrottleRate 120

    RackAutoDetect Off

    RailsAutoDetect Off

    Listen 8140
    ```

2. These lines are tuning settings for passenger. The file then instructs apache to listen on port 8140, the Puppet master port. Next a `VirtualHost` definition is created that loads the Puppet CA certificates and the Puppet master's certificate:

    ```
    <VirtualHost *:8140>
            SSLEngine on
            SSLProtocol            ALL -SSLv2 -SSLv3
            SSLCertificateFile     /var/lib/puppet/ssl/certs/puppet.
    pem
            SSLCertificateKeyFile  /var/lib/puppet/ssl/private_keys/
    puppet.pem
            SSLCertificateChainFile /var/lib/puppet/ssl/certs/ca.pem
            SSLCACertificateFile   /var/lib/puppet/ssl/certs/ca.pem
            SSLCARevocationFile    /var/lib/puppet/ssl/ca/ca_crl.pem
    ```

```
SSLVerifyClient optional
SSLVerifyDepth  1
SSLOptions +StdEnvVars +ExportCertData
```

 You may have more or less lines of SSL configuration here depending on your version of the puppetmaster-passenger package.

3. Next, a few important headers are set so that the passenger process has access to the SSL information sent by the client node:

```
RequestHeader unset X-Forwarded-For
RequestHeader set X-SSL-Subject %{SSL_CLIENT_S_DN}e
RequestHeader set X-Client-DN %{SSL_CLIENT_S_DN}e
RequestHeader set X-Client-Verify %{SSL_CLIENT_VERIFY}e
```

4. Finally, the location of the passenger configuration file `config.ru` is given with the `DocumentRoot` location as follows:

```
DocumentRoot /usr/share/puppet/rack/puppetmasterd/public/
RackBaseURI /
```

5. The `config.ru` file should exist at `/usr/share/puppet/rack/puppetmasterd/` and should have the following content:

```
$0 = "master"
ARGV << "--rack"
ARGV << "--confdir" << "/etc/puppet"
ARGV << "--vardir"  << "/var/lib/puppet"
require 'puppet/util/command_line'
run Puppet::Util::CommandLine.new.execute
```

6. With the passenger apache configuration file in place and the `config.ru` file correctly configured, start the apache server and verify that apache is listening on the Puppet master port (if you configured the standalone Puppet master previously, you must stop that process now using `service puppetmaster stop`):

```
root@puppet:~ # service apache2 start
[ ok ] Starting web server: apache2
root@puppet:~ # lsof -i :8140
COMMAND  PID     USER    FD    TYPE DEVICE SIZE/OFF NODE NAME
apache2 9048    root    8u   IPv6  16842      0t0  TCP *:8140
(LISTEN)
```

```
apache2 9069 www-data    8u  IPv6  16842     0t0  TCP *:8140
(LISTEN)

apache2 9070 www-data    8u  IPv6  16842     0t0  TCP *:8140
(LISTEN)
```

How it works...

The passenger configuration file uses the existing Puppet master certificates to listen on port 8140 and handles all the SSL communication between the server and the client. Once the certificate information has been dealt with, the connection is handed off to a ruby process started from passenger using the command line arguments from the config.ru file.

In this case, the $0 variable is set to master and the arguments variable is set to --rack --confdir /etc/puppet --vardir /var/lib/puppet; this is equivalent to running the following from the command line:

```
puppet master --rack --confdir /etc/puppet --vardir /var/lib/puppet
```

There's more...

You can add additional configuration parameters to the config.ru file to further alter how Puppet runs when it's running through passenger. For instance, to enable debugging on the passenger Puppet master, add the following line to config.ru before the run Puppet::Util::CommandLine.new.execute line:

```
ARGV << "--debug"
```

Setting up the environment

Environments in Puppet are directories holding different versions of your Puppet manifests. Environments prior to Version 3.6 of Puppet were not a default configuration for Puppet. In newer versions of Puppet, environments are configured by default.

Whenever a node connects to a Puppet master, it informs the Puppet master of its environment. By default, all nodes report to the production environment. This causes the Puppet master to look in the production environment for manifests. You may specify an alternate environment with the --environment setting when running puppet agent or by setting environment = newenvironment in /etc/puppet/puppet.conf in the [agent] section.

Getting ready

Set the `environmentpath` function of your installation by adding a line to the `[main]` section of `/etc/puppet/puppet.conf` as follows:

```
[main]
...
environmentpath=/etc/puppet/environments
```

How to do it...

The steps are as follows:

1. Create a `production` directory at `/etc/puppet/environments` that contains both a `modules` and `manifests` directory. Then create a `site.pp` which creates a file in `/tmp` as follows:

   ```
   root@puppet:~# cd /etc/puppet/environments/
   root@puppet:/etc/puppet/environments# mkdir -p production/
   {manifests,modules}
   root@puppet:/etc/puppet/environments# vim production/manifests/
   site.pp
   node default {
     file {'/tmp/production':
       content => "Hello World!\nThis is production\n",
     }
   }
   ```

2. Run puppet agent on the master to connect to it and verify that the production code was delivered:

   ```
   root@puppet:~# puppet agent -vt
   Info: Retrieving pluginfacts
   Info: Retrieving plugin
   Info: Caching catalog for puppet
   Info: Applying configuration version '1410415538'
   Notice: /Stage[main]/Main/Node[default]/File[/tmp/production]/
   ensure: defined content as '{md5}f7ad9261670b9da33a67a5126933044c'
   Notice: Finished catalog run in 0.04 seconds
   # cat /tmp/production
   Hello World!
   This is production
   ```

3. Configure another environment `devel`. Create a new manifest in the `devel` environment:

```
root@puppet:/etc/puppet/environments# mkdir -p devel/
{manifests,modules}
root@puppet:/etc/puppet/environments# vim devel/manifests/site.pp
node default {
  file {'/tmp/devel':
    content => "Good-bye! Development\n",
  }
}
```

4. Apply the new environment by running the `--environment devel` puppet agent using the following command:

```
root@puppet:/etc/puppet/environments# puppet agent -vt
--environment devel
Info: Retrieving pluginfacts
Info: Retrieving plugin
Info: Caching catalog for puppet
Info: Applying configuration version '1410415890'
Notice: /Stage[main]/Main/Node[default]/File[/tmp/devel]/ensure:
defined content as '{md5}b6313bb89bc1b7d97eae5aa94588eb68'
Notice: Finished catalog run in 0.04 seconds
root@puppet:/etc/puppet/environments# cat /tmp/devel
Good-bye! Development
```

 You may need to restart apache2 to enable your new environment, this depends on your version of Puppet and the `environment_timeout` parameter of `puppet.conf`.

There's more...

Each environment can have its own `modulepath` if you create an `environment.conf` file within the environment directory. More information on environments can be found on the Puppet labs website at `https://docs.puppetlabs.com/puppet/latest/reference/environments.html`.

Configuring PuppetDB

PuppetDB is a database for Puppet that is used to store information about nodes connected to a Puppet master. PuppetDB is also a storage area for exported resources. Exported resources are resources that are defined on nodes but applied to other nodes. The simplest way to install PuppetDB is to use the PuppetDB module from Puppet labs. From this point on, we'll assume you are using the `puppet.example.com` machine and have a passenger-based configuration of Puppet.

Getting ready

Install the PuppetDB module in the production environment you created in the previous recipe. If you didn't create directory environments, don't worry, using `puppet module install` will install the module to the correct location for your installation with the following command:

```
root@puppet:~# puppet module install puppetlabs-puppetdb
Notice: Preparing to install into /etc/puppet/environments/production/
modules ...
Notice: Downloading from https://forgeapi.puppetlabs.com ...
Notice: Installing -- do not interrupt ...
/etc/puppet/environments/production/modules
└─┬ puppetlabs-puppetdb (v3.0.1)
  ├── puppetlabs-firewall (v1.1.3)
  ├── puppetlabs-inifile (v1.1.3)
  └─┬ puppetlabs-postgresql (v3.4.2)
    ├─┬ puppetlabs-apt (v1.6.0)
    | └── puppetlabs-stdlib (v4.3.2)
    └── puppetlabs-concat (v1.1.0)
```

How to do it...

Now that our Puppet master has the PuppetDB module installed, we need to apply the PuppetDB module to our Puppet master, we can do this in the site manifest. Add the following to your (production) `site.pp`:

```
node puppet {
  class { 'puppetdb': }
  class { 'puppetdb::master::config':
    puppet_service_name => 'apache2',
  }
}
```

Run `puppet agent` to apply the `puppetdb` class and the `puppetdb::master::config` class:

```
root@puppet:~# puppet agent -t
Info: Caching catalog for puppet
Info: Applying configuration version '1410416952'
...
Info: Class[Puppetdb::Server::Jetty_ini]: Scheduling refresh of
Service[puppetdb]
Notice: Finished catalog run in 160.78 seconds
```

How it works...

The PuppetDB module is a great example of how a complex configuration task can be puppetized. Simply by adding the `puppetdb` class to our Puppet master node, Puppet installed and configured `postgresql` and `puppetdb`.

When we called the `puppetdb::master::config` class, we set the `puppet_service_name` variable to `apache2`, this is because we are running Puppet through passenger. Without this line our agent would try to start the puppetmaster process instead of `apache2`.

The agent then set up the configuration files for PuppetDB and configured Puppet to use PuppetDB. If you look at `/etc/puppet/puppet.conf`, you'll see the following two new lines:

```
storeconfigs = true
storeconfigs_backend = puppetdb
```

There's more...

Now that PuppetDB is configured and we've had a successful agent run, PuppetDB will have data we can query:

```
root@puppet:~# puppet node status puppet
puppet
Currently active
Last catalog: 2014-09-11T06:45:25.267Z
Last facts: 2014-09-11T06:45:22.351Z
```

Configuring Hiera

Hiera is an information repository for Puppet. Using Hiera you can have a hierarchical categorization of data about your nodes that is maintained outside of your manifests. This is very useful for sharing code and dealing with exceptions that will creep into any Puppet deployment.

Getting ready

Hiera should have already been installed as a dependency on your Puppet master. If it has not already, install it using Puppet:

```
root@puppet:~# puppet resource package hiera ensure=installed
package { 'hiera':
  ensure => '1.3.4-1puppetlabs1',
}
```

How to do it...

1. Hiera is configured from a yaml file, `/etc/puppet/hiera.yaml`. Create the file and add the following as a minimal configuration:

   ```
   ---
   :hierarchy:
     - common
   :backends:
     - yaml
   :yaml:
     :datadir: '/etc/puppet/hieradata'
   ```

2. Create the `common.yaml` file referenced in the hierarchy:

   ```
   root@puppet:/etc/puppet# mkdir hieradata
   root@puppet:/etc/puppet# vim hieradata/common.yaml
   ---
   message: 'Default Message'
   ```

3. Edit the `site.pp` file and add a notify resource based on the Hiera value:

   ```
   node default {
     $message = hiera('message','unknown')
     notify {"Message is $message":}
   }
   ```

4. Apply the manifest to a test node:

   ```
   t@ckbk:~$ sudo puppet agent -t
   Info: Retrieving pluginfacts
   Info: Retrieving plugin
   ...
   Info: Caching catalog for cookbook-test
   Info: Applying configuration version '1410504848'
   Notice: Message is Default Message
   ```

```
Notice: /Stage[main]/Main/Node[default]/Notify[Message is Default
Message]/message: defined 'message' as 'Message is Default
Message'

Notice: Finished catalog run in 0.06 seconds
```

How it works...

Hiera uses a hierarchy to search through a set of yaml files to find the appropriate values. We defined this hierarchy in `hiera.yaml` with the single entry for `common.yaml`. We used the `hiera` function in `site.pp` to lookup the value for message and store that value in the variable `$message`. The values used for the definition of the hierarchy can be any facter facts defined about the system. A common hierarchy is shown as:

```
:hierarchy:
    - hosts/%{hostname}
    - os/%{operatingsystem}
    - network/%{network_eth0}
    - common
```

There's more...

Hiera can be used for automatic parameter lookup with parameterized classes. For example, if you have a class named `cookbook::example` with a parameter named `publisher`, you can include the following in a Hiera yaml file to automatically set this parameter:

```
cookbook::example::publisher: 'PacktPub'
```

Another often used fact is `environment` you may reference the `environment` of the client node using `%{environment}` as shown in the following hierarchy:

```
:hierarchy:
hosts/%{hostname}
os/%{operatingsystem}
environment/%{environment}
common
```

 A good rule of thumb is to limit the hierarchy to 8 levels or less. Keep in mind that each time a parameter is searched with Hiera, all the levels are searched until a match is found.

The default Hiera function returns the first match to the search key, you can also use `hiera_array` and `hiera_hash` to search and return all values stored in Hiera.

Hiera can also be searched from the command line as shown in the following command line (note that currently the command line Hiera utility uses `/etc/hiera.yaml` as its configuration file whereas the Puppet master uses `/etc/puppet/hiera.yaml`):

```
root@puppet:/etc/puppet# rm /etc/hiera.yaml
root@puppet:/etc/puppet# ln -s /etc/puppet/hiera.yaml /etc/
root@puppet:/etc/puppet# hiera message
Default Message
```

 For more information, consult the Puppet labs website at `https://docs.puppetlabs.com/hiera/1/`.

Setting node-specific data with Hiera

In our hierarchy defined in `hiera.yaml`, we created an entry based on the hostname fact; in this section, we'll create yaml files in the `hosts` subdirectory of Hiera data with information specific to a particular host.

Getting ready

Install and configure Hiera as in the last section and use the hierarchy defined in the previous recipe that includes a `hosts/%{hostname}` entry.

How to do it...

The following are the steps:

1. Create a file at `/etc/puppet/hieradata/hosts` that is the hostname of your test node. For example if your host is named `cookbook-test`, then the file would be named `cookbook-test.yaml`.

2. Insert a specific message in this file:

    ```
    message: 'This is the test node for the cookbook'
    ```

3. Run Puppet on two different test nodes to note the difference:

    ```
    t@ckbk:~$ sudo puppet agent -t
    Info: Caching catalog for cookbook-test
    Notice: Message is This is the test node for the cookbook
    [root@hiera-test ~]# puppet agent -t
    Info: Caching catalog for hiera-test.example.com
    Notice: Message is Default Message
    ```

How it works...

Hiera searches the hierarchy for files that match the values returned by facter. In this case, the `cookbook-test.yaml` file is found by substituting the hostname of the node into the search path `/etc/puppet/hieradata/hosts/%{hostname}.yaml`.

Using Hiera, it is possible to greatly reduce the complexity of your Puppet code. We will use `yaml` files for separate values, where previously you had large `case` statements or nested `if` statements.

Storing secret data with hiera-gpg

If you're using Hiera to store your configuration data, there's a gem available called **hiera-gpg** that adds an encryption backend to Hiera to allow you to protect values stored in Hiera.

Getting ready

To set up hiera-gpg, follow these steps:

1. Install the `ruby-dev` package; it will be required to build the `hiera-gpg` gem as follows:

   ```
   root@puppet:~# puppet resource package ruby-dev ensure=installed
   Notice: /Package[ruby-dev]/ensure: ensure changed 'purged' to
   'present'
   package { 'ruby-dev':
     ensure => '1:1.9.3',
   }
   ```

2. Install the `hiera-gpg` gem using the gem provider:

   ```
   root@puppet:~# puppet resource package hiera-gpg ensure=installed
   provider=gem
   Notice: /Package[hiera-gpg]/ensure: created
   package { 'hiera-gpg':
     ensure => ['1.1.0'],
   }
   ```

3. Modify your `hiera.yaml` file as follows:

   ```
   :hierarchy:
       - secret
       - common
   :backends:
       - yaml
   ```

```
      - gpg
  :yaml:
      :datadir: '/etc/puppet/hieradata'
  :gpg:
      :datadir: '/etc/puppet/secret'
```

How to do it...

In this example, we'll create a piece of encrypted data and retrieve it using `hiera-gpg` as follows:

1. Create the `secret.yaml` file at `/etc/puppet/secret` with the following contents:

   `top_secret: 'Val Kilmer'`

2. If you don't already have a GnuPG encryption key, follow the steps in the *Using GnuPG to encrypt secrets* recipe in *Chapter 4, Working with Files and Packages*.

3. Encrypt the `secret.yaml` file to this key using the following command (replace the `puppet@puppet.example.com` with the e-mail address you specified when creating the key). This will create the `secret.gpg` file:

   `root@puppet:/etc/puppet/secret# gpg -e -o secret.gpg -r puppet@`
   `puppet.example.com secret.yaml`

   `root@puppet:/etc/puppet/secret# file secret.gpg`

   `secret.gpg: GPG encrypted data`

4. Remove the plaintext `secret.yaml` file:

   `root@puppet:/etc/puppet/secret# rm secret.yaml`

5. Modify your default node in the `site.pp` file as follows:

   ```
   node default {
      $message = hiera('top_secret','Deja Vu')
      notify { "Message is $message": }
   }
   ```

6. Now run Puppet on a node:

   `[root@hiera-test ~]# puppet agent -t`

   `Info: Caching catalog for hiera-test.example.com`

   `Info: Applying configuration version '1410508276'`

   `Notice: Message is Deja Vu`

   `Notice: /Stage[main]/Main/Node[default]/Notify[Message is Deja`
   `Vu]/message: defined 'message' as 'Message is Deja Vu'`

   `Notice: Finished catalog run in 0.08 seconds`

How it works...

When you install `hiera-gpg`, it adds to Hiera, the ability to decrypt `.gpg` files. So you can put any secret data into a `.yaml` file that you then encrypt to the appropriate key with GnuPG. Only machines that have the right secret key will be able to access this data.

For example, you might encrypt the MySQL root password using `hiera-gpg` and install the corresponding key only on your database servers. Although other machines may also have a copy of the `secret.gpg` file, it's not readable to them unless they have the decryption key.

There's more...

You might also like to know about `hiera-eyaml`, another secret-data backend for Hiera that supports encryption of individual values within a Hiera data file. This could be handy if you need to mix encrypted and unencrypted facts within a single file. Find out more about hiera-eyaml at `https://github.com/TomPoulton/hiera-eyaml`.

See also

▸   The *Using GnuPG to encrypt secrets* recipe in *Chapter 4, Working with Files and Packages*.

Using MessagePack serialization

Running Puppet in a centralized architecture creates a lot of traffic between nodes. The bulk of this traffic is JSON and yaml data. An experimental feature of the latest releases of Puppet allow for the serialization of this data using **MessagePack** (**msgpack**).

Getting ready

Install the msgpack gem onto your Puppet master and your nodes. Use Puppet to do the work for you with Puppet resource. You may need to install the `ruby-dev` or `ruby-devel` package on your nodes/server at this point:

```
t@ckbk:~$ sudo puppet resource package msgpack ensure=installed
 provider=gem
Notice: /Package[msgpack]/ensure: created
package { 'msgpack':
  ensure => ['0.5.8'],
}
```

How to do it...

Set the `preferred_serialization_format` to `msgpack` in the `[agent]` section of your nodes `puppet.conf` file:

```
[agent]
preferred_serialization_format=msgpack
```

How it works...

The master will be sent this option when the node begins communicating with the master. Any classes that support serialization with `msgpack` will be transmitted with `msgpack`. `Serialization` of the data between nodes and the master will in theory increase the speed at which nodes communicate by optimizing the data that is travelling between them. This feature is still experimental.

Automatic syntax checking with Git hooks

It would be nice if we knew there was a syntax error in the manifest before we even committed it. You can have Puppet check the manifest using the `puppet parser validate` command:

```
t@ckbk:~$ puppet parser validate bootstrap.pp
Error: Could not parse for environment production: Syntax error at
 'File'; expected '}' at /home/thomas/bootstrap.pp:3
```

This is especially useful because a mistake anywhere in the manifest will stop Puppet from running on any node, even on nodes that don't use that particular part of the manifest. So checking in a bad manifest can cause Puppet to stop applying updates to production for some time, until the problem is discovered, and this could potentially have serious consequences. The best way to avoid this is to automate the syntax check, by using a precommit hook in your version control repo.

How to do it...

Follow these steps:

1. In your Puppet repo, create a new `hooks` directory:

    ```
    t@mylaptop:~/puppet$ mkdir hooks
    ```

2. Create the file `hooks/check_syntax.sh` with the following contents (based on a script by Puppet Labs):

```sh
#!/bin/sh

syntax_errors=0
error_msg=$(mktemp /tmp/error_msg.XXXXXX)

if git rev-parse --quiet --verify HEAD > /dev/null
then
    against=HEAD
else
    # Initial commit: diff against an empty tree object
    against=4b825dc642cb6eb9a060e54bf8d69288fbee4904
fi

# Get list of new/modified manifest and template files
  to check (in git index)
for indexfile in 'git diff-index --diff-filter=AM --
  name-only --cached $against | egrep '\.(pp|erb)''
do
    # Don't check empty files
    if [ 'git cat-file -s :0:$indexfile' -gt 0 ]
    then
        case $indexfile in
            *.pp )
                # Check puppet manifest syntax
                git cat-file blob :0:$indexfile |
                   puppet parser validate > $error_msg ;;
            *.erb )
                # Check ERB template syntax
                git cat-file blob :0:$indexfile |
                   erb -x -T - | ruby -c 2> $error_msg >
                     /dev/null ;;
        esac
        if [ "$?" -ne 0 ]
        then
            echo -n "$indexfile: "
            cat $error_msg
            syntax_errors='expr $syntax_errors + 1'
        fi
    fi
done

rm -f $error_msg

if [ "$syntax_errors" -ne 0 ]
```

```
then
    echo "Error: $syntax_errors syntax errors found,
      aborting commit."
    exit 1
fi
```

3. Set execute permission for the `hook` script with the following command:

    t@mylaptop:~/puppet$ chmod a+x hooks/check_syntax.sh

4. Now either symlink or copy the script to the precommit hook in your hooks directory. If your Git repo is checked out in `~/puppet`, then create the symlink at `~/puppet/hooks/pre-commit` as follows:

    t@mylaptop:~/puppet$ ln -s ~/puppet/hooks/check_syntax.sh .git/hooks/pre-commit

How it works...

The `check_syntax.sh` script will prevent you from committing any files with syntax errors when it is used as the pre-commit hook for Git:

t@mylaptop:~/puppet$ git commit -m "test commit"

Error: Could not parse for environment production: Syntax error at '}' at line 3

Error: Try 'puppet help parser validate' for usage

manifests/nodes.pp: Error: 1 syntax errors found, aborting commit.

If you add the `hooks` directory to your Git repo, anyone who has a checkout can copy the script into their local `hooks` directory to get this syntax checking behavior.

Pushing code around with Git

As we have already seen in the decentralized model, Git can be used to transfer files between machines using a combination of `ssh` and `ssh` keys. It can also be useful to have a Git hook do the same on each successful commit to the repository.

There exists a hook called post-commit that can be run after a successful commit to the repository. In this recipe, we'll create a hook that updates the code on our Puppet master with code from our Git repository on the Git server.

Getting ready

Follow these steps to get started:

1. Create an `ssh` key that can access your Puppet user on your Puppet master and install this key into the Git user's account on `git.example.com`:

    ```
    [git@git ~]$ ssh-keygen -f ~/.ssh/puppet_rsa
    Generating public/private rsa key pair.
    Your identification has been saved in /home/git/.ssh/puppet_rsa.
    Your public key has been saved in /home/git/.ssh/puppet_rsa.pub.
    Copy the public key into the authorized_keys file of the puppet
    user on your puppetmaster
    puppet@puppet:~/.ssh$ cat puppet_rsa.pub >>authorized_keys
    ```

2. Modify the Puppet account to allow the Git user to log in as follows:

    ```
    root@puppet:~# chsh puppet -s /bin/bash
    ```

How to do it...

Perform the following steps:

1. Now that the Git user can log in to the Puppet master as the Puppet user, modify the Git user's `ssh` configuration to use the newly created `ssh` key by default:

    ```
    [git@git ~]$ vim .ssh/config
    Host puppet.example.com
        IdentityFile ~/.ssh/puppet_rsa
    ```

2. Add the Puppet master as a remote location for the Puppet repository on the Git server with the following command:

    ```
    [git@git puppet.git]$ git remote add puppetmaster puppet@puppet.
    example.com:/etc/puppet/environments/puppet.git
    ```

3. On the Puppet master, move the `production` directory out of the way and check out your Puppet repository:

    ```
    root@puppet:~# chown -R puppet:puppet /etc/puppet/environments
    root@puppet:~# sudo -iu puppet
    puppet@puppet:~$ cd /etc/puppet/environments/
    puppet@puppet:/etc/puppet/environments$ mv production production.
    orig
    puppet@puppet:/etc/puppet/environments$ git clone git@git.example.
    com:repos/puppet.git
    ```

```
Cloning into 'puppet.git'...
remote: Counting objects: 63, done.
remote: Compressing objects: 100% (52/52), done.
remote: Total 63 (delta 10), reused 0 (delta 0)
Receiving objects: 100% (63/63), 9.51 KiB, done.
Resolving deltas: 100% (10/10), done.
```

4. Now we have a local bare repository on the Puppet server that we can push to, to remotely clone this into the `production` directory:

```
puppet@puppet:/etc/puppet/environments$ git clone puppet.git
production
Cloning into 'production'...
done.
```

5. Now perform a Git push from the Git server to the Puppet master:

```
[git@git ~]$ cd repos/puppet.git/
[git@git puppet.git]$ git push puppetmaster
Everything up-to-date
```

6. Create a post-commit file in the `hooks` directory of the repository on the Git server with the following contents:

```
[git@git puppet.git]$ vim hooks/post-commit
#!/bin/sh
git push puppetmaster
ssh puppet@puppet.example.com "cd /etc/puppet/environments/
production && git pull"
[git@git puppet.git]$ chmod 755 hooks/post-commit
```

7. Commit a change to the repository from your laptop and verify that the change is propagated to the Puppet master as follows:

```
t@mylaptop puppet$ vim README
t@mylaptop puppet$ git add README
t@mylaptop puppet$ git commit -m "Adding README"
[master 8148902] Adding README
 1 file changed, 4 deletions(-)
t@mylaptop puppet$ git push
X11 forwarding request failed on channel 0
Counting objects: 5, done.
Delta compression using up to 4 threads.
```

```
Compressing objects: 100% (3/3), done.
Writing objects: 100% (3/3), 371 bytes | 0 bytes/s, done.
Total 3 (delta 1), reused 0 (delta 0)
remote: To puppet@puppet.example.com:/etc/puppet/environments/
puppet.git
remote:    377ed44..8148902  master -> master
remote: From /etc/puppet/environments/puppet
remote:    377ed44..8148902  master      -> origin/master
remote: Updating 377ed44..8148902
remote: Fast-forward
remote:  README |    4 ----
remote:  1 file changed, 4 deletions(-)
To git@git.example.com:repos/puppet.git
    377ed44..8148902  master -> master
```

How it works...

We created a bare repository on the Puppet master that we then use as a remote for the repository on `git.example.com` (remote repositories must be bare). We then clone that bare repository into the `production` directory. We add the bare repository on `puppet.example.com` as a remote to the bare repository on `git.example.com`. We then create a post-receive hook in the repository on `git.example.com`.

The hook issues a Git push to the Puppet master bare repository. We then update the `production` directory from the updated bare repository on the Puppet master. In the next section, we'll modify the hook to use branches.

Managing Environments with Git

Branches are a way of keeping several different tracks of development within a single source repository. Puppet environments are a lot like Git branches. You can have the same code with slight variations between branches, just as you can have different modules for different environments. In this section, we'll show how to use Git branches to define environments on the Puppet master.

Getting ready

In the previous section, we created a `production` directory that was based on the master branch; we'll remove that directory now:

```
puppet@puppet:/etc/puppet/environments$ mv production production.master
```

How to do it...

Modify the `post-receive` hook to accept a branch variable. The hook will use this variable to create a directory on the Puppet master as follows:

```
#!/bin/sh

read oldrev newrev refname
branch=${refname#*\/*\/}

git push puppetmaster $branch
ssh puppet@puppet.example.com "if [ ! -d
/etc/puppet/environments/$branch ]; then git clone
 /etc/puppet/environments/puppet.git
 /etc/puppet/environments/$branch; fi; cd
 /etc/puppet/environments/$branch; git checkout $branch; git pull"
```

Modify your README file again and push to the repository on `git.example.com`:

```
t@mylaptop puppet$ git add README
t@mylaptop puppet$ git commit -m "Adding README"
[master 539d9f8] Adding README
 1 file changed, 1 insertion(+)
t@mylaptop puppet$ git push
Counting objects: 5, done.
Delta compression using up to 4 threads.
Compressing objects: 100% (3/3), done.
Writing objects: 100% (3/3), 374 bytes | 0 bytes/s, done.
Total 3 (delta 1), reused 0 (delta 0)
remote: To puppet@puppet.example.com:/etc/puppet/environments/puppet.git
remote:    0d6b49f..539d9f8  master -> master
remote: Cloning into '/etc/puppet/environments/master'...
remote: done.
remote: Already on 'master'
remote: Already up-to-date.
To git@git.example.com:repos/puppet.git
   0d6b49f..539d9f8  master -> master
```

How it works...

The hook now reads in the `refname` and parses out the branch that is being updated. We use that branch variable to clone the repository into a new directory and check out the branch.

There's more...

Now when we want to create a new environment, we can create a new branch in the Git repository. The branch will create a directory on the Puppet master. Each branch of the Git repository represents an environment on the Puppet master:

1. Create the production branch as shown in the following command line:

```
t@mylaptop puppet$ git branch production
t@mylaptop puppet$ git checkout production
Switched to branch 'production'
```

2. Update the production branch and push to the Git server as follows:

```
t@mylaptop puppet$ vim README
t@mylaptop puppet$ git add README
t@mylaptop puppet$ git commit -m "Production Branch"
t@mylaptop puppet$ git push origin production
Counting objects: 7, done.
Delta compression using up to 4 threads.
Compressing objects: 100% (3/3), done.
Writing objects: 100% (3/3), 372 bytes | 0 bytes/s, done.
Total 3 (delta 1), reused 0 (delta 0)
remote: To puppet@puppet.example.com:/etc/puppet/environments/
puppet.git
remote:    11db6e5..832f6a9  production -> production
remote: Cloning into '/etc/puppet/environments/production'...
remote: done.
remote: Switched to a new branch 'production'
remote: Branch production set up to track remote branch production
from origin.
remote: Already up-to-date.
To git@git.example.com:repos/puppet.git
   11db6e5..832f6a9  production -> production
```

Now whenever we create a new branch, a corresponding directory is created in our environment's directory. A one-to-one mapping is established between environments and branches.

3
Writing Better Manifests

"Measuring programming progress by lines of code is like measuring aircraft building progress by weight."

— *Bill Gates*

In this chapter, we will cover:

- Using arrays of resources
- Using resource defaults
- Using defined types
- Using tags
- Using run stages
- Using roles and profiles
- Passing parameters to classes
- Passing parameters from Hiera
- Writing reusable, cross-platform manifests
- Getting information about the environment
- Importing dynamic information
- Passing arguments to shell commands

Introduction

Your Puppet manifests are the living documentation for your entire infrastructure. Keeping them tidy and well organized is a great way to make it easier to maintain and understand. Puppet gives you a number of tools to do this, as follows:

- ▸ Arrays
- ▸ Defaults
- ▸ Defined types
- ▸ Dependencies
- ▸ Class parameters

We'll see how to use all of these and more. As you read through the chapter, try out the examples and look through your own manifests to see where these features might help you simplify and improve your Puppet code.

Using arrays of resources

Anything that you can do to a resource, you can do to an array of resources. Use this idea to refactor your manifests to make them shorter and clearer.

How to do it...

Here are the steps to refactor using arrays of resources:

1. Identify a class in your manifest where you have several instances of the same kind of resource, for example, packages:

```
package { 'sudo' : ensure => installed }
package { 'unzip' : ensure => installed }
package { 'locate' : ensure => installed }
package { 'lsof' : ensure => installed }
package { 'cron' : ensure => installed }
package { 'rubygems' : ensure => installed }
```

2. Group them together and replace them with a single package resource using an array:

```
package
{
   [ 'cron',
   'locate',
```

```
        'lsof',
        'rubygems',
        'sudo',
        'unzip' ] :
        ensure => installed,
    }
```

How it works...

Most of Puppet's resource types can accept an array instead of a single name, and will create one instance for each of the elements in the array. All the parameters you provide for the resource (for example, `ensure => installed`) will be assigned to each of the new resource instances. This shorthand will only work when all the resources have the same attributes.

See also

▶ The *Iterating over multiple items* recipe in *Chapter 1, Puppet Language and Style*

Using resource defaults

A Puppet module is a group of related resources, usually grouped to configure a specific service. Within a module, you may define multiple resources; resource defaults allow you to specify the default attribute values for a resource. In this example, we'll show you how to specify a resource default for the `File` type.

How to do it...

To show you how to use resource defaults, we'll create an apache module. Within this module we will specify that the default owner and group are the `apache` user as follows:

1. Create an apache module and create a resource default for the `File` type:

```
class apache {
  File {
    owner => 'apache',
    group => 'apache',
    mode => 0644,
  }
}
```

2. Create html files within the `/var/www/html` directory:

```
file {'/var/www/html/index.html':
  content => "<html><body><h1><a
    href='cookbook.html'>Cookbook!
    </a></h1></body></html>\n",
}
file {'/var/www/html/cookbook.html':
  content =>
    "<html><body><h2>PacktPub</h2></body></html>\n",
}
```

3. Add this class to your default node definition, or use `puppet apply` to apply the module to your node. I will use the method we configured in the previous chapter, pushing our code to the Git repository and using a Git hook to have the code deployed to the Puppet master as follows:

```
t@mylaptop ~/puppet $ git pull origin production
From git.example.com:repos/puppet
 * branch              production -> FETCH_HEAD
Already up-to-date.
t@mylaptop ~/puppet $ cd modules
t@mylaptop ~/puppet/modules $ mkdir -p apache/manifests
t@mylaptop ~/puppet/modules $ vim apache/manifests/init.pp
t@mylaptop ~/puppet/modules $ cd ..
t@mylaptop ~/puppet $ vim manifests/site.pp
t@mylaptop ~/puppet $ git status
On branch production
Changes not staged for commit:
modified:   manifests/site.pp
Untracked files:
modules/apache/
t@mylaptop ~/puppet $ git add manifests/site.pp modules/apache
t@mylaptop ~/puppet $ git commit -m 'adding apache module'
[production d639a86] adding apache module
 2 files changed, 14 insertions(+)
 create mode 100644 modules/apache/manifests/init.pp
t@mylaptop ~/puppet $ git push origin production
```

```
Counting objects: 13, done.

Delta compression using up to 4 threads.

Compressing objects: 100% (6/6), done.

Writing objects: 100% (8/8), 885 bytes | 0 bytes/s, done.

Total 8 (delta 0), reused 0 (delta 0)

remote: To puppet@puppet.example.com:/etc/puppet/environments/
puppet.git

remote:    832f6a9..d639a86  production -> production

remote: Already on 'production'

remote: From /etc/puppet/environments/puppet

remote:    832f6a9..d639a86  production -> origin/production

remote: Updating 832f6a9..d639a86

remote: Fast-forward

remote:  manifests/site.pp                    |   1 +

remote:  modules/apache/manifests/init.pp |  13 ++++++++++++++

remote:  2 files changed, 14 insertions(+)

remote:  create mode 100644 modules/apache/manifests/init.pp

To git@git.example.com:repos/puppet.git

   832f6a9..d639a86  production -> production
```

4. Apply the module to a node or run Puppet:

```
Notice: /Stage[main]/Apache/File[/var/www/html/cookbook.html]/
ensure: defined content as '{md5}493473fb5bde778ca93d034900348c5d'

Notice: /Stage[main]/Apache/File[/var/www/html/index.html]/ensure:
defined content as '{md5}184f22c181c5632b86ebf9a0370685b3'

Notice: Finished catalog run in 2.00 seconds

[root@hiera-test ~]# ls -l /var/www/html

total 8

-rw-r--r--. 1 apache apache 44 Sep 15 12:00 cookbook.html

-rw-r--r--. 1 apache apache 73 Sep 15 12:00 index.html
```

How it works...

The resource default we defined specifies the owner, group, and mode for all file resources within this class (also known as within this scope). Unless you specifically override a resource default, the value for an attribute will be taken from the default.

There's more...

You can specify resource defaults for any resource type. You can also specify resource defaults in `site.pp`. I find it useful to specify the default action for `Package` and `Service` resources as follows:

```
Package { ensure => 'installed' }
Service {
  hasrestart => true,
  enable     => true,
  ensure     => true,
}
```

With these defaults, whenever you specify a package, the package will be installed. Whenever you specify a service, the service will be started and enabled to run at boot. These are the usual reasons you specify packages and services, most of the time these defaults will do what you prefer and your code will be cleaner. When you need to disable a service, simply override the defaults.

Using defined types

In the previous example, we saw how to reduce redundant code by grouping identical resources into arrays. However, this technique is limited to resources where all the parameters are the same. When you have a set of resources that have some parameters in common, you need to use a defined type to group them together.

How to do it...

The following steps will show you how to create a definition:

1. Add the following code to your manifest:

   ```
   define tmpfile() {
     file { "/tmp/${name}":
       content => "Hello, world\n",
     }
   }
   tmpfile { ['a', 'b', 'c']: }
   ```

2. Run Puppet:

   ```
   [root@hiera-test ~]# vim tmp.pp
   [root@hiera-test ~]# puppet apply tmp.pp
   ```

```
Notice: Compiled catalog for hiera-test.example.com in environment
production in 0.11 seconds
Notice: /Stage[main]/Main/Tmpfile[a]/File[/tmp/a]/ensure: defined
content as '{md5}a7966bf58e23583c9a5a4059383ff850'
Notice: /Stage[main]/Main/Tmpfile[b]/File[/tmp/b]/ensure: defined
content as '{md5}a7966bf58e23583c9a5a4059383ff850'
Notice: /Stage[main]/Main/Tmpfile[c]/File[/tmp/c]/ensure: defined
content as '{md5}a7966bf58e23583c9a5a4059383ff850'
Notice: Finished catalog run in 0.09 seconds
[root@hiera-test ~]# cat /tmp/{a,b,c}
Hello, world
Hello, world
Hello, world
```

How it works...

You can think of a defined type (introduced with the define keyword) as a cookie-cutter. It describes a pattern that Puppet can use to create lots of similar resources. Any time you declare a tmpfile instance in your manifest, Puppet will insert all the resources contained in the tmpfile definition.

In our example, the definition of tmpfile contains a single file resource whose content is Hello, world\n and whose path is /tmp/${name}. If you declared an instance of tmpfile with the name foo:

```
tmpfile { 'foo': }
```

Puppet will create a file with the path /tmp/foo. In other words, ${name} in the definition will be replaced by the name of any actual instance that Puppet is asked to create. It's almost as though we created a new kind of resource: tmpfile, which has one parameter—its name.

Just like with regular resources, we don't have to pass just one title; as in the preceding example, we can provide an array of titles and Puppet will create as many resources as required.

 A word on name, the namevar: Every resource you create must have a unique name, the namevar. This is different than the title, which is how puppet refers to the resource internally (although they are often the same).

There's more...

In the example, we created a definition where the only parameter that varies between instances is the `name` parameter. But we can add whatever parameters we want, so long as we declare them in the definition in parentheses after the `name` parameter, as follows:

```
define tmpfile($greeting) {
  file { "/tmp/${name}":
    content => $greeting,
  }
}
```

Next, pass values to them when we declare an instance of the resource:

```
tmpfile{ 'foo':
  greeting => "Good Morning\n",
}
```

You can declare multiple parameters as a comma-separated list:

```
define webapp($domain,$path,$platform) {
  ...
}
webapp { 'mywizzoapp':
  domain   => 'mywizzoapp.com',
  path     => '/var/www/apps/mywizzoapp',
  platform => 'Rails',
}
```

You can also declare default values for any parameters that aren't supplied, thus making them optional:

```
define tmpfile($greeting,$mode='0644') {
  ...
}
```

This is a powerful technique for abstracting out everything that's common to certain resources, and keeping it in one place so that you *don't repeat yourself*. In the preceding example, there might be many individual resources contained within `webapp`: packages, config files, source code checkouts, virtual hosts, and so on. But all of them are the same for every instance of `webapp` except the parameters we provide. These might be referenced in a template, for example, to set the domain for a virtual host.

▶ The *Passing parameters to classes* recipe, in this chapter

Using tags

Sometimes one Puppet class needs to know about another or at least to know whether or not it's present. For example, a class that manages the firewall may need to know whether or not the node is a web server.

Puppet's `tagged` function will tell you whether a named class or resource is present in the catalog for this node. You can also apply arbitrary tags to a node or class and check for the presence of these tags. Tags are another metaparameter, similar to `require` and `notify` we introduced in *Chapter 1, Puppet Language and Style*. Metaparameters are used in the compilation of the Puppet catalog but are not an attribute of the resource to which they are attached.

To help you find out if you're running on a particular node or class of nodes all nodes are automatically tagged with the node name and the names of any classes they include. Here's an example that shows you how to use `tagged` to get this information:

1. Add the following code to your `site.pp` file (replacing `cookbook` with your machine's `hostname`):

```
node 'cookbook' {
  if tagged('cookbook') {
    notify { 'tagged cookbook': }
  }
}
```

2. Run Puppet:

```
root@cookbook:~# puppet agent -vt
Info: Caching catalog for cookbook
Info: Applying configuration version '1410848350'
Notice: tagged cookbook
Notice: Finished catalog run in 1.00 seconds
```

Nodes are also automatically tagged with the names of all the classes they include in addition to several other automatic tags. You can use `tagged` to find out what classes are included on the node.

You're not just limited to checking the tags automatically applied by Puppet. You can also add your own. To set an arbitrary tag on a node, use the `tag` function, as in the following example:

3. Modify your `site.pp` file as follows:

```
node 'cookbook' {
  tag('tagging')
  class {'tag_test': }
}
```

4. Add a `tag_test` module with the following `init.pp` (or be lazy and add the following definition to your `site.pp`):

```
class tag_test {
  if tagged('tagging') {
    notify { 'containing node/class was tagged.': }
  }
}
```

5. Run Puppet:

```
root@cookbook:~# puppet agent -vt
Info: Caching catalog for cookbook
Info: Applying configuration version '1410851300'
Notice: containing node/class was tagged.
Notice: Finished catalog run in 0.22 seconds
```

6. You can also use tags to determine which parts of the manifest to apply. If you use the `--tags` option on the Puppet command line, Puppet will apply only those classes or resources tagged with the specific tags you include. For example, we can define our `cookbook` class with two classes:

```
node cookbook {
  class {'first_class': }
  class {'second_class': }
}
class first_class {
  notify { 'First Class': }
}
```

```
class second_class {
  notify {'Second Class': }
}
```

7. Now when we run `puppet agent` on the `cookbook` node, we see both notifies:

    ```
    root@cookbook:~# puppet agent -t
    Notice: Second Class
    Notice: First Class
    Notice: Finished catalog run in 0.22 seconds
    ```

8. Now apply the `first_class` and add `--tags` function to the command line:

    ```
    root@cookbook:~# puppet agent -t --tags first_class
    Notice: First Class
    Notice: Finished catalog run in 0.07 seconds
    ```

There's more...

You can use tags to create a collection of resources, and then make the collection a dependency for some other resource. For example, say some service depends on a config file that is built from a number of file snippets, as in the following example:

```
class firewall::service {
  service { 'firewall':
    ...
  }
  File <| tag == 'firewall-snippet' |> ~> Service['firewall']
}
class myapp {
  file { '/etc/firewall.d/myapp.conf':
    tag => 'firewall-snippet',
    ...
  }
}
```

Here, we've specified that the `firewall` service should be notified if any file resource tagged `firewall-snippet` is updated. All we need to do to add a `firewall` config snippet for any particular application or service is to tag it `firewall-snippet`, and Puppet will do the rest.

Although we could add a `notify => Service["firewall"]` function to each snippet resource if our definition of the `firewall` service were ever to change, we would have to hunt down and update all the snippets accordingly. The tag lets us encapsulate the logic in one place, making future maintenance and refactoring much easier.

 What's `<| tag == 'firewall-snippet' |>` `syntax`? This is called a resource collector, and it's a way of specifying a group of resources by searching for some piece of data about them; in this case, the value of a tag. You can find out more about resource collectors and the `<| |>` operator (sometimes known as the spaceship operator) on the Puppet Labs website: `http://docs.puppetlabs.com/puppet/3/reference/lang_collectors.html`.

Using run stages

A common requirement is to apply a certain group of resources before other groups (for example, installing a package repository or a custom Ruby version), or after others (for example, deploying an application once its dependencies are installed). Puppet's run stages feature allows you to do this.

By default, all resources in your manifest are applied in a single stage named `main`. If you need a resource to be applied before all others, you can assign it to a new run stage that is specified to come before `main`. Similarly, you could define a run stage that comes after `main`. In fact, you can define as many run stages as you need and tell Puppet which order they should be applied in.

In this example, we'll use stages to ensure one class is applied first and another last.

How to do it...

Here are the steps to create an example of using run `stages`:

1. Create the file `modules/admin/manifests/stages.pp` with the following contents:

    ```
    class admin::stages {
      stage { 'first': before => Stage['main'] }
      stage { 'last': require => Stage['main'] }
      class me_first {
        notify { 'This will be done first': }
      }
    ```

```
    class me_last {
      notify { 'This will be done last': }
    }
    class { 'me_first':
      stage => 'first',
    }
    class { 'me_last':
      stage => 'last',
    }
  }
```

2. Modify your `site.pp` file as follows:

```
node 'cookbook' {
  class {'first_class': }
  class {'second_class': }
  include admin::stages
}
```

3. Run Puppet:

```
root@cookbook:~# puppet agent -t
Info: Applying configuration version '1411019225'
Notice: This will be done first
Notice: Second Class
Notice: First Class
Notice: This will be done last
Notice: Finished catalog run in 0.43 seconds
```

How it works...

Let's examine this code in detail to see what's happening. First, we declare the run stages `first` and `last`, as follows:

```
stage { 'first': before => Stage['main'] }
stage { 'last': require => Stage['main'] }
```

For the `first` stage, we've specified that it should come before `main`. That is, every resource marked as being in the `first` stage will be applied before any resource in the `main` stage (the default stage).

The `last` stage requires the `main` stage, so no resource in the `last` stage can be applied until after every resource in the `main` stage.

We then declare some classes that we'll later assign to these run stages:

```
class me_first {
  notify { 'This will be done first': }
}
class me_last {
  notify { 'This will be done last': }
}
```

We can now put it all together and include these classes on the node, specifying the run stages for each as we do so:

```
class { 'me_first':
  stage => 'first',
}
class { 'me_last':
  stage => 'last',
}
```

Note that in the `class` declarations for `me_first` and `me_last`, we didn't have to specify that they take a `stage` parameter. The `stage` parameter is another metaparameter, which means it can be applied to any class or resource without having to be explicitly declared. When we ran `puppet agent` on our Puppet node, the notify from the `me_first` class was applied before the notifies from `first_class` and `second_class`. The notify from `me_last` was applied after the `main` stage, so it comes after the two notifies from `first_class` and `second_class`. If you run `puppet agent` multiple times, you will see that the notifies from `first_class` and `second_class` may not always appear in the same order but the `me_first` class will always come first and the `me_last` class will always come last.

There's more...

You can define as many run stages as you like, and set up any ordering for them. This can greatly simplify a complicated manifest that would otherwise require lots of explicit dependencies between resources. Beware of accidentally introducing dependency cycles, though; when you assign something to a run stage you're automatically making it dependent on everything in prior stages.

You may like to define your stages in the `site.pp` file instead, so that at the top level of the manifest, it's easy to see what stages are available.

Gary Larizza has written a helpful introduction to using run stages, with some real-world examples, on his website:

```
http://garylarizza.com/blog/2011/03/11/using-run-stages-with-puppet/
```

A caveat: many people don't like to use run stages, feeling that Puppet already provides sufficient resource ordering control, and that using run stages indiscriminately can make your code very hard to follow. The use of run stages should be kept to a minimum wherever possible. There are a few key examples where the use of stages creates less complexity. The most notable is when a resource modifies the system used to install packages on the system. It helps to have a package management stage that comes before the main stage. When packages are defined in the `main` (default) stage, your manifests can count on the updated package management configuration information being present. For instance, for a Yum-based system, you would create a `yumrepos` stage that comes before `main`. You can specify this dependency using chaining arrows as shown in the following code snippet:

```
stage {'yumrepos': }
Stage['yumrepos'] -> Stage['main']
```

We can then create a class that creates a Yum repository (`yumrepo`) resource and assign it to the `yumrepos` stage as follows:

```
class {'yums':
  stage => 'yumrepos',
}
class yums {
  notify {'always before the rest': }
  yumrepo {'testrepo':
    baseurl => 'file:///var/yum',
    ensure  => 'present',
  }
}
```

For Apt-based systems, the same example would be a stage where Apt sources are defined. The key with stages is to keep their definitions in your `site.pp` file where they are highly visible and to only use them sparingly where you can guarantee that you will not introduce dependency cycles.

See also

- The *Using tags* recipe, in this chapter
- The *Drawing dependency graphs* recipe in *Chapter 10, Monitoring, Reporting, and Troubleshooting*

Using roles and profiles

Well organized Puppet manifests are easy to read; the purpose of a module should be evident in its name. The purpose of a node should be defined in a single class. This single class should include all classes that are required to perform that purpose. Craig Dunn wrote a post about such a classification system, which he dubbed "roles and profiles" (`http://www.craigdunn.org/2012/05/239/`). In this model, roles are the single purpose of a node, a node may only have one role, a role may contain more than one profile, and a profile contains all the resources related to a single service. In this example, we will create a web server role that uses several profiles.

How to do it...

We'll create two modules to store our roles and profiles. Roles will contain one or more profiles. Each role or profile will be defined as a subclass, such as `profile::base`

1. Decide on a naming strategy for your roles and profiles. In our example, we will create two modules, `roles` and `profiles` that will contain our roles and profiles respectively:

```
$ puppet module generate thomas-profiles
$ ln -s thomas-profiles profiles
$ puppet module generate thomas-roles
$ ln -s thomas-roles roles
```

2. Begin defining the constituent parts of our `webserver` role as profiles. To keep this example simple, we will create two profiles. First, a `base` profile to include our basic server configuration classes. Second, an `apache` class to install and configure the apache web server (`httpd`) as follows:

```
$ vim profiles/manifests/base.pp

class profiles::base {

  include base

}
$ vim profiles/manifests/apache.pp

class profiles::apache {

  $apache = $::osfamily ? {

    'RedHat' => 'httpd',

    'Debian' => 'apache2',

  }

  service { "$apache":
```

```
        enable => true,

        ensure => true,

    }

    package { "$apache":

        ensure => 'installed',

    }

}
```

3. Define a `roles::webserver` class for our `webserver` role as follows:

    `$ vim roles/manifests/webserver.pp`

    ```
    class roles::webserver {

      include profiles::apache

      include profiles::base

    }
    ```

4. Apply the `roles::webserver` class to a node. In a centralized installation, you would use either an **External Node Classifier** (**ENC**) to apply the class to the node, or you would use Hiera to define the role:

    ```
    node 'webtest' {
      include roles::webserver
    }
    ```

How it works...

Breaking down the parts of the web server configuration into different profiles allows us to apply those parts independently. We created a base profile that we can expand to include all the resources we would like applied to all nodes. Our `roles::webserver` class simply includes the `base` and `apache` classes.

There's more...

As we'll see in the next section, we can pass parameters to classes to alter how they work. In our `roles::webserver` class, we can use the class instantiation syntax instead of `include`, and override it with `parameters` in the classes. For instance, to pass a parameter to the `base` class, we would use:

```
class {'profiles::base':
  parameter => 'newvalue'
}
```

where we previously used:

```
include profiles::base
```

 In previous versions of this book, node and class inheritance were used to achieve a similar goal, code reuse. Node inheritance is deprecated in Puppet Version 3.7 and higher. Node and class inheritance should be avoided. Using roles and profiles achieves the same level of readability and is much easier to follow.

Passing parameters to classes

Sometimes it's very useful to parameterize some aspect of a class. For example, you might need to manage different versions of a gem package, and rather than making separate classes for each that differ only in the version number, you can pass in the version number as a parameter.

How to do it...

In this example, we'll create a definition that accepts parameters:

1. Declare the parameter as a part of the class definition:

```
class eventmachine($version) {
  package { 'eventmachine':
    provider => gem,
    ensure   => $version,
  }
}
```

2. Use the following syntax to include the class on a node:

```
class { 'eventmachine':
  version => '1.0.3',
}
```

How it works...

The class definition `class eventmachine($version)` { is just like a normal class definition except it specifies that the class takes one parameter: $version. Inside the class, we've defined a package resource:

```
package { 'eventmachine':
  provider => gem,
  ensure   => $version,
}
```

This is a `gem` package, and we're requesting to install version `$version`.

Include the class on a node, instead of the usual `include` syntax:

```
include eventmachine
```

On doing so, there will be a `class` statement:

```
class { 'eventmachine':
  version => '1.0.3',
}
```

This has the same effect but also sets a value for the parameter as `version`.

There's more...

You can specify multiple parameters for a class as:

```
class mysql($package, $socket, $port) {
```

Then supply them in the same way:

```
class { 'mysql':
  package => 'percona-server-server-5.5',
  socket  => '/var/run/mysqld/mysqld.sock',
  port    => '3306',
}
```

Specifying default values

You can also give default values for some of your parameters. When you include the class without setting a parameter, the default value will be used. For instance, if we created a `mysql` class with three parameters, we could provide default values for any or all of the parameters as shown in the code snippet:

```
class mysql($package, $socket, $port='3306') {
```

or all:

```
class mysql(
  package = "percona-server-server-5.5",
  socket  = '/var/run/mysqld/mysqld.sock',
  port    = '3306') {
```

Defaults allow you to use a default value and override that default where you need it.

Unlike a definition, only one instance of a parameterized class can exist on a node. So where you need to have several different instances of the resource, use `define` instead.

Passing parameters from Hiera

Like the parameter `defaults` we introduced in the previous chapter, Hiera may be used to provide default values to classes. This feature requires Puppet Version 3 and higher.

Getting ready

Install and configure `hiera` as we did in *Chapter 2, Puppet Infrastructure*. Create a global or common `yaml` file; this will serve as the default for all values.

How to do it...

1. Create a class with parameters and no default values:

   ```
   t@mylaptop ~/puppet $ mkdir -p modules/mysql/manifests t@mylaptop
   ~/puppet $ vim modules/mysql/manifests/init.pp

   class mysql ( $port, $socket, $package ) {

     notify {"Port: $port Socket: $socket Package: $package": }

   }
   ```

2. Update your common `.yaml` file in Hiera with the default values for the `mysql` class:

   ```
   ---
   mysql::port: 3306

   mysql::package: 'mysql-server'

   mysql::socket: '/var/lib/mysql/mysql.sock'
   ```

   Apply the class to a node, you can add the mysql class to your default node for now.

   ```
   node default {

     class {'mysql': }

   }
   ```

3. Run `puppet agent` and verify the output:

   ```
   [root@hiera-test ~]# puppet agent -t

   Info: Caching catalog for hiera-test.example.com

   Info: Applying configuration version '1411182251'

   Notice: Port: 3306 Socket: /var/lib/mysql/mysql.sock Package:
   mysql-server
   ```

```
Notice: /Stage[main]/Mysql/Notify[Port: 3306 Socket: /var/lib/
mysql/mysql.sock Package: mysql-server]/message: defined 'message'
as 'Port: 3306 Socket: /var/lib/mysql/mysql.sock Package: mysql-
server'

Notice: Finished catalog run in 1.75 seconds
```

How it works...

When we instantiate the `mysql` class in our manifest, we provided no values for any of the attributes. Puppet knows to look for a value in Hiera that matches `class_name::parameter_name:` or `::class_name::parameter_name:`.

When Puppet finds a value, it uses it as the parameter for the class. If Puppet fails to find a value in Hiera and no default is defined, a catalog failure will result in the following command line:

```
Error: Could not retrieve catalog from remote server: Error 400 on
SERVER: Must pass package to Class[Mysql] at /etc/puppet/environments/
production/manifests/site.pp:6 on node hiera-test.example.com
```

This error indicates that Puppet would like a value for the parameter `package`.

There's more...

You can define a Hiera hierarchy and supply different values for parameters based on facts. You could, for instance, have `%{::osfamily}` in your hierarchy and have different `yaml` files based on the `osfamily` parameter (RedHat, Suse, and Debian).

Writing reusable, cross-platform manifests

Every system administrator dreams of a unified, homogeneous infrastructure of identical machines all running the same version of the same OS. As in other areas of life, however, the reality is often messy and doesn't conform to the plan.

You are probably responsible for a bunch of assorted servers of varying age and architecture running different kernels from different OS distributions, often scattered across different data centers and ISPs.

This situation should strike terror into the hearts of the sysadmins of the SSH in a `for` loop persuasion, because executing the same commands on every server can have different, unpredictable, and even dangerous results.

We should certainly strive to bring older servers up to date and get working as far as possible on a single reference platform to make administration simpler, cheaper, and more reliable. But until we get there, Puppet makes coping with heterogeneous environments slightly easier.

How to do it...

Here are some examples of how to make your manifests more portable:

1. Where you need to apply the same manifest to servers with different OS distributions, the main differences will probably be the names of packages and services, and the location of config files. Try to capture all these differences into a single class by using selectors to set global variables:

    ```
    $ssh_service = $::operatingsystem? {
       /Ubuntu|Debian/ => 'ssh',
       default          => 'sshd',
    }
    ```

    You needn't worry about the differences in any other part of the manifest; when you refer to something, use the variable with confidence that it will point to the right thing in each environment:

    ```
    service { $ssh_service:
       ensure => running,
    }
    ```

2. Often we need to cope with mixed architectures; this can affect the paths to shared libraries, and also may require different versions of packages. Again, try to encapsulate all the required settings in a single architecture class that sets global variables:

    ```
    $libdir = $::architecture ? {
       /amd64|x86_64/   => '/usr/lib64',
       default => '/usr/lib',
    }
    ```

    Then you can use these wherever an architecture-dependent value is required in your manifests or even in templates:

    ```
    ; php.ini
    [PHP]
    ; Directory in which the loadable extensions (modules) reside.
    extension_dir = <%= @libdir %>/php/modules
    ```

How it works...

The advantage of this approach (which could be called top-down) is that you only need to make your choices once. The alternative, bottom-up approach would be to have a selector or `case` statement everywhere a setting is used:

```
service { $::operatingsystem? {
  /Ubuntu|Debian/ => 'ssh',
  default         => 'sshd' }:
  ensure => running,
}
```

This not only results in lots of duplication, but makes the code harder to read. And when a new operating system is added to the mix, you'll need to make changes throughout the whole manifest, instead of just in one place.

There's more...

If you are writing a module for public distribution (for example, on Puppet Forge), making your module as cross-platform as possible will make it more valuable to the community. As far as you can, test it on many different distributions, platforms, and architectures, and add the appropriate variables so that it works everywhere.

If you use a public module and adapt it to your own environment, consider updating the public version with your changes if you think they might be helpful to other people.

Even if you are not thinking of publishing a module, bear in mind that it may be in production use for a long time and may have to adapt to many changes in the environment. If it's designed to cope with this from the start, it'll make life easier for you or whoever ends up maintaining your code.

> *"Always code as if the guy who ends up maintaining your code will be a violent psychopath who knows where you live."*

> — *Dave Carhart*

See also

- ▶ The *Using public modules* recipe in *Chapter 7, Managing Applications*
- ▶ The *Configuring Hiera* recipe in *Chapter 2, Puppet Infrastructure*

Getting information about the environment

Often in a Puppet manifest, you need to know some local information about the machine you're on. Facter is the tool that accompanies Puppet to provide a standard way of getting information (facts) from the environment about things such as these:

- Operating system
- Memory size
- Architecture
- Processor count

To see a complete list of the facts available on your system, run:

```
$ sudo facter
architecture => amd64
augeasversion => 0.10.0
domain => compute-1.internal
ec2_ami_id => ami-137bcf7a
ec2_ami_launch_index => 0
```

 While it can be handy to get this information from the command line, the real power of Facter lies in being able to access these facts in your Puppet manifests.

Some modules define their own facts; to see any facts that have been defined locally, add the `-p (pluginsync)` option to facter as follows:

```
$ sudo facter -p
```

How to do it...

Here's an example of using Facter facts in a manifest:

1. Reference a Facter fact in your manifest like any other variable. Facts are global variables in Puppet, so they should be prefixed with a double colon (: :), as in the following code snippet:

   ```
   notify { "This is $::operatingsystem version
   $::operatingsystemrelease, on $::architecture architecture, kernel
   version $::kernelversion": }
   ```

2. When Puppet runs, it will fill in the appropriate values for the current node:

```
[root@hiera-test ~]# puppet agent -t
...
Info: Applying configuration version '1411275985'Notice: This is
RedHat version 6.5, on x86_64 architecture, kernel version 2.6.32
...
Notice: Finished catalog run in 0.40 seconds
```

How it works...

Facter provides a standard way for manifests to get information about the nodes to which they are applied. When you refer to a fact in a manifest, Puppet will query Facter to get the current value and insert it into the manifest. Facter facts are top scope variables.

 Always refer to facts with leading double colons to ensure that you are using the fact and not a local variable:

$::hostname NOT $hostname

There's more...

You can also use facts in ERB templates. For example, you might want to insert the node's hostname into a file, or change a configuration setting for an application based on the memory size of the node. When you use fact names in templates, remember that they don't need a dollar sign because this is Ruby, not Puppet:

```
$KLogPath <%= case @kernelversion when '2.6.31' then
'/var/run/rsyslog/kmsg' else '/proc/kmsg' end %>
```

When referring to facts, use the @ syntax. Variables that are defined at the same scope as the function call to template can also be referenced with the @ syntax. Out of scope variables should use the scope function. For example, to reference the mysql::port variable we defined earlier in the mysql modules, use the following:

```
MySQL Port = <%= scope['::mysql::port'] %>
```
NOTE

Applying this template results in the following file:

```
[root@hiera-test ~]# puppet agent -t
...
Info: Caching catalog for hiera-test.example.com
Notice: /Stage[main]/Erb/File[/tmp/template-test]/ensure: defined content
as '{md5}96edacaf9747093f73084252c7ca7e67'
Notice: Finished catalog run in 0.41 seconds [root@hiera-test ~]# cat /
tmp/template-test
MySQL Port = 3306
```

See also

▶ The *Creating custom facts* recipe in *Chapter 9, External Tools and the Puppet Ecosystem*

Importing dynamic information

Even though some system administrators like to wall themselves off from the rest of the office using piles of old printers, we all need to exchange information with other departments from time to time. For example, you may want to insert data into your Puppet manifests that is derived from some outside source. The generate function is ideal for this. Functions are executed on the machine compiling the catalog (the master for centralized deployments); an example like that shown here will only work in a masterless configuration.

Getting ready

Follow these steps to prepare to run the example:

1. Create the script /usr/local/bin/message.rb with the following contents:

   ```
   #!/usr/bin/env ruby
   puts "This runs on the master if you are centralized"
   ```

2. Make the script executable:

   ```
   $ sudo chmod a+x /usr/local/bin/message.rb
   ```

How to do it...

This example calls the external script we created previously and gets its output:

1. Create a `message.pp` manifest containing the following:

    ```
    $message = generate('/usr/local/bin/message.rb')
    notify { $message: }
    ```

2. Run Puppet:

    ```
    $ puppet apply message.pp
    ...
    Notice: /Stage[main]/Main/Notify[This runs on the master if you
    are centralized
    ]/message: defined 'message' as 'This runs on the master if you
    are centralized
    ```

How it works...

The `generate` function runs the specified script or program and returns the result, in this case, a cheerful message from Ruby.

This isn't terribly useful as it stands but you get the idea. Anything a script can do, print, fetch, or calculate, for example, the results of a database query, can be brought into your manifest using `generate`. You can also, of course, run standard UNIX utilities such as `cat` and `grep`.

There's more...

If you need to pass arguments to the executable called by generate, add them as extra arguments to the function call:

```
$message = generate('/bin/cat', '/etc/motd')
```

Puppet will try to protect you from malicious shell calls by restricting the characters you can use in a call to generate, so shell pipes and redirection aren't allowed, for example. The simplest and safest thing to do is to put all your logic into a script and then call that script.

See also

▶ The *Creating custom facts* recipe in *Chapter 9, External Tools and the Puppet Ecosystem*

▶ The *Configuring Hiera* recipe in *Chapter 2, Puppet Infrastructure*

Passing arguments to shell commands

If you want to insert values into a command line (to be run by an `exec` resource, for example), they often need to be quoted, especially if they contain spaces. The `shellquote` function will take any number of arguments, including arrays, and quote each of the arguments and return them all as a space-separated string that you can pass to commands.

In this example, we would like to set up an `exec` resource that will rename a file; but both the source and the target name contain spaces, so they need to be correctly quoted in the command line.

How to do it...

Here's an example of using the `shellquote` function:

1. Create a `shellquote.pp` manifest with the following command:

```
$source = 'Hello Jerry'
$target = 'Hello... Newman'
$argstring = shellquote($source, $target)
$command = "/bin/mv ${argstring}"
notify { $command: }
```

2. Run Puppet:

```
$ puppet apply shellquote.pp
...
Notice: /bin/mv "Hello Jerry" "Hello... Newman"
Notice: /Stage[main]/Main/Notify[/bin/mv "Hello Jerry" "Hello...
Newman"]/message: defined 'message' as '/bin/mv "Hello Jerry"
"Hello... Newman"'
```

How it works...

First we define the $source and $target variables, which are the two filenames we want to use in the command line:

```
$source = 'Hello Jerry'
$target = 'Hello... Newman'
```

Then we call shellquote to concatenate these variables into a quoted, space-separated string as follows:

```
$argstring = shellquote($source, $target)
```

Then we put together the final command line:

```
$command = "/bin/mv ${argstring}"
```

The result will be:

```
/bin/mv "Hello Jerry" "Hello... Newman"
```

This command line can now be run with an exec resource. What would happen if we didn't use shellquote?

```
$source = 'Hello Jerry'
$target = 'Hello... Newman'
$command = "/bin/mv ${source} ${target}"
notify { $command: }
```

```
Notice: /bin/mv Hello Jerry Hello... Newman
```

This won't work because mv expects space-separated arguments, so it will interpret this as a request to move three files Hello, Jerry, and Hello... into a directory named Newman, which probably isn't what we want.

4
Working with Files and Packages

"A writer has the duty to be good, not lousy; true, not false; lively, not dull; accurate, not full of error."

— E.B. White

In this chapter, we will cover the following recipes:

- ▸ Making quick edits to config files
- ▸ Editing INI style files with puppetlabs-inifile
- ▸ Using Augeas to reliably edit config files
- ▸ Building config files using snippets
- ▸ Using ERB templates
- ▸ Using array iteration in templates
- ▸ Using EPP templates
- ▸ Using GnuPG to encrypt secrets
- ▸ Installing packages from a third-party repository
- ▸ Comparing package versions

Introduction

In this chapter, we'll see how to make small edits to files, how to make larger changes in a structured way using the **Augeas** tool, how to construct files from concatenated snippets, and how to generate files from templates. We'll also learn how to install packages from additional repositories, and how to manage those repositories. In addition, we'll see how to store and decrypt secret data with Puppet.

Making quick edits to config files

When you need to have Puppet change a particular setting in a config file, it's common to simply deploy the whole file with Puppet. This isn't always possible, though; especially if it's a file that several different parts of your Puppet manifest may need to modify.

What would be useful is a simple recipe to add a line to a config file if it's not already present, for example, adding a module name to `/etc/modules` to tell the kernel to load that module at boot. There are several ways to do this, the simplest is to use the `file_line` type provided by the `puppetlabs-stdlib` module. In this example, we install the `stdlib` module and use this type to append a line to a text file.

Getting ready

Install the `puppetlabs-stdlib` module using puppet:

```
t@mylaptop ~ $ puppet module install puppetlabs-stdlib
Notice: Preparing to install into /home/thomas/.puppet/modules ...
Notice: Downloading from https://forgeapi.puppetlabs.com ...
Notice: Installing -- do not interrupt ...
/home/thomas/.puppet/modules
└── puppetlabs-stdlib (v4.5.1)
```

This installs the module from the forge into my user's puppet directory; to install into the system directory, run the command as root or use `sudo`. For the purpose of this example, we'll continue working as our own user.

How to do it...

Using the `file_line` resource type, we can ensure that a line exists or is absent in a config file. Using `file_line` we can quickly make edits to files without controlling the entire file.

1. Create a manifest named `oneline.pp` that will use `file_line` on a file in `/tmp`:

    ```
    file {'/tmp/cookbook':
      ensure => 'file',
    }
    file_line {'cookbook-hello':
    ```

```
      path    => '/tmp/cookbook',
      line    => 'Hello World!',
      require => File['/tmp/cookbook'],
    }
```

2. Run `puppet apply` on the `oneline.pp` manifest:

    t@mylaptop ~/.puppet/manifests $ puppet apply oneline.pp

    Notice: Compiled catalog for mylaptop in environment production in 0.39 seconds

    Notice: /Stage[main]/Main/File[/tmp/cookbook]/ensure: created

    Notice: /Stage[main]/Main/File_line[cookbook-hello]/ensure: created

    Notice: Finished catalog run in 0.02 seconds

3. Now verify that `/tmp/cookbook` contains the line we defined:

    t@mylaptop ~/.puppet/manifests $ cat /tmp/cookbook

    Hello World!

How it works...

We installed the `puppetlabs-stdlib` module into the default module path for Puppet, so when we ran `puppet apply`, Puppet knew where to find the `file_line` type definition. Puppet then created the `/tmp/cookbook` file if it didn't exist. The line `Hello World!` was not found in the file, so Puppet added the line to the file.

There's more...

We can define more instances of `file_line` and add more lines to the file; we can have multiple resources modifying a single file.

Modify the `oneline.pp` file and add another `file_line` resource:

```
file {'/tmp/cookbook':
  ensure => 'file',
}
file_line {'cookbook-hello':
  path    => '/tmp/cookbook',
  line    => 'Hello World!',
  require => File['/tmp/cookbook'],
}
file_line {'cookbook-goodbye':
  path    => '/tmp/cookbook',
```

```
        line    => 'So long, and thanks for all the fish.',
        require => File['/tmp/cookbook'],
    }
```

Now apply the manifest again and verify whether the new line is appended to the file:

t@mylaptop ~/.puppet/manifests $ puppet apply oneline.pp

Notice: Compiled catalog for mylaptop in environment production in 0.36 seconds

Notice: /Stage[main]/Main/File_line[cookbook-goodbye]/ensure: created

Notice: Finished catalog run in 0.02 seconds

t@mylaptop ~/.puppet/manifests $ cat /tmp/cookbook

Hello World!

So long, and thanks for all the fish.

The file_line type also supports pattern matching and line removal as we'll show you in the following example:

```
        file {'/tmp/cookbook':
          ensure => 'file',
        }
        file_line {'cookbook-remove':
          ensure  => 'absent',
          path    => '/tmp/cookbook',
          line    => 'Hello World!',
          require => File['/tmp/cookbook'],
        }
        file_line {'cookbook-match':
          path    => '/tmp/cookbook',
          line    => 'Oh freddled gruntbuggly, thanks for all the
            fish.',
          match   => 'fish.$',
          require => File['/tmp/cookbook'],
        }
```

Verify the contents of /tmp/cookbook before your Puppet run:

t@mylaptop ~/.puppet/manifests $ cat /tmp/cookbook

Hello World!

So long, and thanks for all the fish.

Apply the updated manifest:

```
t@mylaptop ~/.puppet/manifests $ puppet apply oneline.pp
Notice: Compiled catalog for mylaptop in environment production in 0.30
seconds
Notice: /Stage[main]/Main/File_line[cookbook-match]/ensure: created
Notice: /Stage[main]/Main/File_line[cookbook-remove]/ensure: removed
Notice: Finished catalog run in 0.02 seconds
```

Verify that the line has been removed and the goodbye line has been replaced:

```
t@mylaptop ~/.puppet/manifests $ cat /tmp/cookbook
Oh freddled gruntbuggly, thanks for all the fish.
```

Editing files with `file_line` works well if the file is unstructured. Structured files may have similar lines in different sections that have different meanings. In the next section, we'll show you how to deal with one particular type of structured file, a file using **INI syntax**.

Editing INI style files with puppetlabs-inifile

INI files are used throughout many systems, Puppet uses INI syntax for the `puppet.conf` file. The `puppetlabs-inifile` module creates two types, `ini_setting` and `ini_subsetting`, which can be used to edit INI style files.

Getting ready

Install the module from the forge as follows:

```
t@mylaptop ~ $ puppet module install puppetlabs-inifile
Notice: Preparing to install into /home/tuphill/.puppet/modules ...
Notice: Downloading from https://forgeapi.puppetlabs.com ...
Notice: Installing -- do not interrupt ...
/home/tuphill/.puppet/modules
└── puppetlabs-inifile (v1.1.3)
```

How to do it...

In this example, we will create a /tmp/server.conf file and ensure that the server_true setting is set in that file:

1. Create an initest.pp manifest with the following contents:

   ```
   ini_setting {'server_true':
     path    => '/tmp/server.conf',
     section => 'main',
     setting => 'server',
     value   => 'true',
   }
   ```

2. Apply the manifest:

   ```
   t@mylaptop ~/.puppet/manifests $ puppet apply initest.pp
   Notice: Compiled catalog for burnaby in environment production in
   0.14 seconds
   Notice: /Stage[main]/Main/Ini_setting[server_true]/ensure: created
   Notice: Finished catalog run in 0.02 seconds
   ```

3. Verify the contents of the /tmp/server.conf file:

   ```
   t@mylaptop ~/.puppet/manifests $ cat /tmp/server.conf

   [main]
   server = true
   ```

How it works...

The inifile module defines two types, ini_setting and ini_subsetting. Our manifest defines an ini_setting resource that creates a server = true setting within the main section of the ini file. In our case, the file didn't exist, so Puppet created the file, then created the main section, and finally added the setting to the main section.

There's more...

Using ini_subsetting, you can have several resources added to a setting. For instance, our server.conf file has a server's line, we could have each node append its own hostname to a server's line. Add the following to the end of the initest.pp file:

```
ini_subsetting {'server_name':
  path    => '/tmp/server.conf',
  section => 'main',
```

```
    setting => 'server_host',
    subsetting => "$hostname",
}
```

Apply the manifest:

```
t@mylaptop ~/.puppet/manifests $ puppet apply initest.pp
Notice: Compiled catalog for mylaptop in environment production in 0.34
seconds
Notice: /Stage[main]/Main/Ini_subsetting[server_name]/ensure: created
Notice: Finished catalog run in 0.02 seconds
t@mylaptop ~/.puppet/manifests $ cat /tmp/server.conf
[main]
server = true
server_host = mylaptop
```

Now temporarily change your hostname and rerun Puppet:

```
t@mylaptop ~/.puppet/manifests $ sudo hostname inihost
t@mylaptop ~/.puppet/manifests $ puppet apply initest.pp
Notice: Compiled catalog for inihost in environment production in 0.43
seconds
Notice: /Stage[main]/Main/Ini_subsetting[server_name]/ensure: created
Notice: Finished catalog run in 0.02 seconds
t@mylaptop ~/.puppet/manifests $ cat /tmp/server.conf
[main]
server = true
server_host = mylaptop inihost
```

 When working with INI syntax files, using the `inifile` module is an excellent choice.

If your configuration files are not in INI syntax, another tool, Augeas, can be used. In the following section, we will use `augeas` to modify files.

Using Augeas to reliably edit config files

Sometimes it seems like every application has its own subtly different config file format, and writing regular expressions to parse and modify all of them can be a tiresome business.

Thankfully, Augeas is here to help. Augeas is a system that aims to simplify working with different config file formats by presenting them all as a simple tree of values. Puppet's Augeas support allows you to create augeas resources that can make the required config changes intelligently and automatically.

How to do it...

Follow these steps to create an example augeas resource:

1. Modify your base module as follows:

```
class base {
  augeas { 'enable-ip-forwarding':
    incl    => '/etc/sysctl.conf',
    lens    => 'Sysctl.lns',
    changes => ['set net.ipv4.ip_forward 1'],
  }
}
```

2. Run Puppet:

```
[root@cookbook ~]# puppet agent -t
Info: Applying configuration version '1412130479'
Notice: Augeas[enable-ip-forwarding] (provider=augeas):
--- /etc/sysctl.conf        2014-09-04 03:41:09.000000000 -0400
+++ /etc/sysctl.conf.augnew       2014-09-30 22:28:03.503000039 -0400
@@ -4,7 +4,7 @@
 # sysctl.conf(5) for more details.

 # Controls IP packet forwarding
-net.ipv4.ip_forward = 0
+net.ipv4.ip_forward = 1

 # Controls source route verification
 net.ipv4.conf.default.rp_filter = 1
```

Notice: /Stage[main]/Base/Augeas[enable-ip-forwarding]/returns:
executed successfully

Notice: Finished catalog run in 2.27 seconds

3. Check whether the setting has been correctly applied:

```
[root@cookbook ~]# sysctl -p |grep ip_forward
net.ipv4.ip_forward = 1
```

How it works...

We declare an `augeas` resource named `enable-ip-forwarding`:

```
augeas { 'enable-ip-forwarding':
```

We specify that we want to make changes in the file `/etc/sysctl.conf`:

```
incl => '/etc/sysctl.conf',
```

Next we specify the lens to use on this file. Augeas uses files called lenses to translate a configuration file into an object representation. Augeas ships with several lenses, they are located in `/usr/share/augeas/lenses` by default. When specifying the lens in an `augeas` resource, the name of the lens is capitalized and has the `.lns` suffix. In this case, we will specify the `Sysctl` lens as follows:

```
lens => 'Sysctl.lns',
```

The `changes` parameter specifies the changes we want to make. Its value is an array, because we can supply several changes at once. In this example, there is only change, so the value is an array of one element:

```
changes => ['set net.ipv4.ip_forward 1'],
```

In general, Augeas changes take the following form:

```
set <parameter> <value>
```

In this case, the setting will be translated into a line like this in `/etc/sysctl.conf`:

```
net.ipv4.ip_forward=1
```

There's more...

I've chosen `/etc/sysctl.conf` as the example because it can contain a wide variety of kernel settings and you may want to change these settings for all sorts of different purposes and in different Puppet classes. You might want to enable IP forwarding, as in the example, for a router class but you might also want to tune the value of `net.core.somaxconn` for a load-balancer class.

This means that simply puppetizing the `/etc/sysctl.conf` file and distributing it as a text file won't work because you might have several different and conflicting versions depending on the setting you want to modify. Augeas is the right solution here because you can define `augeas` resources in different places, which modify the same file and they won't conflict.

For more information about using Puppet and Augeas, see the page on the Puppet Labs website `http://projects.puppetlabs.com/projects/1/wiki/Puppet_Augeas`.

Another project that uses Augeas is **Augeasproviders**. Augeasproviders uses Augeas to define several types. One of these types is `sysctl`, using this type you can make sysctl changes without knowing how to write the changes in Augeas. More information is available on the forge at `https://forge.puppetlabs.com/domcleal/augeasproviders`.

Learning how to use Augeas can be a little confusing at first. Augeas provides a command line tool, `augtool`, which can be used to get acquainted with making changes in Augeas.

Building config files using snippets

Sometimes you can't deploy a whole config file in one piece, yet making line by line edits isn't enough. Often, you need to build a config file from various bits of configuration managed by different classes. You may run into a situation where local information needs to be imported into the file as well. In this example, we'll build a config file using a local file as well as snippets defined in our manifests.

Getting ready

Although it's possible to create our own system to build files from pieces, we'll use the puppetlabs supported `concat` module. We will start by installing the `concat` module, in a previous example we installed the module to our local machine. In this example, we'll modify the Puppet server configuration and download the module to the Puppet server.

In your Git repository create an `environment.conf` file with the following contents:

```
modulepath = public:modules
manifest = manifests/site.pp
```

Create the public directory and download the module into that directory as follows:

```
t@mylaptop ~/puppet $ mkdir public && cd public
t@mylaptop ~/puppet/public $ puppet module install puppetlabs-concat
--modulepath=.
Notice: Preparing to install into /home/thomas/puppet/public ...
Notice: Downloading from https://forgeapi.puppetlabs.com ...
Notice: Installing -- do not interrupt ...
```

```
/home/thomas/puppet/public
└─┬ puppetlabs-concat (v1.1.1)
  └── puppetlabs-stdlib (v4.3.2)
```

Now add the new modules to our Git repository:

```
t@mylaptop ~/puppet/public $ git add .
t@mylaptop ~/puppet/public $ git commit -m "adding concat"
[production 50c6fca] adding concat
 407 files changed, 20089 insertions(+)
```

Then push to our Git server:

```
t@mylaptop ~/puppet/public $ git push origin production
```

How to do it...

Now that we have the concat module available on our server, we can create a concat container resource in our base module:

```
concat {'hosts.allow':
  path => '/etc/hosts.allow',
  mode => 0644
}
```

Create a concat::fragment module for the header of the new file:

```
concat::fragment {'hosts.allow header':
  target  => 'hosts.allow',
  content => "# File managed by puppet\n",
  order   => '01'
}
```

Create a concat::fragment that includes a local file:

```
concat::fragment {'hosts.allow local':
  target => 'hosts.allow',
  source => '/etc/hosts.allow.local',
  order  => '10',
}
```

Create a concat::fragment module that will go at the end of the file:

```
concat::fragment {'hosts.allow tftp':
  target  => 'hosts.allow',
  content => "in.ftpd: .example.com\n",
  order   => '50',
}
```

On the node, create `/etc/hosts.allow.local` with the following contents:

```
in.tftpd: .example.com
```

Run Puppet to have the file created:

```
[root@cookbook ~]# puppet agent -t
Info: Caching catalog for cookbook.example.com
Info: Applying configuration version '1412138600'
Notice: /Stage[main]/Base/Concat[hosts.allow]/File[hosts.allow]/ensure:
defined content as '{md5}b151c8bbc32c505f1c4a98b487f7d249'
Notice: Finished catalog run in 0.29 seconds
```

Verify the contents of the new file as:

```
[root@cookbook ~]# cat /etc/hosts.allow
# File managed by puppet
in.tftpd: .example.com
in.ftpd: .example.com
```

How it works...

The `concat` resource defines a container that will hold all the subsequent `concat::fragment` resources. Each `concat::fragment` resource references the `concat` resource as the target. Each `concat::fragment` also includes an `order` attribute. The `order` attribute is used to specify the order in which the fragments are added to the final file. Our `/etc/hosts.allow` file is built with the header line, the contents of the local file, and finally the `in.tftpd` line we defined.

Using ERB templates

While you can deploy config files easily with Puppet as simple text files, templates are much more powerful. A template file can do calculations, execute Ruby code, or reference the values of variables from your Puppet manifests. Anywhere you might deploy a text file using Puppet, you can use a template instead.

In the simplest case, a template can just be a static text file. More usefully, you can insert variables into it using the ERB (embedded Ruby) syntax. For example:

```
<%= @name %>, this is a very large drink.
```

If the template is used in a context where the variable $name contains Zaphod Beeblebrox, the template will evaluate to:

```
Zaphod Beeblebrox, this is a very large drink.
```

This simple technique is very useful to generate lots of files that only differ in the values of one or two variables, for example, virtual hosts, and for inserting values into a script such as database names and passwords.

How to do it...

In this example, we'll use an ERB template to insert a password into a backup script:

1. Create the file modules/admin/templates/backup-mysql.sh.erb with the following contents:

   ```
   #!/bin/sh
   /usr/bin/mysqldump -uroot \
     -p<%= @mysql_password %> \
     --all-databases | \
     /bin/gzip > /backup/mysql/all-databases.sql.gz
   ```

2. Modify your site.pp file as follows:

   ```
   node 'cookbook' {
     $mysql_password = 'secret'
     file { '/usr/local/bin/backup-mysql':
       content => template('admin/backup-mysql.sh.erb'),
       mode    => '0755',
     }
   }
   ```

3. Run Puppet:

   ```
   [root@cookbook ~]# puppet agent -t
   Info: Caching catalog for cookbook.example.com
   Info: Applying configuration version '1412140971'
   Notice: /Stage[main]/Main/Node[cookbook]/File[/usr/local/
   bin/backup-mysql]/ensure: defined content as '{md5}
   c12af56559ef36529975d568ff52dca5'
   Notice: Finished catalog run in 0.31 seconds
   ```

4. Check whether Puppet has correctly inserted the password into the template:

   ```
   [root@cookbook ~]# cat /usr/local/bin/backup-mysql
   #!/bin/sh
   /usr/bin/mysqldump -uroot \
   ```

```
-psecret \
--all-databases | \
/bin/gzip > /backup/mysql/all-databases.sql.gz
```

How it works...

Wherever a variable is referenced in the template, for example `<%= @mysql_password %>`, Puppet will replace it with the corresponding value, `secret`.

There's more...

In the example, we only used one variable in the template, but you can have as many as you like. These can also be facts:

```
ServerName <%= @fqdn %>
```

Or Ruby expressions:

```
MAILTO=<%= @emails.join(',') %>
```

Or any Ruby code you want:

```
ServerAdmin <%= @sitedomain == 'coldcomfort.com' ?
  'seth@coldcomfort.com' : 'flora@poste.com' %>
```

See also

▶ The *Using GnuPG to encrypt secrets* recipe in this chapter

▶ `https://docs.puppetlabs.com/guides/templating.html`

Using array iteration in templates

In the previous example, we saw that you can use Ruby to interpolate different values in templates depending on the result of an expression. But you're not limited to getting one value at a time. You can put lots of them in a Puppet array and then have the template generate some content for each element of the array using a loop.

How to do it...

Follow these steps to build an example of iterating over arrays:

1. Modify your `site.pp` file as follows:

```
node 'cookbook' {
  $ipaddresses = ['192.168.0.1',
    '158.43.128.1', '10.0.75.207' ]
  file { '/tmp/addresslist.txt':
    content => template('base/addresslist.erb')
  }
}
```

2. Create the file `modules/base/templates/addresslist.erb` with the following contents:

```
<% @ipaddresses.each do |ip| -%>
IP address <%= ip %> is present
<% end -%>
```

3. Run Puppet:

```
[root@cookbook ~]# puppet agent -t
Info: Caching catalog for cookbook.example.com
Info: Applying configuration version '1412141917'
Notice: /Stage[main]/Main/Node[cookbook]/File[/tmp/addresslist.
txt]/ensure: defined content as '{md5}073851229d7b2843830024afb2b3
902d'
Notice: Finished catalog run in 0.30 seconds
```

4. Check the contents of the generated file:

```
[root@cookbook ~]# cat /tmp/addresslist.txt
  IP address 192.168.0.1 is present.
  IP address 158.43.128.1 is present.
  IP address 10.0.75.207 is present.
```

How it works...

In the first line of the template, we reference the array `ipaddresses`, and call its `each` method:

```
<% @ipaddresses.each do |ip| -%>
```

In Ruby, this creates a loop that will execute once for each element of the array. Each time round the loop, the variable `ip` will be set to the value of the current element.

In our example, the `ipaddresses` array contains three elements, so the following line will be executed three times, once for each element:

```
IP address <%= ip %> is present.
```

This will result in three output lines:

```
IP address 192.168.0.1 is present.
IP address 158.43.128.1 is present.
IP address 10.0.75.207 is present.
```

The final line ends the loop:

```
<% end -%>
```

Note that the first and last lines end with `-%>` instead of just `%>` as we saw before. The effect of the `-` is to suppress the new line that would otherwise be generated on each pass through the loop, giving us unwanted blank lines in the file.

There's more...

Templates can also iterate over hashes, or arrays of hashes:

```
$interfaces = [ {name => 'eth0', ip => '192.168.0.1'},
  {name => 'eth1', ip => '158.43.128.1'},
  {name => 'eth2', ip => '10.0.75.207'} ]

<% @interfaces.each do |interface| -%>
Interface <%= interface['name'] %> has the address <%= interface['ip']
%>.
<% end -%>

Interface eth0 has the address 192.168.0.1.
Interface eth1 has the address 158.43.128.1.
Interface eth2 has the address 10.0.75.207.
```

See also

▶ The *Using ERB templates* recipe in this chapter

Using EPP templates

EPP templates are a new feature in Puppet 3.5 and newer versions. EPP templates use a syntax similar to ERB templates but are not compiled through Ruby. Two new functions are defined to call EPP templates, `epp`, and `inline_epp`. These functions are the EPP equivalents of the ERB functions `template` and `inline_template`, respectively. The main difference with EPP templates is that variables are referenced using the Puppet notation, `$variable` instead of `@variable`.

How to do it...

1. Create an EPP template in `~/puppet/epp-test.epp` with the following content:

   ```
   This is <%= $message %>.
   ```

2. Create an `epp.pp` manifest, which uses the `epp` and `inline_epp` functions:

   ```
   $message = "the message"
   file {'/tmp/epp-test':
     content => epp('/home/thomas/puppet/epp-test.epp')
   }
   notify {inline_epp('Also prints <%= $message %>'):}
   ```

3. Apply the manifest making sure to use the future parser (the future parser is required for the `epp` and `inline_epp` functions to be defined):

   ```
   t@mylaptop ~/puppet $ puppet apply epp.pp --parser=future
   Notice: Compiled catalog for mylaptop in environment production in
   1.03 seconds
   Notice: /Stage[main]/Main/File[/tmp/epp-test]/ensure: defined
   content as '{md5}999ccc2507d79d50fae0775d69b63b8c'
   Notice: Also prints the message
   ```

4. Verify that the template worked as intended:

   ```
   t@mylaptop ~/puppet $ cat /tmp/epp-test
   This is the message.
   ```

How it works...

Using the future parser, the `epp` and `inline_epp` functions are defined. The main difference between EPP templates and ERB templates is that variables are referenced in the same way they are within Puppet manifests.

There's more...

Both `epp` and `inline_epp` allow for variables to be overridden within the function call. A second parameter to the function call can be used to specify values for variables used within the scope of the function call. For example, we can override the value of $message with the following code:

```
file {'/tmp/epp-test':
  content => epp('/home/tuphill/puppet/epp-test.epp',
    { 'message' => "override $message"} )
}
notify {inline_epp('Also prints <%= $message %>',
  { 'message' => "inline override $message"}):}
```

Now when we run Puppet and verify the output we see that the value of $message has been overridden:

```
t@mylaptop ~/puppet $ puppet apply epp.pp --parser=future
Notice: Compiled catalog for mylaptop.pan.costco.com in environment
production in 0.85 seconds
Notice: Also prints inline override the message
Notice: Finished catalog run in 0.05 seconds
t@mylaptop ~/puppet $ cat /tmp/epp-test
This is override the message.
```

Using GnuPG to encrypt secrets

We often need Puppet to have access to secret information, such as passwords or crypto keys, for it to configure systems properly. But how do you avoid putting such secrets directly into your Puppet code, where they're visible to anyone who has read access to your repository?

It's a common requirement for third-party developers and contractors to be able to make changes via Puppet, but they definitely shouldn't see any confidential information. Similarly, if you're using a distributed Puppet setup like that described in *Chapter 2, Puppet Infrastructure*, every machine has a copy of the whole repo, including secrets for other machines that it doesn't need and shouldn't have. How can we prevent this?

One answer is to encrypt the secrets using the **GnuPG** tool, so that any secret information in the Puppet repo is undecipherable (for all practical purposes) without the appropriate key. Then we distribute the key securely to the people or machines that need it.

Getting ready

First you'll need an encryption key, so follow these steps to generate one. If you already have a GnuPG key that you'd like to use, go on to the next section. To complete this section, you will need to install the gpg command:

1. Use `puppet` resource to install gpg:

   ```
   # puppet resource package gnupg ensure=installed
   ```

    You may need to use gnupg2 as the package name, depending on your target OS.

2. Run the following command. Answer the prompts as shown, except to substitute your name and e-mail address for mine. When prompted for a passphrase, just hit *Enter*:

   ```
   t@mylaptop ~/puppet $ gpg --gen-key

   gpg (GnuPG) 1.4.18; Copyright (C) 2014 Free Software Foundation,
   Inc.

   This is free software: you are free to change and redistribute it.

   There is NO WARRANTY, to the extent permitted by law.

   Please select what kind of key you want:
       (1) RSA and RSA (default)
       (2) DSA and Elgamal
       (3) DSA (sign only)
       (4) RSA (sign only)
   Your selection? 1

   RSA keys may be between 1024 and 4096 bits long.

   What keysize do you want? (2048) 2048

   Requested keysize is 2048 bits

   Please specify how long the key should be valid.
           0 = key does not expire
         <n>  = key expires in n days
         <n>w = key expires in n weeks
         <n>m = key expires in n months
         <n>y = key expires in n years
   Key is valid for? (0) 0

   Key does not expire at all

   Is this correct? (y/N) y
   ```

You need a user ID to identify your key; the software constructs the user ID

from the Real Name, Comment and Email Address in this form:

    "Heinrich Heine (Der Dichter) <heinrichh@duesseldorf.de>"

Real name: Thomas Uphill

Email address: thomas@narrabilis.com

Comment: <enter>

You selected this USER-ID:

    "Thomas Uphill <thomas@narrabilis.com>"

Change (N)ame, (C)omment, (E)mail or (O)kay/(Q)uit? o

You need a Passphrase to protect your secret key.

Hit enter twice here to have an empty passphrase

You don't want a passphrase - this is probably a *bad* idea!

I will do it anyway. You can change your passphrase at any time,

using this program with the option "--edit-key".

gpg: key F1C1EE49 marked as ultimately trusted

public and secret key created and signed.

gpg: checking the trustdb

gpg: 3 marginal(s) needed, 1 complete(s) needed, PGP trust model

gpg: depth: 0 valid: 1 signed: 0 trust: 0-, 0q, 0n, 0m, 0f, 1u

pub   2048R/F1C1EE49 2014-10-01

       Key fingerprint = 461A CB4C 397F 06A7 FB82 3BAD 63CF 50D8 F1C1 EE49

uid   Thomas Uphill <thomas@narrabilis.com>

sub   2048R/E2440023 2014-10-01

3. You may see a message like this if your system is not configured with a source of randomness:

We need to generate a lot of random bytes. It is a good idea to perform

some other action (type on the keyboard, move the mouse, utilize the disks) during the prime generation; this gives the random number generator a better chance to gain enough entropy.

4. In this case, install and start a random number generator daemon such as `haveged` or `rng-tools`. Copy the gpg key you just created into the `puppet` user's account on your Puppet master:

```
t@mylaptop ~ $ scp -r .gnupg puppet@puppet.example.com:
gpg.conf                                    100% 7680
7.5KB/s     00:00
random_seed                                 100%  600
0.6KB/s     00:00
pubring.gpg                                 100% 1196
1.2KB/s     00:00
secring.gpg                                 100% 2498
2.4KB/s     00:00
trustdb.gpg                                 100% 1280
1.3KB/s     00:00
```

How to do it...

With your encryption key installed on the `puppet` user's keyring (the key generation process described in the previous section will do this for you), you're ready to set up Puppet to decrypt secrets.

1. Create the following directory:

   t@cookbook:~/puppet$ mkdir -p modules/admin/lib/puppet/parser/ functions

2. Create the file `modules/admin/lib/puppet/parser/functions/secret.rb` with the following contents:

```
module Puppet::Parser::Functions
  newfunction(:secret, :type => :rvalue) do |args|
    'gpg --no-tty -d #{args[0]}'
  end
end
```

3. Create the file `secret_message` with the following contents:

```
For a moment, nothing happened.
Then, after a second or so, nothing continued to happen.
```

4. Encrypt this file with the following command (use the e-mail address you supplied when creating the GnuPG key):

   t@mylaptop ~/puppet $ gpg -e -r thomas@narrabilis.com secret_ message

5. Move the resulting encrypted file into your Puppet repo:

```
t@mylaptop:~/puppet$ mv secret_message.gpg modules/admin/files/
```

6. Remove the original (plaintext) file:

```
t@mylaptop:~/puppet$ rm secret_message
```

7. Modify your `site.pp` file as follows:

```
node 'cookbook' {
  $message = secret('
    /etc/puppet/environments/production/
    modules/admin/files/secret_message.gpg')
  notify { "The secret message is: ${message}": }
}
```

8. Run Puppet:

```
[root@cookbook ~]# puppet agent -t
Info: Caching catalog for cookbook.example.com
Info: Applying configuration version '1412145910'
Notice: The secret message is: For a moment, nothing happened.
Then, after a second or so, nothing continued to happen.
Notice: Finished catalog run in 0.27 seconds
```

How it works...

First, we've created a custom function to allow Puppet to decrypt the secret files using GnuPG:

```
module Puppet::Parser::Functions
  newfunction(:secret, :type => :rvalue) do |args|
    'gpg --no-tty -d #{args[0]}'
  end
end
```

The preceding code creates a function named `secret` that takes a file path as an argument and returns the decrypted text. It doesn't manage encryption keys so you need to ensure that the `puppet` user has the necessary key installed. You can check this with the following command:

```
puppet@puppet:~ $ gpg --list-secret-keys
/var/lib/puppet/.gnupg/secring.gpg
---------------------------------
sec   2048R/F1C1EE49 2014-10-01
uid                  Thomas Uphill <thomas@narrabilis.com>
ssb   2048R/E2440023 2014-10-01
```

Having set up the `secret` function and the required key, we now encrypt a message to this key:

```
tuphill@mylaptop ~/puppet $ gpg -e -r thomas@narrabilis.com secret_
message
```

This creates an encrypted file that can only be read by someone with access to the secret key (or Puppet running on a machine that has the secret key).

We then call the `secret` function to decrypt this file and get the contents:

```
$message = secret(' /etc/puppet/environments/production/modules/admin/
files/secret_message.gpg')
```

There's more...

You should use the `secret` function, or something like it, to protect any confidential data in your Puppet repo: passwords, AWS credentials, license keys, even other secret keys such as SSL host keys.

You may decide to use a single key, which you push to machines as they're built, perhaps as part of a bootstrap process like that described in the *Bootstrapping Puppet with Bash* recipe in *Chapter 2, Puppet Infrastructure*. For even greater security, you might like to create a new key for each machine, or group of machines, and encrypt a given secret only for the machines that need it.

For example, your web servers might need a certain secret that you don't want to be accessible on any other machine. You could create a key for web servers, and encrypt the data only for this key.

If you want to use encrypted data with Hiera, there is a GnuPG backend for Hiera available at `http://www.craigdunn.org/2011/10/secret-variables-in-puppet-with-hiera-and-gpg/`.

See also

- ▸ The *Configuring Hiera* recipe in *Chapter 2, Puppet Infrastructure*
- ▸ The *Storing secret data with hiera-gpg* recipe in *Chapter 2, Puppet Infrastructure*

Installing packages from a third-party repository

Most often you will want to install packages from the main distribution repo, so a simple package resource will do:

```
package { 'exim4': ensure => installed }
```

Sometimes, you need a package that is only found in a third-party repository (an Ubuntu PPA, for example), or it might be that you need a more recent version of a package than that provided by the distribution, which is available from a third party.

On a manually-administered machine, you would normally do this by adding the repo source configuration to `/etc/apt/sources.list.d` (and, if necessary, a gpg key for the repo) before installing the package. We can automate this process easily with Puppet.

How to do it...

In this example, we'll use the popular Percona APT repo (Percona is a MySQL consulting firm who maintain and release their own specialized version of MySQL, more information is available at `http://www.percona.com/software/repositories`):

1. Create the file `modules/admin/manifests/percona_repo.pp` with the following contents:

```
# Install Percona APT repo
class admin::percona_repo {
  exec { 'add-percona-apt-key':
    unless  => '/usr/bin/apt-key list |grep percona',
    command => '/usr/bin/gpg --keyserver
      hkp://keys.gnupg.net --recv-keys 1C4CBDCDCD2EFD2A
      && /usr/bin/gpg -a --export CD2EFD2A |
      apt-key add -',
    notify  => Exec['percona-apt-update'],
  }

  exec { 'percona-apt-update':
    command     => '/usr/bin/apt-get update',
    require     => [File['/etc/apt/sources.list.d/percona.list'],
File['/etc/apt/preferences.d/00percona.pref']],
    refreshonly => true,
  }

  file { '/etc/apt/sources.list.d/percona.list':
```

```
      content => 'deb http://repo.percona.com/apt wheezy
        main',
      notify  => Exec['percona-apt-update'],
  }

    file { '/etc/apt/preferences.d/00percona.pref':
      content => "Package: *\nPin: release o=Percona
      Development Team\nPin-Priority: 1001",
      notify  => Exec['percona-apt-update'],
    }
  }
```

2. Modify your `site.pp` file as follows:

```
node 'cookbook' {
  include admin::percona_repo

  package { 'percona-server-server-5.5':
    ensure  => installed,
    require => Class['admin::percona_repo'],
  }
}
```

3. Run Puppet:

```
root@cookbook-deb:~# puppet agent -t

Info: Caching catalog for cookbook-deb

Notice: /Stage[main]/Admin::Percona_repo/Exec[add-percona-apt-
key]/returns: executed successfully

Info: /Stage[main]/Admin::Percona_repo/Exec[add-percona-apt-key]:
Scheduling refresh of Exec[percona-apt-update]

Notice: /Stage[main]/Admin::Percona_repo/File[/etc/apt/
sources.list.d/percona.list]/ensure: defined content as '{md5}
b8d479374497255804ffbf0a7bcdf6c2'

Info: /Stage[main]/Admin::Percona_repo/File[/etc/apt/sources.
list.d/percona.list]: Scheduling refresh of Exec[percona-apt-
update]

Notice: /Stage[main]/Admin::Percona_repo/File[/etc/apt/
preferences.d/00percona.pref]/ensure: defined content as '{md5}1d8
ca6c1e752308a9bd3018713e2d1ad'

Info: /Stage[main]/Admin::Percona_repo/File[/etc/apt/
preferences.d/00percona.pref]: Scheduling refresh of Exec[percona-
apt-update]

Notice: /Stage[main]/Admin::Percona_repo/Exec[percona-apt-update]:
Triggered 'refresh' from 3 events
```

How it works...

In order to install any Percona package, we first need to have the repository configuration installed on the machine. This is why the `percona-server-server-5.5` package (Percona's version of the standard MySQL server) requires the `admin::percona_repo` class:

```
package { 'percona-server-server-5.5':
  ensure  => installed,
  require => Class['admin::percona_repo'],
}
```

So, what does the `admin::percona_repo` class do? It:

- Installs the Percona APT key with which the packages are signed
- Configures the Percona repo URL as a file in `/etc/apt/sources.list.d`
- Runs `apt-get update` to retrieve the repo metadata
- Adds an APT pin configuration in `/etc/apt/preferences.d`

First of all, we install the APT key:

```
exec { 'add-percona-apt-key':
  unless  => '/usr/bin/apt-key list |grep percona',
  command => '/usr/bin/gpg --keyserver  hkp://keys.gnupg.net --
    recv-keys 1C4CBDCDCD2EFD2A && /usr/bin/gpg -a --export
    CD2EFD2A | apt-key add -',
  notify  => Exec['percona-apt-update'],
}
```

The `unless` parameter checks the output of `apt-key list` to make sure that the Percona key is not already installed, in which case we need not do anything. Assuming it isn't, the `command` runs:

```
/usr/bin/gpg --keyserver  hkp://keys.gnupg.net --recv-keys
1C4CBDCDCD2EFD2A && /usr/bin/gpg -a --export CD2EFD2A | apt-key add -
```

This command retrieves the key from the GnuPG keyserver, exports it in the ASCII format, and pipes this into the `apt-key add` command, which adds it to the system keyring. You can use a similar pattern for most third-party repos that require an APT signing key.

Having installed the key, we add the repo configuration:

```
file { '/etc/apt/sources.list.d/percona.list':
  content => 'deb http://repo.percona.com/apt wheezy main',
  notify  => Exec['percona-apt-update'],
}
```

Then run `apt-get update` to update the system's APT cache with the metadata from the new repo:

```
exec { 'percona-apt-update':
  command     => '/usr/bin/apt-get update',
  require     => [File['/etc/apt/sources.list.d/percona.list'],
File['/etc/apt/preferences.d/00percona.pref']],
  refreshonly => true,
}
```

Finally, we configure the APT pin priority for the repo:

```
file { '/etc/apt/preferences.d/00percona.pref':
  content => "Package: *\nPin: release o=Percona Development Team\
nPin-Priority: 1001",
  notify  => Exec['percona-apt-update'],
}
```

This ensures that packages installed from the Percona repo will never be superseded by packages from somewhere else (the main Ubuntu distro, for example). Otherwise, you could end up with broken dependencies and be unable to install the Percona packages automatically.

There's more...

The APT package framework is specific to the Debian and Ubuntu systems. There is a forge module for managing apt repos, `https://forge.puppetlabs.com/puppetlabs/apt`. If you're on a Red Hat or CentOS-based system, you can use the `yumrepo` resources to manage RPM repositories directly:

`http://docs.puppetlabs.com/references/latest/type.html#yumrepo`

Comparing package versions

Package version numbers are odd things. They look like decimal numbers, but they're not: a version number is often in the form of `2.6.4`, for example. If you need to compare one version number with another, you can't do a straightforward string comparison: `2.6.4` would be interpreted as greater than `2.6.12`. And a numeric comparison won't work because they're not valid numbers.

Puppet's `versioncmp` function comes to the rescue. If you pass two things that look like version numbers, it will compare them and return a value indicating which is greater:

```
versioncmp( A, B )
```

returns:

- ▸ 0 if A and B are equal
- ▸ Greater than 1 if A is higher than B
- ▸ Less than 0 if A is less than B

How to do it...

Here's an example using the `versioncmp` function:

1. Modify your `site.pp` file as follows:

```
node 'cookbook' {
  $app_version = '1.2.2'
  $min_version = '1.2.10'

  if versioncmp($app_version, $min_version) >= 0 {
    notify { 'Version OK': }
  } else {
    notify { 'Upgrade needed': }
  }
}
```

2. Run Puppet:

```
[root@cookbook ~]# puppet agent -t
Info: Caching catalog for cookbook.example.com
Notice: Upgrade needed
```

3. Now change the value of `$app_version`:

```
$app_version = '1.2.14'
```

4. Run Puppet again:

```
[root@cookbook ~]# puppet agent -t
Info: Caching catalog for cookbook.example.com
Notice: Version OK
```

How it works...

We've specified that the minimum acceptable version ($min_version) is 1.2.10. So, in the first example, we want to compare it with $app_version of 1.2.2. A simple alphabetic comparison of these two strings (in Ruby, for example) would give the wrong result, but versioncmp correctly determines that 1.2.2 is less than 1.2.10 and alerts us that we need to upgrade.

In the second example, $app_version is now 1.2.14, which versioncmp correctly recognizes as greater than $min_version and so we get the message **Version OK**.

5

Users and Virtual Resources

"Nothing is a problem, until it's a problem."

In this chapter, we will cover the following recipes:

- ▸ Using virtual resources
- ▸ Managing users with virtual resources
- ▸ Managing users' SSH access
- ▸ Managing users' customization files
- ▸ Using exported resources

Introduction

Users can be a real pain. I don't mean the people, though doubtless that's sometimes true. But keeping UNIX user accounts and file permissions in sync across a network of machines, some of them running different operating systems, can be very challenging without some kind of centralized configuration management.

Each new developer who joins the organization needs an account on every machine, along with sudo privileges and group memberships, and needs their SSH key authorized for a bunch of different accounts. The system administrator who has to take care of this manually will be at the job all day, while the system administrator who uses Puppet will be done in minutes, and head out for an early lunch.

In this chapter, we'll look at some handy patterns and techniques to manage users and their associated resources. Users are also one of the most common applications for virtual resources, so we'll find out all about those. In the final section, we'll introduce exported resources, which are related to virtual resources.

Using virtual resources

Virtual resources in Puppet might seem complicated and confusing but, in fact, they're very simple. They're exactly like regular resources, but they don't actually take effect until they're realized (in the sense of "made real"); whereas a regular resource can only be declared once per node (so two classes can't declare the same resource, for example). A virtual resource can be realized as many times as you like.

This comes in handy when you need to move applications and services between machines. If two applications that use the same resource end up sharing a machine, they would cause a conflict unless you make the resource virtual.

To clarify this, let's look at a typical situation where virtual resources might come in handy.

You are responsible for two popular web applications: WordPress and Drupal. Both are web apps running on Apache, so they both require the Apache package to be installed. The definition for WordPress might look something like the following:

```
class wordpress {
  package {'httpd':
    ensure => 'installed',
  }
  service {'httpd':
    ensure => 'running',
    enable => true,
  }
}
```

The definition for Drupal might look like this:

```
class drupal {
  package {'httpd':
    ensure => 'installed',
  }
  service {'httpd':
    ensure => 'running',
    enable => true,
  }
}
```

All is well until you need to consolidate both apps onto a single server:

```
node 'bigbox' {
    include wordpress
    include drupal
}
```

Now Puppet will complain because you tried to define two resources with the same name:
httpd.

```
root@bigbox:~                                                         x
[root@bigbox ~]# puppet agent -t
Info: Retrieving pluginfacts
Info: Retrieving plugin
Info: Loading facts
Error: Could not retrieve catalog from remote server: Error 400 on SERVER: Dupli
cate declaration: Package[httpd] is already declared in file /etc/puppet/environ
ments/production/modules/wordpress/manifests/init.pp:4; cannot redeclare at /etc
/puppet/environments/production/modules/drupal/manifests/init.pp:4 on node bigbo
x.example.com
Warning: Not using cache on failed catalog
Error: Could not retrieve catalog; skipping run
[root@bigbox ~]#
```

You could remove the duplicate Apache package definition from one of the classes, but then nodes without the class including Apache would fail. You can get around this problem by putting the Apache package in its own class and then using `include apache` everywhere it's needed; Puppet doesn't mind you including the same class multiple times. In reality, putting Apache in its own class solves most problems but, in general, this method has the disadvantage that every potentially conflicting resource must have its own class.

Virtual resources can be used to solve this problem. A virtual resource is just like a normal resource, except that it starts with an `@` character:

```
@package { 'httpd': ensure => installed }
```

You can think of it as being like a placeholder resource; you want to define it but you aren't sure you are going to use it yet. Puppet will read and remember virtual resource definitions, but won't actually create the resource until you realize the resource.

To create the resource, use the `realize` function:

```
realize(Package['httpd'])
```

You can call `realize` as many times as you want on the resource and it won't result in a conflict. So virtual resources are the way to go when several different classes all require the same resource, and they may need to coexist on the same node.

How to do it...

Here's how to build the example using virtual resources:

1. Create the virtual module with the following contents:

```
class virtual {
  @package {'httpd': ensure => installed }
  @service {'httpd':
    ensure  => running,
    enable  => true,
    require => Package['httpd']
  }
}
```

2. Create the Drupal module with the following contents:

```
class drupal {
  include virtual
  realize(Package['httpd'])
  realize(Service['httpd'])
}
```

3. Create the WordPress module with the following contents:

```
class wordpress {
  include virtual
  realize(Package['httpd'])
  realize(Service['httpd'])
}
```

4. Modify your `site.pp` file as follows:

```
node 'bigbox' {
  include drupal
  include wordpress
}
```

5. Run Puppet:

```
bigbox# puppet agent -t
Info: Caching catalog for bigbox.example.com
Info: Applying configuration version '1413179615'
Notice: /Stage[main]/Virtual/Package[httpd]/ensure: created
Notice: /Stage[main]/Virtual/Service[httpd]/ensure: ensure changed
'stopped' to 'running'
```

```
Info: /Stage[main]/Virtual/Service[httpd]: Unscheduling refresh on
Service[httpd]

Notice: Finished catalog run in 6.67 seconds
```

How it works...

You define the package and service as virtual resources in one place: the `virtual` class. All nodes can include this class and you can put all your virtual services and packages in it. None of the packages will actually be installed on a node or services started until you call `realize`:

```
class virtual {
  @package { 'httpd': ensure => installed }
}
```

Every class that needs the Apache package can call `realize` on this virtual resource:

```
class drupal {
  include virtual
  realize(Package['httpd'])
}
```

Puppet knows, because you made the resource virtual, that you intended to have multiple references to the same package, and didn't just accidentally create two resources with the same name. So it does the right thing.

There's more...

To realize virtual resources, you can also use the collection *spaceship* syntax:

```
Package <| title = 'httpd' |>
```

The advantage of this syntax is that you're not restricted to the resource name; you could also use a tag, for example:

```
Package <| tag = 'web' |>
```

Alternatively, you can just specify all instances of the resource type, by leaving the query section blank:

```
Package <| |>
```

Managing users with virtual resources

Users are a great example of a resource that may need to be realized by multiple classes. Consider the following situation. To simplify administration of a large number of machines, you defined classes for two kinds of users: `developers` and `sysadmins`. All machines need to include `sysadmins`, but only some machines need `developers`:

```
node 'server' {
  include user::sysadmins
}

node 'webserver' {
  include user::sysadmins
  include user::developers
}
```

However, some users may be members of both groups. If each group simply declares its members as regular `user` resources, this will lead to a conflict when a node includes both `developers` and `sysadmins`, as in the `webserver` example.

To avoid this conflict, a common pattern is to make all users virtual resources, defined in a single class `user::virtual` that every machine includes, and then realizing the users where they are needed. This way, there will be no conflict if a user is a member of multiple groups.

How to do it...

Follow these steps to create a `user::virtual` class:

1. Create the file `modules/user/manifests/virtual.pp` with the following contents:

    ```
    class user::virtual {
      @user { 'thomas':  ensure => present }
      @user { 'theresa': ensure => present }
      @user { 'josko':   ensure => present }
      @user { 'nate':    ensure => present }
    }
    ```

2. Create the file `modules/user/manifests/developers.pp` with the following contents:

    ```
    class user::developers {
      realize(User['theresa'])
      realize(User['nate'])
    }
    ```

3. Create the file `modules/user/manifests/sysadmins.pp` with the following contents:

```
class user::sysadmins {
  realize(User['thomas'])
  realize(User['theresa'])
  realize(User['josko'])
}
```

4. Modify your `nodes.pp` file as follows:

```
node 'cookbook' {
  include user::virtual
  include user::sysadmins
  include user::developers
}
```

5. Run Puppet:

```
cookbook# puppet agent -t
Info: Caching catalog for cookbook.example.com
Info: Applying configuration version '1413180590'
Notice: /Stage[main]/User::Virtual/User[theresa]/ensure: created
Notice: /Stage[main]/User::Virtual/User[nate]/ensure: created
Notice: /Stage[main]/User::Virtual/User[thomas]/ensure: created
Notice: /Stage[main]/User::Virtual/User[josko]/ensure: created
Notice: Finished catalog run in 0.47 seconds
```

How it works...

When we include the `user::virtual` class, all the users are declared as virtual resources (because we included the @ symbol):

```
@user { 'thomas':  ensure => present }
@user { 'theresa': ensure => present }
@user { 'josko':   ensure => present }
@user { 'nate':    ensure => present }
```

That is to say, the resources exist in Puppet's catalog; they can be referred to by and linked with other resources, and they are in every respect identical to regular resources, except that Puppet doesn't actually create the corresponding users on the machine.

In order for that to happen, we need to call `realize` on the virtual resources. When we include the `user::sysadmins` class, we get the following code:

```
realize(User['thomas'])
realize(User['theresa'])
realize(User['josko'])
```

Calling `realize` on a virtual resource tells Puppet, "I'd like to use that resource now". This is what it does, as we can see from the run output:

Notice: /Stage[main]/User::Virtual/User[theresa]/ensure: created

However, Theresa is in both the `developers` and `sysadmins` classes! Won't that mean we end up calling `realize` twice on the same resource?

```
realize(User['theresa'])
...
realize(User['theresa'])
```

Yes, it does, and that's fine. You're explicitly allowed to realize resources multiple times, and there will be no conflict. So long as some class, somewhere, calls `realize` on Theresa's account, it will be created. Unrealized resources are simply discarded during catalog compilation.

There's more...

When you use this pattern to manage your own users, every node should include the `user::virtual` class, as a part of your basic housekeeping configuration. This class will declare all users (as virtual) in your organization or site. This should also include any users who exist only to run applications or services (such as `Apache`, `www-data`, or `deploy`, for example). Then, you can realize them as needed on individual nodes or in specific classes.

For production use, you'll probably also want to specify a UID and GID for each user or group, so that these numeric identifiers are synchronized across your network. You can do this using the `uid` and `gid` parameters for the `user` resource.

 If you don't specify a user's UID, for example, you'll just get whatever is the next ID number available on a given machine, so the same user on different machines will have a different UID. This can lead to permission problems when using shared storage, or moving files between machines.

A common pattern when defining users as virtual resources is to assign tags to the users based on their assigned roles within your organization. You can then use the `collector` syntax instead of `realize` to collect users with specific tags applied.

For example, see the following code snippet:

```
@user { 'thomas':  ensure => present, tag => 'sysadmin' }
@user { 'theresa': ensure => present, tag => 'sysadmin' }
@user { 'josko':   ensure => present, tag => 'dev' }
User <| tag == 'sysadmin' |>
```

In the previous example, only users `thomas` and `theresa` would be included.

See also

▸ The *Using virtual resources* recipe in this chapter

▸ The *Managing users' customization files* recipe in this chapter

Managing users' SSH access

A sensible approach to access control for servers is to use named user accounts with passphrase-protected SSH keys, rather than having users share an account with a widely known password. Puppet makes this easy to manage thanks to the built-in `ssh_authorized_key` type.

To combine this with virtual users, as described in the previous section, you can create a `define`, which includes both the `user` and `ssh_authorized_key` resources. This will also come in handy when adding customization files and other resources to each user.

How to do it...

Follow these steps to extend your virtual users' class to include SSH access:

1. Create a new module `ssh_user` to contain our `ssh_user` definition. Create the `modules/ssh_user/manifests/init.pp` file as follows:

```
define ssh_user($key,$keytype) {
  user { $name:
    ensure      => present,
  }

  file { "/home/${name}":
    ensure => directory,
    mode    => '0700',
    owner   => $name,
    require => User["$name"]
  }
  file { "/home/${name}/.ssh":
```

```
      ensure => directory,
      mode   => '0700',
      owner  => "$name",
      require => File["/home/${name}"],
    }

    ssh_authorized_key { "${name}_key":
      key      => $key,
      type     => "$keytype",
      user     => $name,
      require => File["/home/${name}/.ssh"],
    }
  }
```

2. Modify your `modules/user/manifests/virtual.pp` file, comment out the previous definition for user `thomas`, and replace it with the following:

```
@ssh_user { 'thomas':
  key     => 'AAAAB3NzaC1yc2E...XaWM5sX0z',
  keytype => 'ssh-rsa'
}
```

3. Modify your `modules/user/manifests/sysadmins.pp` file as follows:

```
class user::sysadmins {
    realize(Ssh_user['thomas'])
}
```

4. Modify your `site.pp` file as follows:

```
node 'cookbook' {
  include user::virtual
  include user::sysadmins
}
```

5. Run Puppet:

```
cookbook# puppet agent -t
Info: Caching catalog for cookbook.example.com
Info: Applying configuration version '1413254461'
Notice: /Stage[main]/User::Virtual/Ssh_user[thomas]/File[/home/
thomas/.ssh]/ensure: created
Notice: /Stage[main]/User::Virtual/Ssh_user[thomas]/Ssh_
authorized_key[thomas_key]/ensure: created
Notice: Finished catalog run in 0.11 seconds
```

How it works...

For each user in our `user::virtual` class, we need to create:

- The user account itself
- The user's home directory and `.ssh` directory
- The user's `.ssh/authorized_keys` file

We could declare separate resources to implement all of these for each user, but it's much easier to create a definition instead, which wraps them into a single resource. By creating a new module for our definition, we can refer to `ssh_user` from anywhere (in any scope):

```
define ssh_user ($key, $keytype) {
  user { $name:
    ensure      => present,
  }
```

After we create the user, we can then create the home directory; we need the user first so that when we assign ownership, we can use the username, `owner => $name`:

```
file { "/home/${name}":
  ensure => directory,
  mode => '0700',
  owner => $name,
  require => User["$name"]
}
```

> Puppet can create the users' home directory using the `managehome` attribute to the user resource. Relying on this mechanism is problematic in practice, as it does not account for users that were created outside of Puppet without home directories.

Next, we need to ensure that the `.ssh` directory exists within the home directory of the user. We require the home directory, `File["/home/${name}"]`, since that needs to exist before we create this subdirectory. This implies that the user already exists because the home directory required the user:

```
file { "/home/${name}/.ssh":
  ensure => directory,
  mode     => '0700',
  owner   => $name ,
  require => File["/home/${name}"],
}
```

Finally, we create the `ssh_authorized_key` resource, again requiring the containing folder (`File["/home/${name}/.ssh"]`). We use the `$key` and `$keytype` variables to assign the key and type parameters to the `ssh_authorized_key` type as follows:

```
ssh_authorized_key { "${name}_key":
  key     => $key,
  type    => "$keytype",
  user    => $name,
  require => File["/home/${name}/.ssh"],
  }
}
```

We passed the `$key` and `$keytype` variables when we defined the `ssh_user` resource for `thomas`:

```
@ssh_user { 'thomas':
  key => 'AAAAB3NzaC1yc2E...XaWM5sX0z',
  keytype => 'ssh-rsa'
}
```

 The value for `key`, in the preceding code snippet, is the ssh key's public key value; it is usually stored in an `id_rsa.pub` file.

Now, with everything defined, we just need to call `realize` on `thomas` for all these resources to take effect:

```
realize(Ssh_user['thomas'])
```

Notice that this time the virtual resource we're realizing is not simply the `user` resource, as before, but the `ssh_user` defined type we created, which includes the user and the related resources needed to set up the SSH access:

`Notice: /Stage[main]/User::Virtual/Ssh_user[thomas]/User[thomas]/ensure: created`

`Notice: /Stage[main]/User::Virtual/Ssh_user[thomas]/File[/home/thomas]/ensure: created`

`Notice: /Stage[main]/User::Virtual/Ssh_user[thomas]/File[/home/thomas/.ssh]/ensure: created`

`Notice: /Stage[main]/User::Virtual/Ssh_user[thomas]/Ssh_authorized_key[thomas_key]/ensure: created`

There's more...

Of course, you can add whatever resources you like to the `ssh_user` definition to have Puppet automatically create them for new users. We'll see an example of this in the next recipe, _Managing users' customization files_.

Managing users' customization files

Users tend to customize their shell environments, terminal colors, aliases, and so forth. This is usually achieved by a number of **dotfiles** in their home directory, for example, `.bash_profile` or `.vimrc`.

You can use Puppet to synchronize and update each user's dotfiles across a number of machines by extending the virtual user setup we developed throughout this chapter. We'll start a new module, `admin_user` and use the file types, `recurse` attribute to copy files into each user's home directory.

How to do it...

Here's what you need to do:

1. Create the `admin_user` defined type (`define admin_user`) in the `modules/admin_user/manifests/init.pp` file as follows:

```
define admin_user ($key, $keytype, $dotfiles = false) {
  $username = $name
  user { $username:
    ensure      => present,
  }
  file { "/home/${username}/.ssh":
    ensure  => directory,
    mode    => '0700',
    owner   => $username,
    group   => $username,
    require => File["/home/${username}"],
  }
  ssh_authorized_key { "${username}_key":
    key     => $key,
    type    => "$keytype",
    user    => $username,
    require => File["/home/${username}/.ssh"],
  }
  # dotfiles
  if $dotfiles == false {
```

```
    # just create the directory
    file { "/home/${username}":
      ensure  => 'directory',
      mode    => '0700',
      owner   => $username,
      group   => $username,
      require => User["$username"]
    }
  } else {
    # copy in all the files in the subdirectory
    file { "/home/${username}":
      recurse => true,
      mode    => '0700',
      owner   => $username,
      group   => $username,
      source  => "puppet:///modules/admin_user/${username}",
      require => User["$username"]
    }
  }
}
```

2. Modify the file `modules/user/manifests/sysadmins.pp` as follows:

```
class user::sysadmins {
  realize(Admin_user['thomas'])
}
```

3. Alter the definition of `thomas` in `modules/user/manifests/virtual.pp` as follows:

```
@ssh_user { 'thomas':
  key => 'AAAAB3NzaC1yc2E...XaWM5sX0z',
  keytype => 'ssh-rsa',
  dotfiles => true
}
```

4. Create a subdirectory in the `admin_user` module for the file of user `thomas`:

```
$ mkdir -p modules/admin_user/files/thomas
```

5. Create dotfiles for the user `thomas` in the directory you just created:

```
$ echo "alias vi=vim" > modules/admin_user/files/thomas/.bashrc

$ echo "set tabstop=2" > modules/admin_user/files/thomas/.vimrc
```

6. Make sure your `site.pp` file reads as follows:

```
node 'cookbook' {
  include user::virtual
```

```
    include user::sysadmins
}
```

7. Run Puppet:

cookbook# puppet agent -t

Info: Caching catalog for cookbook.example.com

Info: Applying configuration version '1413266235'

**Notice: /Stage[main]/User::Virtual/Admin_user[thomas]/
User[thomas]/ensure: created**

**Notice: /Stage[main]/User::Virtual/Admin_user[thomas]/File[/home/
thomas]/ensure: created**

**Notice: /Stage[main]/User::Virtual/Admin_user[thomas]/
File[/home/thomas/.vimrc]/ensure: defined content as '{md5}
cb2af2d35b18b5ac2539057bd429d3ae'**

**Notice: /Stage[main]/User::Virtual/Admin_user[thomas]/File[/home/
thomas/.bashrc]/ensure: defined content as '{md5}033c3484e4b276e06
41becc3aa268a3a'**

**Notice: /Stage[main]/User::Virtual/Admin_user[thomas]/File[/home/
thomas/.ssh]/ensure: created**

**Notice: /Stage[main]/User::Virtual/Admin_user[thomas]/Ssh_
authorized_key[thomas_key]/ensure: created**

Notice: Finished catalog run in 0.36 seconds

How it works...

We created a new admin_user definition, which defines the home directory recursively if
$dotfiles is not false (the default value):

```
if $dotfiles == 'false' {
  # just create the directory
  file { "/home/${username}":
    ensure  => 'directory',
    mode    => '0700',
    owner   => $username,
    group   => $username,
    require => User["$username"]
  }
} else {
  # copy in all the files in the subdirectory
  file { "/home/${username}":
    recurse => true,
    mode    => '0700',
    owner   => $username,
```

```
        group   => $username,
        source  => "puppet:///modules/admin_user/${username}",
        require => User["$username"]
    }
}
```

We created a directory to hold the user's dotfiles within the `admin_user` module; all the files within that directory will be copied into the user's home directory, as shown in the puppet run output in the following command line:

```
Notice: /Stage[main]/User::Virtual/Admin_user[thomas]/File[/home/thomas/.
vimrc]/ensure: defined content as '{md5}cb2af2d35b18b5ac2539057bd429d3ae'
```

```
Notice: /Stage[main]/User::Virtual/Admin_user[thomas]/File[/home/thomas/.
bashrc]/ensure: defined content as '{md5}033c3484e4b276e0641becc3aa268a
3a'
```

Using the `recurse` option allows us to add as many dotfiles as we wish for each user without having to modify the definition of the user.

There's more...

We could specify that the `source` attribute of the home directory is a directory where users can place their own dotfiles. This way, each user could modify their own dotfiles and have them transferred to all the nodes in the network without our involvement.

See also

▶ The *Managing users with virtual resources* recipe in this chapter

Using exported resources

All our recipes up to this point have dealt with a single machine. It is possible with Puppet to have resources from one node affect another node. This interaction is managed with **exported resources**. Exported resources are just like any resource you might define for a node but instead of applying to the node on which they were created, they are exported for use by all nodes in the environment. Exported resources can be thought of as virtual resources that go one step further and exist beyond the node on which they were defined.

There are two actions with exported resources. When an exported resource is created, it is said to be defined. When all the exported resources are harvested, they are said to be collected. Defining exported resources is similar to virtual resources; the resource in question has two @ symbols prepended. For example, to define a file resource as external, use `@@file`. Collecting resources is done with the space ship operator, `<<|  |>>`; this is thought to look like a spaceship. To collect the exported file resource (`@@file`), you would use `File <<| |>>`.

There are many examples that use exported resources; the most common one involves SSH host keys. Using exported resources, it is possible to have every machine that is running Puppet share their SSH host keys with the other connected nodes. The idea here is that each machine exports its own host key and then collects all the keys from the other machines. In our example, we will create two classes; first, a class that exports the SSH host key from every node. We will include this class in our base class. The second class will be a collector class, which collects the SSH host keys. We will apply this class to our Jumpboxes or SSH login servers.

> Jumpboxes are machines that have special firewall rules to allow them to log in to different locations.

Getting ready

To use exported resources, you will need to enable storeconfigs on your Puppet masters. It is possible to use exported resources with a masterless (decentralized) deployment; however, we will assume you are using a centralized model for this example. In *Chapter 2, Puppet Infrastructure*, we configured puppetdb using the puppetdb module from the forge. It is possible to use other backends if you desire; however, all of these except puppetdb are deprecated. More information is available at the following link: `http://projects.puppetlabs.com/projects/puppet/wiki/Using_Stored_Configuration`.

Ensure your Puppet masters are configured to use puppetdb as a storeconfigs container.

How to do it...

We'll create an `ssh_host` class to export the `ssh` keys of a host and ensure that it is included in our base class.

1. Create the first class, `base::ssh_host`, which we will include in our base class:

```
class base::ssh_host {
  @@sshkey{"$::fqdn":
    ensure       => 'present',
    host_aliases => ["$::hostname","$::ipaddress"],
    key          => $::sshdsakey,
    type         => 'dsa',
  }
}
```

2. Remember to include this class from inside the base class definition:

```
class base {
  ...
  include ssh_host
}
```

3. Create a definition for `jumpbox`, either in a class or within the node definition for `jumpbox`:

```
node 'jumpbox' {
  Sshkey <<| |>>
}
```

4. Now run Puppet on a few nodes to create the exported resources. In my case, I ran Puppet on my Puppet server and my second example node (`node2`). Finally, run Puppet on `jumpbox` to verify that the SSH host keys for our other nodes are collected:

```
[root@jumpbox ~]# puppet agent -t

Info: Caching catalog for jumpbox.example.com

Info: Applying configuration version '1413176635'

Notice: /Stage[main]/Main/Node[jumpbox]/Sshkey[node2.example.com]/
ensure: created

Notice: /Stage[main]/Main/Node[jumpbox]/Sshkey[puppet]/ensure:
created

Notice: Finished catalog run in 0.08 seconds
```

How it works...

We created an `sshkey` resource for the node using the facter facts `fqdn`, `hostname`, `ipaddress`, and `sshdsakey`. We use the `fqdn` as the title for our exported resource because each exported resource must have a unique name. We can assume the `fqdn` of a node will be unique within our organization (although sometimes they may not be; Puppet can be good at finding out such things when you least expect it). We then go on to define aliases by which our node may be known. We use the hostname variable for one alias and the main IP address of the machine as the other. If you had other naming conventions for your nodes, you could include other aliases here. We assume that hosts are using DSA keys, so we use the `sshdsakey` variable in our definition. In a large installation, you would wrap this definition in tests to ensure the DSA keys existed. You would also use the RSA keys if they existed as well.

With the `sshkey` resource defined and exported, we then created a `jumpbox` node definition. In this definition, we used the spaceship syntax `Sshkey <<| |>>` to collect all defined exported `sshkey` resources.

There's more...

When defining the exported resources, you can add tag attributes to the resource to create subsets of exported resources. For example, if you had a development and production area of your network, you could create different groups of `sshkey` resources for each area as shown in the following code snippet:

```
@@sshkey{"$::fqdn":
    host_aliases => ["$::hostname","$::ipaddress"],
    key          => $::sshdsakey,
    type         => 'dsa',
    tag          => "$::environment",
}
```

You could then modify `jumpbox` to only collect resources for production, for example, as follows:

```
Sshkey <<| tag == 'production' |>>
```

Two important things to remember when working with exported resources: first, every resource must have a unique name across your installation. Using the `fqdn` domain name within the title is usually enough to keep your definitions unique. Second, any resource can be made virtual. Even defined types that you created may be exported. Exported resources can be used to achieve some fairly complex configurations that automatically adjust when machines change.

One word of caution when working with an extremely large number of nodes (more than 5,000) is that exported resources can take a long time to collect and apply, particularly if each exported resource creates a file.

6
Managing Resources and Files

"The art of simplicity is a puzzle of complexity".

– Douglas Horton

In this chapter, we will cover the following recipes:

- ▶ Distributing cron jobs efficiently
- ▶ Scheduling when resources are applied
- ▶ Using host resources
- ▶ Using exported host resources
- ▶ Using multiple file sources
- ▶ Distributing and merging directory trees
- ▶ Cleaning up old files
- ▶ Auditing resources
- ▶ Temporarily disabling resources

Introduction

In the previous chapter, we introduced virtual and exported resources. Virtual and exported resources are ways to manage the way in which resources are applied to a node. In this chapter, we will deal with when and how to apply resources. In some cases, you may only wish to apply a resource off hours, while in others, you may wish to only audit the resource but change nothing. In other cases, you may wish to apply completely different resources based on which node is using the code. As we will see, Puppet has the flexibility to deal with all these scenarios.

Distributing cron jobs efficiently

When you have many servers executing the same cron job, it's usually a good idea not to run them all at the same time. If all the jobs access a common server (for example, when running backups), it may put too much load on that server, and even if they don't, all the servers will be busy at the same time, which may affect their capacity to provide other services.

As usual, Puppet can help; this time, using the `inline_template` function to calculate a unique time for each job.

How to do it...

Here's how to have Puppet schedule the same job at a different time for each machine:

1. Modify your `site.pp` file as follows:

```
node 'cookbook' {
  cron { 'run-backup':
    ensure  => present,
    command => '/usr/local/bin/backup',
    hour    => inline_template('<%= @hostname.sum % 24 %>'),
    minute  => '00',
  }
}
```

2. Run Puppet:

```
[root@cookbook ~]# puppet agent -t
Info: Caching catalog for cookbook.example.com
Info: Applying configuration version '1413730771'
Notice: /Stage[main]/Main/Node[cookbook]/Cron[run-backup]/ensure:
created
Notice: Finished catalog run in 0.11 seconds
```

3. Run `crontab` to see how the job has been configured:

```
[root@cookbook ~]# crontab -l
# HEADER: This file was autogenerated at Sun Oct 19 10:59:32 -0400
2014 by puppet.
# HEADER: While it can still be managed manually, it is definitely
not recommended.
# HEADER: Note particularly that the comments starting with
'Puppet Name' should
# HEADER: not be deleted, as doing so could cause duplicate cron
jobs.
# Puppet Name: run-backup
0 15 * * * /usr/local/bin/backup
```

How it works...

We want to distribute the hour of the cron job runs across all our nodes. We choose something that is unique across all the machines and convert it to a number. This way, the value will be distributed across the nodes and will not change per node.

We can do the conversion using Ruby's `sum` method, which computes a numerical value from a string that is unique to the machine (in this case, the machine's hostname). The `sum` function will generate a large integer (in the case of the string `cookbook`, the sum is 855), and we want values for `hour` between 0 and 23, so we use Ruby's `%` (modulo) operator to restrict the result to this range. We should get a reasonably good (though not statistically uniform) distribution of values, depending on your hostnames. Another option here is to use the `fqdn_rand()` function, which works in much the same way as our example.

If all your machines have the same name (it does happen), don't expect this trick to work! In this case, you can use some other string that is unique to the machine, such as `ipaddress` or `fqdn`.

There's more...

If you have several cron jobs per machine and you want to run them a certain number of hours apart, add this number to the `hostname.sum` resource before taking the modulus. Let's say we want to run the `dump_database` job at some arbitrary time and the `run_backup` job an hour later, this can be done using the following code snippet:

```
cron { 'dump-database':
  ensure  => present,
  command => '/usr/local/bin/dump_database',
  hour    => inline_template('<%= @hostname.sum % 24 %>'),
  minute  => '00',
```

```
  }

cron { 'run-backup':
  ensure  => present,
  command => '/usr/local/bin/backup',
  hour    => inline_template('<%= ( @hostname.sum + 1) % 24 %>'),
  minute  => '00',
}
```

The two jobs will end up with different `hour` values for each machine Puppet runs on, but `run_backup` will always be one hour after `dump_database`.

Most cron implementations have directories for hourly, daily, weekly, and monthly tasks. The directories `/etc/cron.hourly`, `/etc/cron.daily`, `/etc/cron.weekly`, and `/etc/cron.monthly` exist on both our Debian and Enterprise Linux machines. These directories hold executables, which will be run on the referenced schedule (hourly, daily, weekly, or monthly). I find it better to describe all the jobs in these folders and push the jobs as `file` resources. An admin on the box searching for your script will be able to find it with `grep` in these directories. To use the same trick here, we would push a cron task into `/etc/cron.hourly` and then verify that the hour is the correct hour for the task to run. To create the cron jobs using the cron directories, follow these steps:

1. First, create a `cron` class in `modules/cron/init.pp`:

   ```
   class cron {
     file { '/etc/cron.hourly/run-backup':
       content => template('cron/run-backup'),
       mode    => 0755,
     }
   }
   ```

2. Include the `cron` class in your cookbook node in `site.pp`:

   ```
   node cookbook {
     include cron
   }
   ```

3. Create a template to hold the cron task:

   ```
   #!/bin/bash

   runhour=<%= @hostname.sum%24 %>
   hour=$(date +%H)
   if [ "$runhour" -ne "$hour" ]; then
     exit 0
   fi

   echo run-backup
   ```

4. Then, run Puppet:

```
[root@cookbook ~]# puppet agent -t
Info: Caching catalog for cookbook.example.com
Info: Applying configuration version '1413732254'
Notice: /Stage[main]/Cron/File[/etc/cron.hourly/run-backup]/
ensure: defined content as '{md5}5e50a7b586ce774df23301ee72904dda'
Notice: Finished catalog run in 0.11 seconds
```

5. Verify that the script has the same value we calculated before, 15:

```
#!/bin/bash

runhour=15
hour=$(date +%H)
if [ "$runhour" -ne "$hour" ]; then
  exit 0
fi

echo run-backup
```

Now, this job will run every hour but only when the hour, returned by $(date +%H), is equal to 15 will the rest of the script run. Creating your cron jobs as file resources in a large organization makes it easier for your fellow administrators to find them. When you have a very large number of machines, it can be advantageous to add another random wait at the beginning of your job. You would need to modify the line before echo run-backup and add the following:

```
MAXWAIT=600
sleep $((RANDOM%MAXWAIT))
```

This will sleep a maximum of 600 seconds but will sleep a different amount each time it runs (assuming your random number generator is working). This sort of random wait is useful when you have thousands of machines, all running the same task and you need to stagger the runs as much as possible.

See also

▶ The *Running Puppet from cron* recipe in *Chapter 2, Puppet Infrastructure*

Scheduling when resources are applied

So far, we looked at what Puppet can do, and the order that it does things in, but not when it does them. One way to control this is to use the `schedule` metaparameter. When you need to limit the number of times a resource is applied within a specified period, `schedule` can help. For example:

```
exec { "/usr/bin/apt-get update":
    schedule => daily,
}
```

The most important thing to understand about `schedule` is that it can only stop a resource being applied. It doesn't guarantee that the resource will be applied with a certain frequency. For example, the `exec` resource shown in the preceding code snippet has `schedule =>` `daily`, but this just represents an upper limit on the number of times the `exec` resource can run per day. It won't be applied more than once a day. If you don't run Puppet at all, the resource won't be applied at all. Using the hourly schedule, for instance, is meaningless on a machine configured to run the agent every 4 hours (via the `runinterval` configuration setting).

That being said, `schedule` is best used to restrict resources from running when they shouldn't, or don't need to; for example, you might want to make sure that `apt-get update` isn't run more than once an hour. There are some built-in schedules available for you to use:

- `hourly`
- `daily`
- `weekly`
- `monthly`
- `never`

However, you can modify these and create your own custom schedules, using the `schedule` resource. We'll see how to do this in the following example. Let's say we want to make sure that an `exec` resource representing a maintenance job won't run during office hours, when it might interfere with production.

How to do it...

In this example, we'll create a custom `schedule` resource and assign this to the resource:

1. Modify your `site.pp` file as follows:

```
schedule { 'outside-office-hours':
  period => daily,
  range  => ['17:00-23:59','00:00-09:00'],
  repeat => 1,
```

```
  }
node 'cookbook' {
  notify { 'Doing some maintenance':
    schedule => 'outside-office-hours',
  }
}
```

2. Run Puppet. What you'll see will depend on the time of the day. If it's currently outside the office hours period you defined, Puppet will apply the resource as follows:

```
[root@cookbook ~]# date
Fri Jan  2 23:59:01 PST 2015
[root@cookbook ~]# puppet agent -t
Info: Caching catalog for cookbook.example.com
Info: Applying configuration version '1413734477'
Notice: Doing some maintenance
Notice: /Stage[main]/Main/Node[cookbook]/Notify[Doing some
maintenance]/message: defined 'message' as 'Doing some
maintenance'
Notice: Finished catalog run in 0.07 seconds
```

3. If the time is within the office hours period, Puppet will do nothing:

```
[root@cookbook ~]# date
Fri Jan  2 09:59:01 PST 2015
[root@cookbook ~]# puppet agent -t
Info: Caching catalog for cookbook.example.com
Info: Applying configuration version '1413734289'
Notice: Finished catalog run in 0.09 seconds
```

How it works...

A schedule consists of three bits of information:

- The period (hourly, daily, weekly, or monthly)
- The range (defaults to the whole period, but can be a smaller part of it)
- The repeat count (how often the resource is allowed to be applied within the range; the default is 1 or once per period)

Our custom schedule named `outside-office-hours` supplies these three parameters:

```
schedule { 'outside-office-hours':
  period => daily,
  range  => ['17:00-23:59','00:00-09:00'],
  repeat => 1,
}
```

The `period` is `daily`, and `range` is defined as an array of two time intervals:

```
17:00-23:59
00:00-09:00
```

The schedule named `outside-office-hours` is now available for us to use with any resource, just as though it were built into Puppet such as the `daily` or `hourly` schedules. In our example, we assign this schedule to the `exec` resource using the `schedule` metaparameter:

```
notify { 'Doing some maintenance':
  schedule => 'outside-office-hours',
}
```

Without this `schedule` parameter, the resource would be applied every time Puppet runs. With it, Puppet will check the following parameters to decide whether or not to apply the resource:

- ▶ Whether the time is in the permitted range
- ▶ Whether the resource has already been run the maximum permitted number of times in this period

For example, let's consider what happens if Puppet runs at 4 p.m., 5 p.m., and 6 p.m. on a given day:

- ▶ **4 p.m.**: It's outside the permitted time range, so Puppet will do nothing
- ▶ **5 p.m.**: It's inside the permitted time range, and the resource hasn't been run yet in this period, so Puppet will apply the resource
- ▶ **6 p.m.**: It's inside the permitted time range, but the resource has already been run the maximum number of times in this period, so Puppet will do nothing

And so on until the next day.

There's more...

The `repeat` parameter governs how many times the resource will be applied given the other constraints of the schedule. For example, to apply a resource no more than six times an hour, use a schedule as follows:

```
period => hourly,
repeat => 6,
```

Remember that this won't guarantee that the job is run six times an hour. It just sets an upper limit; no matter how often Puppet runs or anything else happens, the job won't be run if it has already run six times this hour. If Puppet only runs once a day, the job will just be run once. So `schedule` is best used to make sure things don't happen at certain times (or don't exceed a given frequency).

Using host resources

It's not always practical or convenient to use DNS to map your machine names to IP addresses, especially in cloud infrastructures, where those addresses may change all the time. However, if you use entries in the `/etc/hosts` file instead, you then have the problem of how to distribute these entries to all machines and keep them up to date.

Here's a better way to do it; Puppet's host resource type controls a single `/etc/hosts` entry, and you can use this to map a hostname to an IP address easily across your whole network. For example, if all your machines need to know the address of the main database server, you can manage it with a `host` resource.

How to do it...

Follow these steps to create an example `host` resource:

1. Modify your `site.pp` file as follows:

   ```
   node 'cookbook' {
     host { 'packtpub.com':
       ensure => present,
       ip      => '83.166.169.231',
     }
   }
   ```

2. Run Puppet:

   ```
   [root@cookbook ~]# puppet agent -t
   Info: Caching catalog for cookbook.example.com
   Info: Applying configuration version '1413781153'
   Notice: /Stage[main]/Main/Node[cookbook]/Host[packtpub.com]/
   ensure: created
   Info: Computing checksum on file /etc/hosts
   Notice: Finished catalog run in 0.12 seconds
   ```

How it works...

Puppet will check the `target` file (usually `/etc/hosts`) to see whether the host entry already exists, and if not, add it. If an entry for that hostname already exists with a different address, Puppet will change the address to match the manifest.

There's more...

Organizing your host resources into classes can be helpful. For example, you could put the host resources for all your DB servers into one class called `admin::dbhosts`, which is included by all web servers.

Where machines may need to be defined in multiple classes (for example, a database server might also be a repository server), virtual resources can solve this problem. For example, you could define all your hosts as virtual in a single class:

```
class admin::allhosts {
  @host { 'db1.packtpub.com':
    tag => 'database'
    ...
  }
}
```

You could then realize the hosts you need in the various classes:

```
class admin::dbhosts {
  Host <| tag=='database' |>
}

class admin::webhosts {
  Host <| tag=='web' |>
}
```

Using exported host resources

In the previous example, we used the spaceship syntax to collect virtual host resources for hosts of type database or type web. You can use the same trick with exported resources. The advantage to using exported resources is that as you add more database servers, the collector syntax will automatically pull in the newly created exported host entries for those servers. This makes your `/etc/hosts` entries more dynamic.

Getting ready

We will be using exported resources. If you haven't already done so, set up puppetdb and enable storeconfigs to use puppetdb as outlined in *Chapter 2, Puppet Infrastructure*.

How to do it...

In this example, we will configure database servers and clients to communicate with each other. We'll make use of exported resources to do the configuration.

1. Create a new database module, db:

    ```
    t@mylaptop ~/puppet/modules $ mkdir -p db/manifests
    ```

2. Create a new class for your database servers, db::server:

    ```
    class db::server {
      @@host {"$::fqdn":
        host_aliases => $::hostname,
        ip           => $::ipaddress,
        tag          => 'db::server',
      }
      # rest of db class
    }
    ```

3. Create a new class for your database clients:

    ```
    class db::client {
      Host <<| tag == 'db::server' |>>
    }
    ```

4. Apply the database server module to some nodes, in site.pp, for example:

    ```
    node 'dbserver1.example.com' {
      class {'db::server': }
    }
    node 'dbserver2.example.com' {
      class {'db::server': }
    }
    ```

5. Run Puppet on the nodes with the database server module to create the exported resources.

6. Apply the database client module to cookbook:

    ```
    node 'cookbook' {
      class {'db::client': }
    }
    ```

7. Run Puppet:

```
[root@cookbook ~]# puppet agent -t
Info: Caching catalog for cookbook.example.com
Info: Applying configuration version '1413782501'
Notice: /Stage[main]/Db::Client/Host[dbserver2.example.com]/
ensure: created
Info: Computing checksum on file /etc/hosts
Notice: /Stage[main]/Db::Client/Host[dbserver1.example.com]/
ensure: created
Notice: Finished catalog run in 0.10 seconds
```

8. Verify the host entries in /etc/hosts:

```
[root@cookbook ~]# cat /etc/hosts
# HEADER: This file was autogenerated at Mon Oct 20 01:21:42 -0400
2014
# HEADER: by puppet.  While it can still be managed manually, it
# HEADER: is definitely not recommended.
127.0.0.1    localhost  localhost.localdomain localhost4
localhost4.localdomain4
::1  localhost  localhost.localdomain localhost6 localhost6.
localdomain6
83.166.169.231  packtpub.com
192.168.122.150  dbserver2.example.com   dbserver2
192.168.122.151  dbserver1.example.com   dbserver1
```

How it works...

In the db::server class, we create an exported host resource:

```
@@host {"$::fqdn":
  host_aliases => $::hostname,
  ip           => $::ipaddress,
  tag          => 'db::server',
}
```

This resource uses the fully qualified domain name ($::fqdn) of the node on which it is applied. We also use the short hostname ($::hostname) as an alias of the node. Aliases are printed after fqdn in /etc/hosts. We use the node's $::ipaddress fact as the IP address for the host entry. Finally, we add a tag to the resource so that we can collect based on that tag later.

The important thing to remember here is that if the IP address should change for the host, the exported resource will be updated, and nodes that collect the exported resource will update their host records accordingly.

We created a collector in `db::client`, which only collects exported host resources that have been tagged with `'db::server'`:

```
Host <<| tag == 'db::server' |>>
```

We applied the `db::server` class for a couple of nodes, dbserver1 and dbserver2, which we then collected on cookbook by applying the `db::client` class. The host entries were placed in `/etc/hosts` (the default file). We can see that the host entry contains both the fqdn and the short hostname for dbserver1 and dbserver2.

There's more...

Using exported resources in this manner is very useful. Another similar system would be to create an NFS server class, which creates exported resources for the mount points that it exports (via NFS). You can then use tags to have clients collect the appropriate mount points from the server. In the previous example, we made use of a tag to aid in our collection of exported resources. It is worth noting that there are several tags automatically added to resources when they are created, one of which is the scope where the resource was created.

Using multiple file sources

A neat feature of Puppet's `file` resource is that you can specify multiple values for the `source` parameter. Puppet will search them in order. If the first source isn't found, it moves on to the next, and so on. You can use this to specify a default substitute if the particular file isn't present, or even a series of increasingly generic substitutes.

How to do it...

This example demonstrates using multiple file sources:

1. Create a new greeting module as follows:

```
class greeting {
  file { '/tmp/greeting':
    source => [ 'puppet:///modules/greeting/hello.txt',
                'puppet:///modules/greeting/universal.txt'],
  }
}
```

2. Create the file `modules/greeting/files/hello.txt` with the following contents:

   ```
   Hello, world.
   ```

3. Create the file `modules/greeting/files/universal.txt` with the following contents:

   ```
   Bah-weep-Graaaaagnah wheep ni ni bong
   ```

4. Add the class to a node:

   ```
   node cookbook {
     class {'greeting': }
   }
   ```

5. Run Puppet:

   ```
   [root@cookbook ~]# puppet agent -t
   Info: Caching catalog for cookbook.example.com
   Info: Applying configuration version '1413784347'
   Notice: /Stage[main]/Greeting/File[/tmp/greeting]/ensure: defined
   content as '{md5}54098b367d2e87b078671fad4afb9dbb'
   Notice: Finished catalog run in 0.43 seconds
   ```

6. Check the contents of the `/tmp/greeting` file:

   ```
   [root@cookbook ~]# cat /tmp/greeting
   Hello, world.
   ```

7. Now remove the `hello.txt` file from your Puppet repository and rerun the agent:

   ```
   [root@cookbook ~]# puppet agent -t
   Info: Caching catalog for cookbook.example.com
   Info: Applying configuration version '1413784939'
   Notice: /Stage[main]/Greeting/File[/tmp/greeting]/content:
   --- /tmp/greeting    2014-10-20 01:52:28.117999991 -0400
   +++ /tmp/puppet-file20141020-4960-1o9g344-0    2014-10-20
   02:02:20.695999979 -0400
   @@ -1 +1 @@
   -Hello, world.
   +Bah-weep-Graaaaagnah wheep ni ni bong

   Info: Computing checksum on file /tmp/greeting
   Info: /Stage[main]/Greeting/File[/tmp/greeting]: Filebucketed /
   tmp/greeting to puppet with sum 54098b367d2e87b078671fad4afb9dbb
   ```

```
Notice: /Stage[main]/Greeting/File[/tmp/greeting]/content: content
changed '{md5}54098b367d2e87b078671fad4afb9dbb' to '{md5}933c7f04d
501b45456e830de299b5521'

Notice: Finished catalog run in 0.77 seconds
```

How it works...

On the first Puppet run, puppet searches for the available file sources in the order given:

```
source => [
  'puppet:///modules/greeting/hello.txt',
  'puppet:///modules/greeting/universal.txt'
],
```

The file `hello.txt` is first in the list, and is present, so Puppet uses that as the source for `/tmp/greeting`:

```
Hello, world.
```

On the second Puppet run, `hello.txt` is missing, so Puppet goes on to look for the next file, `universal.txt`. This is present, so it becomes the source for `/tmp/greeting`:

```
Bah-weep-Graaaaagnah wheep ni ni bong
```

There's more...

You can use this trick anywhere you have a `file` resource. A common example is a service that is deployed on all nodes, such as rsyslog. The `rsyslog` configuration is the same on every host except for the rsyslog server. Create an `rsyslog` class with a file resource for the `rsyslog` configuration file:

```
class rsyslog {
  file { '/etc/rsyslog.conf':
    source => [
      "puppet:///modules/rsyslog/rsyslog.conf.${::hostname}",
      'puppet:///modules/rsyslog/rsyslog.conf' ],
  }
}
```

Then, you put the default configuration in `rsyslog.conf`. For your rsyslog server, `logger`, create an `rsyslog.conf.logger` file. On the machine logger, `rsyslog.conf.logger` will be used before `rsyslog.conf` because it is listed first in the array of sources.

See also

 ▸ The *Passing parameters to classes* recipe in *Chapter 3, Writing Better Manifests*

Distributing and merging directory trees

As we saw in the previous chapter, the file resource has a `recurse` parameter, which allows Puppet to transfer entire directory trees. We used this parameter to copy an admin user's dotfiles into their home directory. In this section, we'll show how to use `recurse` and another parameter `sourceselect` to extend our previous example.

How to do it...

Modify our admin user example as follows:

1. Remove the `$dotfiles` parameter, remove the condition based on `$dotfiles`. Add a second source to the home directory `file` resource:

```
define admin_user ($key, $keytype) {
  $username = $name
  user { $username:
    ensure      => present,
  }
  file { "/home/${username}/.ssh":
    ensure  => directory,
    mode    => '0700',
    owner   => $username,
    group   => $username,
    require => File["/home/${username}"],
  }
  ssh_authorized_key { "${username}_key":
    key     => $key,
    type    => "$keytype",
    user    => $username,
    require => File["/home/${username}/.ssh"],
  }
  # copy in all the files in the subdirectory
  file { "/home/${username}":
    recurse => true,
    mode    => '0700',
    owner   => $username,
    group   => $username,
```

```
        source   => [
          "puppet:///modules/admin_user/${username}",
          'puppet:///modules/admin_user/base' ],
        sourceselect => 'all',
        require       => User["$username"],
      }
    }
```

2. Create a base directory and copy all the system default files from `/etc/skel`:

   `t@mylaptop ~/puppet/modules/admin_user/files $ cp -a /etc/skel base`

3. Create a new `admin_user` resource, one that will not have a directory defined:

```
node 'cookbook' {
  admin_user {'steven':
    key     => 'AAAAB3N...',
    keytype => 'dsa',
  }
}
```

4. Run Puppet:

   `[root@cookbook ~]# puppet agent -t`

   `Info: Caching catalog for cookbook.example.com`

   `Info: Applying configuration version '1413787159'`

   `Notice: /Stage[main]/Main/Node[cookbook]/Admin_user[steven]/User[steven]/ensure: created`

   `Notice: /Stage[main]/Main/Node[cookbook]/Admin_user[steven]/File[/home/steven]/ensure: created`

   `Notice: /Stage[main]/Main/Node[cookbook]/Admin_user[steven]/File[/home/steven/.bash_logout]/ensure: defined content as '{md5}6a5bc1c c5f80a48b540bc09d082b5855'`

   `Notice: /Stage[main]/Main/Node[cookbook]/Admin_user[steven]/File[/home/steven/.emacs]/ensure: defined content as '{md5} de7ee35f4058681a834a99b5d1b048b3'`

   `Notice: /Stage[main]/Main/Node[cookbook]/Admin_user[steven]/File[/home/steven/.bashrc]/ensure: defined content as '{md5}2f8222b4f275 c4f18e69c34f66d2631b'`

   `Notice: /Stage[main]/Main/Node[cookbook]/Admin_user[steven]/File[/home/steven/.bash_profile]/ensure: defined content as '{md5} f939eb71a81a9da364410b799e817202'`

```
Notice: /Stage[main]/Main/Node[cookbook]/Admin_user[steven]/File[/
home/steven/.ssh]/ensure: created

Notice: /Stage[main]/Main/Node[cookbook]/Admin_user[steven]/Ssh_
authorized_key[steven_key]/ensure: created

Notice: Finished catalog run in 1.11 seconds
```

How it works...

If a `file` resource has the `recurse` parameter set on it, and it is a directory, Puppet will deploy not only the directory itself, but all its contents (including subdirectories and their contents). As we saw in the previous example, when a file has more than one source, the first source file found is used to satisfy the request. This applies to directories as well.

There's more...

By specifying the parameter `sourceselect` as 'all', the contents of all the source directories will be combined. For example, add `thomas admin_user` back into your node definition in `site.pp` for cookbook:

```
admin_user {'thomas':
    key     => 'ABBA...',
    keytype => 'rsa',
}
```

Now run Puppet again on cookbook:

```
[root@cookbook thomas]# puppet agent -t
Info: Caching catalog for cookbook.example.com
Info: Applying configuration version '1413787770'
Notice: /Stage[main]/Main/Node[cookbook]/Admin_user[thomas]/File[/home/
thomas/.bash_profile]/content: content changed '{md5}3e8337f44f84b298a8a9
9869ae8ca76a' to '{md5}f939eb71a81a9da364410b799e817202'

Notice: /Stage[main]/Main/Node[cookbook]/Admin_user[thomas]/File[/home/
thomas/.bash_profile]/group: group changed 'root' to 'thomas'

Notice: /Stage[main]/Main/Node[cookbook]/Admin_user[thomas]/File[/home/
thomas/.bash_profile]/mode: mode changed '0644' to '0700'

Notice: /File[/home/thomas/.bash_profile]/seluser: seluser changed
'system_u' to 'unconfined_u'

Notice: /Stage[main]/Main/Node[cookbook]/Admin_user[thomas]/File[/home/
thomas/.bash_logout]/ensure: defined content as '{md5}6a5bc1cc5f80a48b540
bc09d082b5855'
```

```
Notice: /Stage[main]/Main/Node[cookbook]/Admin_user[thomas]/
File[/home/thomas/.bashrc]/content: content changed '{md5}
db2a20b2b9cdf36cca1ca4672622ddd2' to '{md5}033c3484e4b276e0641becc3aa268a
3a'
```

```
Notice: /Stage[main]/Main/Node[cookbook]/Admin_user[thomas]/File[/home/
thomas/.bashrc]/group: group changed 'root' to 'thomas'
```

```
Notice: /Stage[main]/Main/Node[cookbook]/Admin_user[thomas]/File[/home/
thomas/.bashrc]/mode: mode changed '0644' to '0700'
```

```
Notice: /File[/home/thomas/.bashrc]/seluser: seluser changed 'system_u'
to 'unconfined_u'
```

```
Notice: /Stage[main]/Main/Node[cookbook]/Admin_user[thomas]/
File[/home/thomas/.emacs]/ensure: defined content as '{md5}
de7ee35f4058681a834a99b5d1b048b3'
```

```
Notice: Finished catalog run in 0.86 seconds
```

Because we previously applied the `thomas` `admin_user` to cookbook, the user existed. The two files defined in the `thomas` directory on the Puppet server were already in the home directory, so only the additional files, `.bash_logout`, `.bash_profile`, and `.emacs` were created. Using these two parameters together, you can have default files that can be overridden easily.

Sometimes you want to deploy files to an existing directory but remove any files which aren't managed by Puppet. A good example would be if you are using `mcollective` in your environment. The directory holding client credentials should only have certificates that come from Puppet.

The `purge` parameter will do this for you. Define the directory as a resource in Puppet:

```
file { '/etc/mcollective/ssl/clients':
  purge   => true,
  recurse => true,
}
```

The combination of `recurse` and `purge` will remove all files and subdirectories in `/etc/mcollective/ssl/clients` that are not deployed by Puppet. You can then deploy your own files to that location by placing them in the appropriate directory on the Puppet server.

If there are subdirectories that contain files you don't want to purge, just define the subdirectory as a Puppet resource, and it will be left alone:

```
file { '/etc/mcollective/ssl/clients':
  purge => true,
  recurse => true,
}
file { '/etc/mcollective/ssl/clients/local':
  ensure => directory,
}
```

Be aware that, at least in current implementations of Puppet, recursive file copies can be quite slow and place a heavy memory load on the server. If the data doesn't change very often, it might be better to deploy and unpack a `tar` file instead. This can be done with a file resource for the `tar` file and an exec, which requires the file resource and unpacks the archive. Recursive directories are less of a problem when filled with small files. Puppet is not a very efficient file server, so creating large tar files and distributing them with Puppet is not a good idea either. If you need to copy large files around, using the Operating Systems packager is a better solution.

Cleaning up old files

Puppet's `tidy` resource will help you clean up old or out-of-date files, reducing disk usage. For example, if you have Puppet reporting enabled as described in the section on generating reports, you might want to regularly delete old report files.

How to do it...

Let's get started.

1. Modify your `site.pp` file as follows:

```
node 'cookbook' {
  tidy { '/var/lib/puppet/reports':
    age     => '1w',
    recurse => true,
  }
}
```

2. Run Puppet:

```
[root@cookbook clients]# puppet agent -t
Info: Caching catalog for cookbook.example.com
Notice: /Stage[main]/Main/Node[cookbook]/File[/var/lib/puppet/
reports/cookbook.example.com/201409090637.yaml]/ensure: removed
Notice: /Stage[main]/Main/Node[cookbook]/File[/var/lib/puppet/
reports/cookbook.example.com/201409100556.yaml]/ensure: removed
Notice: /Stage[main]/Main/Node[cookbook]/File[/var/lib/puppet/
reports/cookbook.example.com/201409090631.yaml]/ensure: removed
Notice: /Stage[main]/Main/Node[cookbook]/File[/var/lib/puppet/
reports/cookbook.example.com/201408210557.yaml]/ensure: removed
Notice: /Stage[main]/Main/Node[cookbook]/File[/var/lib/puppet/
reports/cookbook.example.com/201409080557.yaml]/ensure: removed
```

```
Notice: /Stage[main]/Main/Node[cookbook]/File[/var/lib/puppet/
reports/cookbook.example.com/201409100558.yaml]/ensure: removed

Notice: /Stage[main]/Main/Node[cookbook]/File[/var/lib/puppet/
reports/cookbook.example.com/201408210546.yaml]/ensure: removed

Notice: /Stage[main]/Main/Node[cookbook]/File[/var/lib/puppet/
reports/cookbook.example.com/201408210539.yaml]/ensure: removed

Notice: Finished catalog run in 0.80 seconds
```

How it works...

Puppet searches the specified path for any files matching the `age` parameter; in this case, `2w` (two weeks). It also searches subdirectories (`recurse => true`).

Any files matching your criteria will be deleted.

There's more...

You can specify file ages in seconds, minutes, hours, days, or weeks by using a single character to specify the time unit, as follows:

- `60s`
- `180m`
- `24h`
- `30d`
- `4w`

You can specify that files greater than a given size should be removed, as follows:

```
size => '100m',
```

This removes files of 100 megabytes and over. For kilobytes, use `k`, and for bytes, use `b`.

> Note that if you specify both age and size parameters, they are treated as independent criteria. For example, if you specify the following, Puppet will remove all files that are either at least one day old, or at least 512 KB in size:
>
> age => "1d",
>
> size => "512k",

Auditing resources

Dry run mode, using the `--noop` switch, is a simple way to audit any changes to a machine under Puppet's control. However, Puppet also has a dedicated audit feature, which can report changes to resources or specific attributes.

How to do it...

Here's an example showing Puppet's auditing capabilities:

1. Modify your `site.pp` file as follows:

```
node 'cookbook' {
  file { '/etc/passwd':
    audit => [ owner, mode ],
  }
}
```

2. Run Puppet:

```
[root@cookbook clients]# puppet agent -t
Info: Caching catalog for cookbook.example.com
Info: Applying configuration version '1413789080'
Notice: /Stage[main]/Main/Node[cookbook]/File[/etc/passwd]/owner:
audit change: newly-recorded value 0
Notice: /Stage[main]/Main/Node[cookbook]/File[/etc/passwd]/mode:
audit change: newly-recorded value 644
Notice: Finished catalog run in 0.55 seconds
```

How it works...

The `audit` metaparameter tells Puppet that you want to record and monitor certain things about the resource. The value can be a list of the parameters that you want to audit.

In this case, when Puppet runs, it will now record the owner and mode of the `/etc/passwd` file. In future runs, Puppet will spot whether either of these has changed. For example, if you run:

```
[root@cookbook ~]# chmod 666 /etc/passwd
```

Puppet will pick up this change and log it on the next run:

```
Notice: /Stage[main]/Main/Node[cookbook]/File[/etc/passwd]/mode: audit
change: previously recorded value 0644 has been changed to 0666
```

There's more...

This feature is very useful to audit large networks for any changes to machines, either malicious or accidental. It's also very handy to keep an eye on things that aren't managed by Puppet, for example, application code on production servers. You can read more about Puppet's auditing capability here:

```
http://puppetlabs.com/blog/all-about-auditing-with-puppet/
```

If you just want to audit everything about a resource, use `all`:

```
file { '/etc/passwd':
  audit => all,
}
```

See also

▶ The *Noop - the don't change anything option* recipe in *Chapter 10, Monitoring, Reporting, and Troubleshooting*

Temporarily disabling resources

Sometimes you want to disable a resource for the time being so that it doesn't interfere with other work. For example, you might want to tweak a configuration file on the server until you have the exact settings you want, before checking it into Puppet. You don't want Puppet to overwrite it with an old version in the meantime, so you can set the `noop` metaparameter on the resource:

```
noop => true,
```

How to do it...

This example shows you how to use the `noop` metaparameter:

1. Modify your `site.pp` file as follows:

```
node 'cookbook' {
  file { '/etc/resolv.conf':
    content => "nameserver 127.0.0.1\n",
    noop    => true,
  }
}
```

2. Run Puppet:

```
[root@cookbook ~]# puppet agent -t
Info: Caching catalog for cookbook.example.com
Info: Applying configuration version '1413789438'
Notice: /Stage[main]/Main/Node[cookbook]/File[/etc/resolv.conf]/
content:
--- /etc/resolv.conf  2014-10-20 00:27:43.095999975 -0400
+++ /tmp/puppet-file20141020-8439-1lhuy1y-0    2014-10-20
03:17:18.969999979 -0400
@@ -1,3 +1 @@
-; generated by /sbin/dhclient-script
-search example.com
-nameserver 192.168.122.1
+nameserver 127.0.0.1


Notice: /Stage[main]/Main/Node[cookbook]/File[/etc/resolv.conf]/
content: current_value {md5}4c0d192511df253826d302bc830a371b,
should be {md5}949343428bded6a653a85910f6bdb48e (noop)
Notice: Node[cookbook]: Would have triggered 'refresh' from 1
events
Notice: Class[Main]: Would have triggered 'refresh' from 1 events
Notice: Stage[main]: Would have triggered 'refresh' from 1 events
Notice: Finished catalog run in 0.50 seconds
```

How it works...

The noop metaparameter is set to true, so for this particular resource, it's as if you had to run Puppet with the --noop flag. Puppet noted that the resource would have been applied, but otherwise did nothing.

The nice thing with running the agent in test mode (-t) is that Puppet output a diff of what it would have done if the `noop` was not present (you can tell puppet to show the diff's without using -t with --show_diff; -t implies many different settings):

```
--- /etc/resolv.conf   2014-10-20 00:27:43.095999975 -0400
+++ /tmp/puppet-file20141020-8439-1lhuy1y-0     2014-10-20
03:17:18.969999979 -0400
@@ -1,3 +1 @@
-; generated by /sbin/dhclient-script
-search example.com
-nameserver 192.168.122.1
+nameserver 127.0.0.1
```

This can be very useful when debugging a template; you can work on your changes and then see what they would look like on the node without actually applying them. Using the diff, you can see whether your updated template produces the correct output.

7
Managing Applications

Everyone knows that debugging is twice as hard as writing a program in the first place. So if you're as clever as you can be when you write it, how will you ever debug it?

— Brian W. Kernighan.

In this chapter, we will cover the following recipes:

- ▸ Using public modules
- ▸ Managing Apache servers
- ▸ Creating Apache virtual hosts
- ▸ Creating nginx virtual hosts
- ▸ Managing MySQL
- ▸ Creating databases and users

Introduction

Without applications, a server is just a very expensive space heater. In this chapter, I'll present some recipes to manage some specific software with Puppet: MySQL, Apache, **nginx**, and Ruby. I hope the recipes will be useful to you in themselves. However, the patterns and techniques they use are applicable to almost any software, so you can adapt them to your own purposes without much difficulty. One thing that is common about these applications, they are common. Most Puppet installations will have to deal with a web server, Apache or nginx. Most, if not all, will have databases and some of those will have MySQL. When everyone has to deal with a problem, community solutions are generally better tested and more thorough than homegrown solutions. We'll use modules from the Puppet Forge in this chapter to manage these applications.

When you are writing your own Apache or nginx modules from scratch, you'll have to pay attention to the nuances of the distributions you support. Some distributions call the apache package `httpd`, while others use `apache2`; the same can be said for MySQL. In addition, Debian-based distributions use an enabled folder method to enable custom sites in Apache, which are virtual sites, whereas RPM based distributions do not. For more information on virtual sites, visit `http://httpd.apache.org/docs/2.2/vhosts/`.

Using public modules

When you write a Puppet module to manage some software or service, you don't have to start from scratch. Community-contributed modules are available at the Puppet Forge site for many popular applications. Sometimes, a community module will be exactly what you need and you can download and start using it straight away. In most cases, you will need to make some modifications to suit your particular needs and environment.

Like all community efforts, there are some excellent and some less than excellent modules on the Forge. You should read the README section of the module and decide whether the module is going to work in your installation. At the least, ensure that your distribution is supported. Puppetlabs has introduced a set of modules that are supported, that is, if you are an enterprise customer, they will support your use of the module in your installation. Additionally, most Forge modules deal with multiple operating systems, distributions, and a great number of use cases. In many cases, not using a forge module is like reinventing the wheel. One caveat though is that Forge modules may be more complex than your local modules. You should read the code and get a sense of what the module is doing. Knowing how the module works will help you debug it later.

How to do it...

In this example, we'll use the `puppet module` command to find and install the useful `stdlib` module, which contains many utility functions to help you develop Puppet code. It is one of the aforementioned supported modules by puppetlabs. I'll download the module into my user's home directory and manually install it in the Git repository. To install puppetlabs stdlib module, follow these steps:

1. Run the following command:

```
t@mylaptop ~ $ puppet module search puppetlabs-stdlib

Notice: Searching https://forgeapi.puppetlabs.com ...

NAME                    DESCRIPTION                    AUTHOR
KEYWORDS

puppetlabs-stdlib    Puppet Module Standard Library    @puppetlabs
stdlib stages
```

2. We verified that we have the right module, so we'll install it with `module install` now:

```
t@mylaptop ~ $ puppet module install puppetlabs-stdlib
Notice: Preparing to install into /home/thomas/.puppet/modules ...
Notice: Downloading from https://forgeapi.puppetlabs.com ...
Notice: Installing -- do not interrupt ...
/home/thomas/.puppet/modules
└── puppetlabs-stdlib (v4.3.2)
```

3. The module is now ready to use in your manifests; most good modules come with a README file to show you how to do this.

How it works...

You can search for modules that match the package or software you're interested in with the `puppet module search` command. To install a specific module, use `puppet module install`. You can add the `-i` option to tell Puppet where to find your module directory.

You can browse the forge to see what's available at `http://forge.puppetlabs.com/`.

More information on supported modules is available at `https://forge.puppetlabs.com/supported`.

The current list of supported modules is available at `https://forge.puppetlabs.com/modules?endorsements=supported`.

There's more...

Modules on the Forge include a `metadata.json` file, which describes the module and which operating systems the module supports. This file also includes a list of modules that are required by the module.

 This file was previously named Modulefile and not in JSON format; the old Modulefile format was deprecated in Version 3.6.

As we will see in our next section, when installing a module from the Forge, the required dependencies will automatically be installed as well.

Not all publically available modules are on Puppet Forge. Some other great places to look at on GitHub are:

- `https://github.com/camptocamp`
- `https://github.com/example42`

Though not a collection of modules as such, the Puppet Cookbook website has many useful and illuminating code examples, patterns, and tips, maintained by the admirable Dean Wilson:

```
http://www.puppetcookbook.com/
```

Managing Apache servers

Apache is the world's favorite web server, so it's highly likely that part of your Puppetly duties will include installing and managing Apache.

How to do it...

We'll install and use the `puppetlabs-apache` module to install and start Apache. This time, when we run `puppet module install`, we'll use the `-i` option to tell Puppet to install the module in our Git repository's module's directory.

1. Install the module using `puppet modules install`:

   ```
   t@mylaptop ~/puppet $ puppet module install -i modules puppetlabs-apache
   Notice: Preparing to install into /home/thomas/puppet/modules ...
   Notice: Downloading from https://forgeapi.puppetlabs.com ...
   Notice: Installing -- do not interrupt ...
   /home/thomas/puppet/modules
   └─┬ puppetlabs-apache (v1.1.1)
     ├── puppetlabs-concat (v1.1.1)
     └── puppetlabs-stdlib (v4.3.2)
   ```

2. Add the modules to your Git repository and push them out:

   ```
   t@mylaptop ~/puppet $ git add modules/apache modules/concat modules/stdlib
   t@mylaptop ~/puppet $ git commit -m "adding puppetlabs-apache module"
   [production 395b079] adding puppetlabs-apache module
    647 files changed, 35017 insertions(+), 13 deletions(-)
    rename modules/{apache => apache.cookbook}/manifests/init.pp (100%)
    create mode 100644 modules/apache/CHANGELOG.md
    create mode 100644 modules/apache/CONTRIBUTING.md
   ...
   t@mylaptop ~/puppet $ git push origin production
   Counting objects: 277, done.
   Delta compression using up to 4 threads.
   ```

```
Compressing objects: 100% (248/248), done.
Writing objects: 100% (266/266), 136.25 KiB | 0 bytes/s, done.
Total 266 (delta 48), reused 0 (delta 0)
remote: To puppet@puppet.example.com:/etc/puppet/environments/
puppet.git
remote:    9faaa16..395b079  production -> production
```

3. Create a web server node definition in `site.pp`:

```
node webserver {
  class {'apache': }
}
```

4. Run Puppet to apply the default Apache module configuration:

```
[root@webserver ~]# puppet agent -t
Info: Caching certificate for webserver.example.com
Notice: /File[/var/lib/puppet/lib/puppet/provider/a2mod]/ensure:
created
...
Info: Caching catalog for webserver.example.com
...
Info: Class[Apache::Service]: Scheduling refresh of Service[httpd]
Notice: /Stage[main]/Apache::Service/Service[httpd]: Triggered
'refresh' from 51 events
Notice: Finished catalog run in 11.73 seconds
```

5. Verify that you can reach `webserver.example.com`:

```
[root@webserver ~]# curl http://webserver.example.com
<!DOCTYPE HTML PUBLIC "-//W3C//DTD HTML 3.2 Final//EN">
<html>
 <head>
  <title>Index of /</title>
 </head>
 <body>
<h1>Index of /</h1>
<table><tr><th><img src="/icons/blank.gif" alt="[ICO]"></
th><th><a href="?C=N;O=D">Name</a></th><th><a href="?C=M;O=A">Last
modified</a></th><th><a href="?C=S;O=A">Size</a></
th><th><a href="?C=D;O=A">Description</a></th></tr><tr><th
colspan="5"><hr></th></tr>
<tr><th colspan="5"><hr></th></tr>
</table>
</body></html>
```

How it works...

Installing the puppetlabs-Apache module from the Forge causes both puppetlabs-concat and puppetlabs-stdlib to be installed into our modules directory. The concat module is used to stitch snippets of files together in a specific order. It is used by the Apache module to create the main Apache configuration files.

We then defined a web server node and applied the Apache class to that node. We used all the default values and let the Apache module configure our server to be an Apache web server.

The Apache module then went and rewrote all our Apache configurations. By default, the module purges all the configuration files from the Apache directory (`/etc/apache2` or `/etc/httpd` depending on the distribution). The module can configure many different distributions and handle the nuances of each distribution. As a user of the module, you don't need to know how your distribution deals with the Apache module configuration.

After purging and rewriting the configuration files, the module ensures that the apache2 service is running (`httpd` on Enterprise Linux (EL)).

We then tested the webserver using curl. There was nothing returned but an empty index page. This is the expected behavior. Normally, when we install Apache on a server, there are some files that display a default page (`welcome.conf` on EL-based systems), since the module purged those configurations, we only see an empty page.

In a production environment, you would modify the defaults applied by the Apache module; the suggested configuration from the README is as follows:

```
class { 'apache':
  default_mods        => false,
  default_confd_files => false,
}
```

Creating Apache virtual hosts

Apache virtual hosts are created with the `apache` module with the defined type `apache::vhost`. We will create a new vhost on our Apache webserver called **navajo**, one of the apache tribes.

How to do it...

Follow these steps to create Apache virtual hosts:

1. Create a navajo `apache::vhost` definition as follows:

```
apache::vhost { 'navajo.example.com':
    port          => '80',
    docroot => '/var/www/navajo',
}
```

2. Create an index file for the new vhost:

```
file {'/var/www/navajo/index.html':
    content => "<html>\nnavajo.example.com\nhttp://en.wikipedia.
org/wiki/Navajo_people\n</html>\n",
    mode       => '0644',
    require => Apache::Vhost['navajo.example.com']
}
```

3. Run Puppet to create the new vhost:

```
[root@webserver ~]# puppet agent -t

Info: Caching catalog for webserver.example.com

Info: Applying configuration version '1414475598'

Notice: /Stage[main]/Main/Node[webserver]/Apache::Vhost[navajo.
example.com]/File[/var/www/navajo]/ensure: created

Notice: /Stage[main]/Main/Node[webserver]/Apache::Vhost[navajo.
example.com]/File[25-navajo.example.com.conf]/ensure: created

Info: /Stage[main]/Main/Node[webserver]/Apache::Vhost[navajo.
example.com]/File[25-navajo.example.com.conf]: Scheduling refresh
of Service[httpd]

Notice: /Stage[main]/Main/Node[webserver]/File[/var/www/navajo/
index.html]/ensure: defined content as '{md5}5212fe215f4c0223fb861
02a34319cc6'

Notice: /Stage[main]/Apache::Service/Service[httpd]: Triggered
'refresh' from 1 events

Notice: Finished catalog run in 2.73 seconds
```

4. Verify that you can reach the new virtual host:

```
[root@webserver ~]# curl http://navajo.example.com

<html>

navajo.example.com

http://en.wikipedia.org/wiki/Navajo_people

</html>
```

How it works...

The `apache::vhost` defined type creates a virtual host configuration file for Apache, `25-navajo.example.com.conf`. The file is created with a template; `25` at the beginning of the filename is the "priority level" of this virtual host. When Apache first starts, it reads through its configuration directory and starts executing files in an alphabetical order. Files that begin with numbers are read before files that start with letters. In this way, the Apache module ensures that the virtual hosts are read in a specific order, which can be specified when you define the virtual host. The contents of this file are as follows:

```
# **********************************
# Vhost template in module puppetlabs-apache
# Managed by Puppet
# **********************************

<VirtualHost *:80>
  ServerName navajo.example.com

  ## Vhost docroot
  DocumentRoot "/var/www/navajo"



  ## Directories, there should at least be a declaration for
    /var/www/navajo


  <Directory "/var/www/navajo">
    Options Indexes FollowSymLinks MultiViews
    AllowOverride None
    Order allow,deny
    Allow from all
  </Directory>

  ## Load additional static includes


  ## Logging
  ErrorLog "/var/log/httpd/navajo.example.com_error.log"
  ServerSignature Off
  CustomLog "/var/log/httpd/navajo.example.com_access.log"
    combined


</VirtualHost>
```

As you can see, the default file has created log files, set up directory access permissions and options, in addition to specifying the listen port and DocumentRoot.

The vhost definition creates the DocumentRoot directory, specified as 'root' to the apache::virtual definition. The directory is created before the virtual host configuration file; after that file has been created, a notify trigger is sent to the Apache process to restart.

Our manifest included a file that required the Apache::Vhost['navajo.example.com'] resource; our file was then created after the directory and the virtual host configuration file.

When we run curl on the new website (if you haven't created a hostname alias in DNS, you will have to create one in your local /etc/hosts file for navajo.example.com, or specify the host as curl -H 'Host: navajo.example.com' <ipaddress of navajo.example. com>), we see the contents of the index file we created:

```
file {'/var/www/navajo/index.html':
    content => "<html>\nnavajo.example.com\nhttp://en.wikipedia.org/
wiki/Navajo_people\n</html>\n",
    mode    => '0644',
    require => Apache::Vhost['navajo.example.com']
  }
[root@webserver ~]# curl http://navajo.example.com
<html>
navajo.example.com
http://en.wikipedia.org/wiki/Navajo_people
<\html>
```

There's more...

Both the defined type and the template take into account a multitude of possible configuration scenarios for virtual hosts. It is highly unlikely that you will find a setting that is not covered by this module. You should look at the definition for apache::virtual and the sheer number of possible arguments.

The module also takes care of several settings for you. For instance, if we change the listen port on our navajo virtual host from 80 to 8080, the module will make the following changes in /etc/httpd/conf.d/ports.conf:

```
 Listen 80
+Listen 8080
  NameVirtualHost *:80
+NameVirtualHost *:8080
```

And in our virtual host file:

```
 -<VirtualHost *:80>
 +<VirtualHost *:8080>
```

So that we can now curl on port 8080 and see the same results:

```
[root@webserver ~]# curl http://navajo.example.com:8080
<html>
navajo.example.com
http://en.wikipedia.org/wiki/Navajo_people
</html>
```

And when we try on port 80:

```
[root@webserver ~]# curl http://navajo.example.com
<!DOCTYPE HTML PUBLIC "-//W3C//DTD HTML 3.2 Final//EN">
<html>
 <head>
  <title>Index of /</title>
 </head>
 <body>
<h1>Index of /</h1>
<table><tr><th><img src="/icons/blank.gif" alt="[ICO]"></
th><th><a href="?C=N;O=D">Name</a></th><th><a href="?C=M;O=A">Last
modified</a></th><th><a href="?C=S;O=A">Size</a></th><th><a
href="?C=D;O=A">Description</a></th></tr><tr><th colspan="5"><hr></th></
tr>
<tr><th colspan="5"><hr></th></tr>
</table>
</body>
</html>
```

As we can see, the virtual host is no longer listening on port 80 and we receive the default empty directory listing we saw in our earlier example.

Creating nginx virtual hosts

Nginx is a fast, lightweight web server that is preferred over Apache in many contexts, especially where high performance is important. Nginx is configured slightly differently than Apache; like Apache though, there is a Forge module that can be used to configure nginx for us. Unlike Apache, however, the module that is suggested for use is not supplied by puppetlabs but by James Fryman. This module uses some interesting tricks to configure itself. Previous versions of this module used R.I. Pienaar's `module_data` package. This package is used to configure hieradata within a module. It's used to supply default values to the nginx module. I wouldn't recommend starting out with this module at this point, but it is a good example of where module configuration may be headed in the future. Giving modules the ability to modify hieradata may prove useful.

How to do it...

In this example, we'll use a Forge module to configure nginx. We'll download the module and use it to configure virtualhosts.

1. Download the `jfryman-nginx` module from the Forge:

```
t@mylaptop ~ $ cd ~/puppet
t@mylaptop ~/puppet $ puppet module install -i modules jfryman-
nginx
Notice: Preparing to install into /home/thomas/puppet/modules ...
Notice: Downloading from https://forgeapi.puppetlabs.com ...
Notice: Installing -- do not interrupt ...
/home/thomas/puppet/modules
└─┬ jfryman-nginx (v0.2.1)
  ├── puppetlabs-apt (v1.7.0)
  ├── puppetlabs-concat (v1.1.1)
  └── puppetlabs-stdlib (v4.3.2)
```

2. Replace the definition for webserver with an nginx configuration:

```
node webserver {
  class {'nginx':}
  nginx::resource::vhost { 'mescalero.example.com':
      www_root => '/var/www/mescalero',
  }
  file {'/var/www/mescalero':
    ensure  => 'directory''directory',
    mode    => '0755',
    require => Nginx::Resource::Vhost['mescalero.example.com'],
  }
  file {'/var/www/mescalero/index.html':
    content => "<html>\nmescalero.example.com\nhttp://
en.wikipedia.org/wiki/Mescalero\n</html>\n",
    mode    => 0644,
    require => File['/var/www/mescalero'],
  }
}
```

3. If apache is still running on your webserver, stop it:

```
[root@webserver ~]# puppet resource service httpd ensure=false
Notice: /Service[httpd]/ensure: ensure changed 'running' to
'stopped'
service { 'httpd':
  ensure => 'stopped',
}
```

```
Run puppet agent on your webserver node:
[root@webserver ~]# puppet agent -t
Info: Caching catalog for webserver.example.com
Info: Applying configuration version '1414561483'
Notice: /Stage[main]/Main/Node[webserver]/Nginx::Resource::Vhost[m
escalero.example.com]/Concat[/etc/nginx/sites-available/mescalero.
example.com.conf]/File[/etc/nginx/sites-available/mescalero.
example.com.conf]/ensure: defined content as '{md5}35bb59bfcd0cf5a
549d152aaec284357'
Info: /Stage[main]/Main/Node[webserver]/Nginx::Resource::Vhost[me
scalero.example.com]/Concat[/etc/nginx/sites-available/mescalero.
example.com.conf]/File[/etc/nginx/sites-available/mescalero.
example.com.conf]: Scheduling refresh of Class[Nginx::Service]
Info: Concat[/etc/nginx/sites-available/mescalero.example.com.
conf]: Scheduling refresh of Class[Nginx::Service]
Notice: /Stage[main]/Main/Node[webserver]/Nginx::Resource::Vhost[
mescalero.example.com]/File[mescalero.example.com.conf symlink]/
ensure: created
Info: /Stage[main]/Main/Node[webserver]/Nginx::Resource::Vhost[m
escalero.example.com]/File[mescalero.example.com.conf symlink]:
Scheduling refresh of Service[nginx]
Notice: /Stage[main]/Main/Node[webserver]/File[/var/www/
mescalero]/ensure: created
Notice: /Stage[main]/Main/Node[webserver]/File[/var/www/mescalero/
index.html]/ensure: defined content as '{md5}2bd618c7dc3a3addc9e27
c2f3cfde294'
Notice: /Stage[main]/Nginx::Config/File[/etc/nginx/conf.d/
proxy.conf]/ensure: defined content as '{md5}1919fd65635d4965327
3e14028888617'
Info: Computing checksum on file /etc/nginx/conf.d/example_ssl.
conf
Info: /Stage[main]/Nginx::Config/File[/etc/nginx/conf.d/example_
ssl.conf]: Filebucketed /etc/nginx/conf.d/example_ssl.conf to
puppet with sum 84724f296c7056157d531d6b1215b507
Notice: /Stage[main]/Nginx::Config/File[/etc/nginx/conf.d/example_
ssl.conf]/ensure: removed
Info: Computing checksum on file /etc/nginx/conf.d/default.conf
Info: /Stage[main]/Nginx::Config/File[/etc/nginx/conf.d/default.
conf]: Filebucketed /etc/nginx/conf.d/default.conf to puppet with
sum 4dce452bf8dbb01f278ec0ea9ba6cf40
Notice: /Stage[main]/Nginx::Config/File[/etc/nginx/conf.d/default.
conf]/ensure: removed
Info: Class[Nginx::Config]: Scheduling refresh of
Class[Nginx::Service]
```

```
Info: Class[Nginx::Service]: Scheduling refresh of Service[nginx]
Notice: /Stage[main]/Nginx::Service/Service[nginx]: Triggered
'refresh' from 2 events
Notice: Finished catalog run in 28.98 seconds
```

4. Verify that you can reach the new virtualhost:

```
[root@webserver ~]# curl mescalero.example.com
<html>
mescalero.example.com
http://en.wikipedia.org/wiki/Mescalero
</html>
```

How it works...

Installing the `jfryman-nginx` module causes the concat, stdlib, and APT modules to be installed. We run Puppet on our master to have the plugins created by these modules added to our running master. The stdlib and concat have facter and Puppet plugins that need to be installed for the nginx module to work properly.

With the plugins synchronized, we can then run puppet agent on our web server. As a precaution, we stop Apache if it was previously started (we can't have nginx and Apache both listening on port `80`). After puppet agent runs, we verified that nginx was running and the virtual host was configured.

There's more...

This nginx module is under active development. There are several interesting solutions employed with the module. Previous releases used the `ripienaar-module_data` module, which allows a module to include default values for its various attributes, via a hiera plugin. Although still in an early stage of development, this system is already usable and represents one of the cutting-edge modules on the Forge.

In the next section, we'll use a supported module to configure and manage MySQL installations.

Managing MySQL

MySQL is a very widely used database server, and it's fairly certain you'll need to install and configure a MySQL server at some point. The `puppetlabs-mysql` module can simplify your MySQL deployments.

How to do it...

Follow these steps to create the example:

1. Install the `puppetlabs-mysql` module:

    ```
    t@mylaptop ~/puppet $ puppet module install -i modules puppetlabs-
    mysql
    Notice: Preparing to install into /home/thomas/puppet/modules ...
    Notice: Downloading from https://forgeapi.puppetlabs.com ...
    Notice: Installing -- do not interrupt ...
    /home/thomas/puppet/modules
    └─┬ puppetlabs-mysql (v2.3.1)
      └── puppetlabs-stdlib (v4.3.2)
    ```

2. Create a new node definition for your MySQL server:

    ```
    node dbserver {
      class { '::mysql::server':
        root_password    => 'PacktPub',
        override_options => {
          'mysqld' => { 'max_connections' => '1024' }
        }
      }
    }
    ```

3. Run Puppet to install the database server and apply the new root password:

    ```
    [root@dbserver ~]# puppet agent -t
    Info: Caching catalog for dbserver.example.com
    Info: Applying configuration version '1414566216'
    Notice: /Stage[main]/Mysql::Server::Install/Package[mysql-server]/
    ensure: created
    Notice: /Stage[main]/Mysql::Server::Service/Service[mysqld]/
    ensure: ensure changed 'stopped' to 'running'
    Info: /Stage[main]/Mysql::Server::Service/Service[mysqld]:
    Unscheduling refresh on Service[mysqld]
    Notice: /Stage[main]/Mysql::Server::Root_password/Mysql_
    user[root@localhost]/password_hash: defined 'password_hash' as
    '*6ABB0D4A7D1381BAEE4D078354557D495ACFC059'
    Notice: /Stage[main]/Mysql::Server::Root_password/File[/root/.
    my.cnf]/ensure: defined content as '{md5}87bc129b137c9d613e9f31c80
    ea5426c'
    Notice: Finished catalog run in 35.50 seconds
    ```

4. Verify that you can connect to the database:

    ```
    [root@dbserver ~]# mysql
    ```

```
Welcome to the MySQL monitor.  Commands end with ; or \g.
Your MySQL connection id is 11
Server version: 5.1.73 Source distribution

Copyright (c) 2000, 2013, Oracle and/or its affiliates. All rights
reserved.

Oracle is a registered trademark of Oracle Corporation and/or its
affiliates. Other names may be trademarks of their respective
owners.

Type 'help;' or '\h' for help. Type '\c' to clear the current
input statement.

mysql>
```

How it works...

The MySQL module installs the MySQL server and ensures that the server is running. It then configures the root password for MySQL. The module does a lot of other things for you as well. It creates a `.my.cnf` file with the root user password. When we run the `mysql` client, the `.my.cnf` file sets all the defaults, so we do not need to supply any arguments.

There's more...

In the next section, we'll show how to create databases and users.

Creating databases and users

Managing a database means more than ensuring that the service is running; a database server is nothing without databases. Databases need users and privileges. Privileges are handled with GRANT statements. We will use the `puppetlabs-mysql` package to create a database and a user with access to that database. We'll create a MySQL user Drupal and a database called Drupal. We'll create a table named nodes and place data into that table.

How to do it...

Follow these steps to create databases and users:

1. Create a database definition within your dbserver class:

```
mysql::db { 'drupal':
    host    => 'localhost',
```

```
    user      => 'drupal',
    password    => 'Cookbook',
    sql      => '/root/drupal.sql',
    require => File['/root/drupal.sql']
}

file { '/root/drupal.sql':
    ensure => present,
    source => 'puppet:///modules/mysql/drupal.sql',
}
```

2. Allow the Drupal user to modify the nodes table:

```
mysql_grant { 'drupal@localhost/drupal.nodes':
    ensure      => 'present',
    options     => ['GRANT'],
    privileges => ['ALL'],
    table       => 'drupal.nodes'nodes',
    user        => 'drupal@localhost',
}
```

3. Create the `drupal.sql` file with the following contents:

```
CREATE TABLE users (id INT PRIMARY KEY AUTO_INCREMENT, title
VARCHAR(255), body TEXT);
INSERT INTO users (id, title, body) VALUES (1,'First
Node','Contents of first Node');
INSERT INTO users (id, title, body) VALUES (2,'Second
Node','Contents of second Node');
```

4. Run Puppet to have user, database, and GRANT created:

```
[root@dbserver ~]# puppet agent -t

Info: Caching catalog for dbserver.example.com

Info: Applying configuration version '1414648818'

Notice: /Stage[main]/Main/Node[dbserver]/File[/root/drupal.sql]/
ensure: defined content as '{md5}780f3946cfc0f373c6d4146394650f6b'

Notice: /Stage[main]/Main/Node[dbserver]/Mysql_grant[drupal@
localhost/drupal.nodes]/ensure: created

Notice: /Stage[main]/Main/Node[dbserver]/Mysql::Db[drupal]/Mysql_
user[drupal@localhost]/ensure: created

Notice: /Stage[main]/Main/Node[dbserver]/Mysql::Db[drupal]/Mysql_
database[drupal]/ensure: created

Info: /Stage[main]/Main/Node[dbserver]/Mysql::Db[drupal]/Mysql_
database[drupal]: Scheduling refresh of Exec[drupal-import]

Notice: /Stage[main]/Main/Node[dbserver]/Mysql::Db[drupal]/Mysql_
grant[drupal@localhost/drupal.*]/ensure: created
```

```
Notice: /Stage[main]/Main/Node[dbserver]/Mysql::Db[drupal]/
Exec[drupal-import]: Triggered 'refresh' from 1 events
Notice: Finished catalog run in 10.06 seconds
```

5. Verify that the database and table have been created:

```
[root@dbserver ~]# mysql drupal
Reading table information for completion of table and column names
You can turn off this feature to get a quicker startup with -A

Welcome to the MySQL monitor.  Commands end with ; or \g.
Your MySQL connection id is 34
Server version: 5.1.73 Source distribution

Copyright (c) 2000, 2013, Oracle and/or its affiliates. All rights
reserved.

Oracle is a registered trademark of Oracle Corporation and/or its
affiliates. Other names may be trademarks of their respective
owners.

Type 'help;' or '\h' for help. Type '\c' to clear the current
input statement.

mysql> show tables;
+------------------+
| Tables_in_drupal |
+------------------+
| users            |
+------------------+
1 row in set (0.00 sec)
```

6. Now, verify that our default data has been loaded into the table:

```
mysql> select * from users;
+----+-------------+-------------------------+
| id | title       | body                    |
+----+-------------+-------------------------+
|  1 | First Node  | Contents of first Node  |
|  2 | Second Node | Contents of second Node |
+----+-------------+-------------------------+
2 rows in set (0.00 sec)
```

How it works...

We start with the definition of the new drupal database:

```
mysql::db { 'drupal':
  host      => 'localhost',
  user      => 'drupal',
  password    => 'Cookbook',
  sql      => '/root/drupal.sql',
  require => File['/root/drupal.sql']
}
```

We specify that we'll connect from localhost (we could connect to the database from another server) using the drupal user. We give the password for the user and specify a SQL file that will be applied to the database after the database has been created. We require that this file already exist and define the file next:

```
file { '/root/drupal.sql':
  ensure => present,
  source => 'puppet:///modules/mysql/drupal.sql',
}
```

We then ensure that the user has the appropriate privileges with a `mysql_grant` statement:

```
mysql_grant { 'drupal@localhost/drupal.nodes':
  ensure     => 'present',
  options    => ['GRANT'],
  privileges => ['ALL'],
  table      => 'drupal.nodes',
  user       => 'drupal@localhost',
}
```

There's more...

Using the puppetlabs-MySQL and puppetlabs-Apache module, we can create an entire functioning web server. The puppetlabs-Apache module will install Apache, and we can include the PHP module and MySQL module as well. We can then use the puppetlabs-Mysql module to install the MySQL server, and then create the required drupal databases and seed the database with the data.

Deploying a new drupal installation would be as simple as including a class on a node.

8

Internode Coordination

"Rest is not idleness, and to lie sometimes on the grass under trees on a summer's day, listening to the murmur of the water, or watching the clouds float across the sky, is by no means a waste of time."

— John Lubbock

In this chapter, we will cover the following recipes:

- ▶ Managing firewalls with iptables
- ▶ Building high-availability services using Heartbeat
- ▶ Managing NFS servers and file shares
- ▶ Using HAProxy to load-balance multiple web servers
- ▶ Managing Docker with Puppet

Introduction

As powerful as Puppet is to manage the configuration of a single server, it's even more useful when coordinating many machines. In this chapter, we'll explore ways to use Puppet to help you create high-availability clusters, share files across your network, set up automated firewalls, and use load-balancing to get more out of the machines you have. We'll use exported resources as the communication between nodes.

Managing firewalls with iptables

In this chapter, we will begin to configure services that require communication between hosts over the network. Most Linux distributions will default to running a host-based firewall, **iptables**. If you want your hosts to communicate with each other, you have two options: turn off iptables or configure iptables to allow the communication.

I prefer to leave iptables turned on and configure access. Keeping iptables is just another layer on your defense across the network. iptables isn't a magic bullet that will make your system secure, but it will block access to services you didn't intend to expose to the network.

Configuring iptables properly is a complicated task, which requires deep knowledge of networking. The example presented here is a simplification. If you are unfamiliar with iptables, I suggest you research iptables before continuing. More information can be found at http://wiki.centos.org/HowTos/Network/IPTables or https://help. ubuntu.com/community/IptablesHowTo.

Getting ready

In the following examples, we'll be using the Puppet Labs Firewall module to configure iptables. Prepare by installing the module into your Git repository with `puppet module install`:

```
t@mylaptop ~ $ puppet module install -i ~/puppet/modules puppetlabs
-firewall
Notice: Preparing to install into /home/thomas/puppet/modules ...
Notice: Downloading from https://forgeapi.puppetlabs.com ...
/home/thomas/puppet/modules
└── puppetlabs-firewall (v1.2.0)
```

How to do it...

To configure the firewall module, we need to create a set of rules, which will be applied before all other rules. As a simple example, we'll create the following rules:

- Allow all traffic on the loopback (lo) interface
- Allow all ICMP traffic
- Allow all traffic that is part of an established connection (ESTABLISHED, RELATED)
- Allow all TCP traffic to port 22 (ssh)

We will create a `myfw` (my firewall) class to configure the firewall module. We will then apply the `myfw` class to a node to have iptables configured on that node:

1. Create a class to contain these rules and call it `myfw::pre`:

```
class myfw::pre {
  Firewall {
    require => undef,
  }
  firewall { '0000 Allow all traffic on loopback':
    proto => 'all',
    iniface => 'lo',
    action => 'accept',
  }
  firewall { '0001 Allow all ICMP':
    proto => 'icmp',
    action => 'accept',
  }
  firewall { '0002 Allow all established traffic':
    proto => 'all',
    state => ['RELATED', 'ESTABLISHED'],
    action => 'accept',
  }
  firewall { '0022 Allow all TCP on port 22 (ssh)':
    proto => 'tcp',
    port => '22',
    action => 'accept',
  }
}
```

2. When traffic doesn't match any of the previous rules, we want a final rule that will drop the traffic. Create the class `myfw::post` to contain the default drop rule:

```
class myfw::post {
  firewall { '9999 Drop all other traffic':
    proto  => 'all',
    action => 'drop',
    before => undef,
  }
}
```

3. Create a `myfw` class, which will include `myfw::pre` and `myfw::post` to configure the firewall:

```
class myfw {
  include firewall
  # our rulesets
  include myfw::post
  include myfw::pre
```

```
# clear all the rules
resources { "firewall":
  purge => true
}

# resource defaults
Firewall {
  before => Class['myfw::post'],
  require => Class['myfw::pre'],
}
}
```

4. Attach the `myfw` class to a node definition; I'll do this to my cookbook node:

```
node cookbook {
  include myfw
}
```

5. Run Puppet on cookbook to see whether the firewall rules have been applied:

```
[root@cookbook ~]# puppet agent -t

Info: Retrieving pluginfacts

Info: Retrieving plugin

Info: Loading facts

Info: Caching catalog for cookbook.example.com

Info: Applying configuration version '1415512948'

Notice: /Stage[main]/Myfw::Pre/Firewall[000 Allow all traffic on
loopback]/ensure: created

Notice: /File[/etc/sysconfig/iptables]/seluser: seluser changed
'unconfined_u' to 'system_u'

Notice: /Stage[main]/Myfw::Pre/Firewall[0001 Allow all ICMP]/
ensure: created

Notice: /Stage[main]/Myfw::Pre/Firewall[0022 Allow all TCP on port
22 (ssh)]/ensure: created

Notice: /Stage[main]/Myfw::Pre/Firewall[0002 Allow all established
traffic]/ensure: created

Notice: /Stage[main]/Myfw::Post/Firewall[9999 Drop all other
traffic]/ensure: created

Notice: /Stage[main]/Myfw/Firewall[9003
49bcd611c61bdd18b235cea46ef04fae]/ensure: removed

Notice: Finished catalog run in 15.65 seconds
```

6. Verify the new rules with `iptables-save`:

```
# Generated by iptables-save v1.4.7 on Sun Nov  9 01:18:30 2014
*filter
:INPUT ACCEPT [0:0]
:FORWARD ACCEPT [0:0]
:OUTPUT ACCEPT [74:35767]
-A INPUT -i lo -m comment --comment "0000 Allow all traffic on
loopback" -j ACCEPT
-A INPUT -p icmp -m comment --comment "0001 Allow all ICMP" -j
ACCEPT
-A INPUT -m comment --comment "0002 Allow all established traffic"
-m state --state RELATED,ESTABLISHED -j ACCEPT
-A INPUT -p tcp -m multiport --ports 22 -m comment --comment "022
Allow all TCP on port 22 (ssh)" -j ACCEPT
-A INPUT -m comment --comment "9999 Drop all other traffic" -j
DROP
COMMIT
# Completed on Sun Nov  9 01:18:30 2014
```

How it works...

This is a great example of how to use metaparameters to achieve a complex ordering with little effort. Our `myfw` module achieves the following configuration:

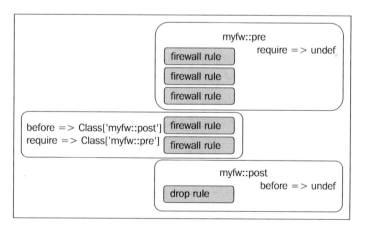

All the rules in the `myfw::pre` class are guaranteed to come before any other firewall rules we define. The rules in `myfw::post` are guaranteed to come after any other firewall rules. So, we have the rules in `myfw::pre` first, then any other rules, followed by the rules in `myfw::post`.

Our definition for the `myfw` class sets up this dependency with resource defaults:

```
# resource defaults
Firewall {
  before => Class['myfw::post'],
  require => Class['myfw::pre'],
}
```

These defaults first tell Puppet that any firewall resource should be executed before anything in the `myfw::post` class. Second, they tell Puppet that any firewall resource should require that the resources in `myfw::pre` already be executed.

When we defined the `myfw::pre` class, we removed the require statement in a resource default for Firewall resources. This ensures that the resources within the myfw::pre-class don't require themselves before executing (Puppet will complain that we created a cyclic dependency otherwise):

```
Firewall {
    require => undef,
}
```

We use the same trick in our `myfw::post` definition. In this case, we only have a single rule in the post class, so we simply remove the `before` requirement:

```
firewall { '9999 Drop all other traffic':
    proto  => 'all',
    action => 'drop',
    before => undef,
}
```

Finally, we include a rule to purge all the existing iptables rules on the system. We do this to ensure we have a consistent set of rules; only rules defined in Puppet will persist:

```
# clear all the rules
resources { "firewall":
  purge => true
}
```

There's more...

As we hinted, we can now define firewall resources in our manifests and have them applied to the iptables configuration after the initialization rules (`myfw::pre`) but before the final drop (`myfw::post`). For example, to allow http traffic on our cookbook machine, modify the node definition as follows:

```
include myfw
firewall {'0080 Allow HTTP':
  proto  => 'tcp',
  action => 'accept',
  port   => 80,
}
```

Run Puppet on cookbook:

```
[root@cookbook ~]# puppet agent -t
Info: Retrieving pluginfacts
Info: Retrieving plugin
Info: Loading facts
Info: Caching catalog for cookbook.example.com
Info: Applying configuration version '1415515392'
Notice: /File[/etc/sysconfig/iptables]/seluser: seluser changed
'unconfined_u' to 'system_u'
Notice: /Stage[main]/Main/Node[cookbook]/Firewall[0080 Allow HTTP]/
ensure: created
Notice: Finished catalog run in 2.74 seconds
```

Verify that the new rule has been added after the last myfw::pre rule (port 22, ssh):

```
[root@cookbook ~]# iptables-save
# Generated by iptables-save v1.4.7 on Sun Nov  9 01:46:38 2014
*filter
:INPUT ACCEPT [0:0]
:FORWARD ACCEPT [0:0]
:OUTPUT ACCEPT [41:26340]
-A INPUT -i lo -m comment --comment "0000 Allow all traffic on loopback"
-j ACCEPT
-A INPUT -p icmp -m comment --comment "0001 Allow all ICMP" -j ACCEPT
-A INPUT -m comment --comment "0002 Allow all established traffic" -m
state --state RELATED,ESTABLISHED -j ACCEPT
```

```
-A INPUT -p tcp -m multiport --ports 22 -m comment --comment "0022 Allow
all TCP on port 22 (ssh)" -j ACCEPT
-A INPUT -p tcp -m multiport --ports 80 -m comment --comment "0080 Allow
HTTP" -j ACCEPT
-A INPUT -m comment --comment "9999 Drop all other traffic" -j DROP
COMMIT
# Completed on Sun Nov  9 01:46:38 2014
```

 The Puppet Labs Firewall module has a built-in notion of order, all our firewall resource titles begin with a number. This is a requirement. The module attempts to order resources based on the title. You should keep this in mind when naming your firewall resources.

In the next section, we'll use our firewall module to ensure that two nodes can communicate as required.

Building high-availability services using Heartbeat

High-availability services are those that can survive the failure of an individual machine or network connection. The primary technique for high availability is redundancy, otherwise known as throwing hardware at the problem. Although the eventual failure of an individual server is certain, the simultaneous failure of two servers is unlikely enough that this provides a good level of redundancy for most applications.

One of the simplest ways to build a redundant pair of servers is to have them share an IP address using Heartbeat. Heartbeat is a daemon that runs on both machines and exchanges regular messages—heartbeats—between the two. One server is the primary one, and normally has the resource; in this case, an IP address (known as a virtual IP, or VIP). If the secondary server fails to detect a heartbeat from the primary server, it can take over the address, ensuring continuity of service. In real-world scenarios, you may want more machines involved in the VIP, but for this example, two machines works well enough.

In this recipe, we'll set up two machines in this configuration using Puppet, and I'll explain how to use it to provide a high-availability service.

Getting ready

You'll need two machines, of course, and an extra IP address to use as the VIP. You can usually request this from your ISP, if necessary. In this example, I'll be using machines named cookbook and cookbook2, with cookbook being the primary. We'll add the hosts to the heartbeat configuration.

How to do it...

Follow these steps to build the example:

1. Create the file `modules/heartbeat/manifests/init.pp` with the following contents:

```
# Manage Heartbeat
class heartbeat {
  package { 'heartbeat':
    ensure => installed,
  }

  service { 'heartbeat':
    ensure  => running,
    enable  => true,
    require => Package['heartbeat'],
  }

  file { '/etc/ha.d/authkeys':
    content => "auth 1\n1 sha1 TopSecret",
    mode    => '0600',
    require => Package['heartbeat'],
    notify  => Service['heartbeat'],
  }
  include myfw
  firewall {'0694 Allow UDP ha-cluster':
    proto  => 'udp',
    port   => 694,
    action => 'accept',
  }
}
```

2. Create the file `modules/heartbeat/manifests/vip.pp` with the following contents:

```
# Manage a specific VIP with Heartbeat
class
  heartbeat::vip($node1,$node2,$ip1,$ip2,$vip,$interface='eth0:1')
{
  include heartbeat

  file { '/etc/ha.d/haresources':
```

```
            content => "${node1} IPaddr::${vip}/${interface}\n",
            require => Package['heartbeat'],
            notify  => Service['heartbeat'],
         }

      file { '/etc/ha.d/ha.cf':
         content => template('heartbeat/vip.ha.cf.erb'),
         require => Package['heartbeat'],
         notify  => Service['heartbeat'],
      }
   }
```

3. Create the file `modules/heartbeat/templates/vip.ha.cf.erb` with the following contents:

```
use_logd yes
udpport 694
autojoin none
ucast eth0 <%= @ip1 %>
ucast eth0 <%= @ip2 %>
keepalive 1
deadtime 10
warntime 5
auto_failback off
node <%= @node1 %>
node <%= @node2 %>
```

4. Modify your `site.pp` file as follows. Replace the `ip1` and `ip2` addresses with the primary IP addresses of your two nodes, `vip` with the virtual IP address you'll be using, and `node1` and `node2` with the hostnames of the two nodes. (Heartbeat uses the fully-qualified domain name of a node to determine whether it's a member of the cluster, so the values for `node1` and `node2` should match what's given by `facter fqdn` on each machine.):

```
node cookbook,cookbook2 {
   class { 'heartbeat::vip':
      ip1   => '192.168.122.132',
      ip2   => '192.168.122.133',
      node1 => 'cookbook.example.com',
      node2 => 'cookbook2.example.com',
```

```
    vip   => '192.168.122.200/24',
  }
}
```

5. Run Puppet on each of the two servers:

```
[root@cookbook2 ~]# puppet agent -t
Info: Retrieving pluginfacts
Info: Retrieving plugin
Info: Loading facts
Info: Caching catalog for cookbook2.example.com
Info: Applying configuration version '1415517914'
Notice: /Stage[main]/Heartbeat/Package[heartbeat]/ensure: created
Notice: /Stage[main]/Myfw::Pre/Firewall[0000 Allow all traffic on
loopback]/ensure: created
Notice: /Stage[main]/Myfw::Pre/Firewall[0001 Allow all ICMP]/
ensure: created
Notice: /File[/etc/sysconfig/iptables]/seluser: seluser changed
'unconfined_u' to 'system_u'
Notice: /Stage[main]/Myfw::Pre/Firewall[0022 Allow all TCP on port
22 (ssh)]/ensure: created
Notice: /Stage[main]/Heartbeat::Vip/File[/etc/ha.d/haresources]/
ensure: defined content as '{md5}fb9f5d9d2b26e3bddf681676d8b2129c'
Info: /Stage[main]/Heartbeat::Vip/File[/etc/ha.d/haresources]:
Scheduling refresh of Service[heartbeat]
Notice: /Stage[main]/Heartbeat::Vip/File[/etc/ha.d/ha.cf]/ensure:
defined content as '{md5}84da22f7ac1a3629f69dcf29ccfd8592'
Info: /Stage[main]/Heartbeat::Vip/File[/etc/ha.d/ha.cf]:
Scheduling refresh of Service[heartbeat]
Notice: /Stage[main]/Heartbeat/Service[heartbeat]/ensure: ensure
changed 'stopped' to 'running'
Info: /Stage[main]/Heartbeat/Service[heartbeat]: Unscheduling
refresh on Service[heartbeat]
Notice: /Stage[main]/Myfw::Pre/Firewall[0002 Allow all established
traffic]/ensure: created
Notice: /Stage[main]/Myfw::Post/Firewall[9999 Drop all other
traffic]/ensure: created
Notice: /Stage[main]/Heartbeat/Firewall[0694 Allow UDP ha
-cluster]/ensure: created
Notice: Finished catalog run in 12.64 seconds
```

6. Verify that the VIP is running on one of the nodes (it should be on cookbook at this point; note that you will need to use the `ip` command, `ifconfig` will not show the address):

```
[root@cookbook ~]# ip addr show dev eth0

2: eth0: <BROADCAST,MULTICAST,UP,LOWER_UP> mtu 1500 qdisc pfifo_
fast state UP qlen 1000
    link/ether 52:54:00:c9:d5:63 brd ff:ff:ff:ff:ff:ff
    inet 192.168.122.132/24 brd 192.168.122.255 scope global eth0
    inet 192.168.122.200/24 brd 192.168.122.255 scope global
secondary eth0:1
    inet6 fe80::5054:ff:fec9:d563/64 scope link
       valid_lft forever preferred_lft forever
```

7. As we can see, cookbook has the `eth0:1` interface active. If you stop heartbeat on cookbook, cookbook2 will create `eth0:1` and take over:

```
[root@cookbook2 ~]# ip a show dev eth0

2: eth0: <BROADCAST,MULTICAST,UP,LOWER_UP> mtu 1500 qdisc pfifo_
fast state UP qlen 1000
    link/ether 52:54:00:ee:9c:fa brd ff:ff:ff:ff:ff:ff
    inet 192.168.122.133/24 brd 192.168.122.255 scope global eth0
    inet 192.168.122.200/24 brd 192.168.122.255 scope global
secondary eth0:1
    inet6 fe80::5054:ff:feee:9cfa/64 scope link
       valid_lft forever preferred_lft forever
```

How it works...

We need to install Heartbeat first of all, using the `heartbeat` class:

```
# Manage Heartbeat
class heartbeat {
  package { 'heartbeat':
    ensure => installed,
  }
  ...
}
```

Next, we use the `heartbeat::vip` class to manage a specific virtual IP:

```
# Manage a specific VIP with Heartbeat
class
```

```
heartbeat::vip($node1,$node2,$ip1,$ip2,$vip,$interface='eth0:1') {
include heartbeat
```

As you can see, the class includes an `interface` parameter; by default, the VIP will be configured on `eth0:1`, but if you need to use a different interface, you can pass it in using this parameter.

Each pair of servers that we configure with a virtual IP will use the `heartbeat::vip` class with the same parameters. These will be used to build the `haresources` file:

```
file { '/etc/ha.d/haresources':
  content => "${node1} IPaddr::${vip}/${interface}\n",
  notify  => Service['heartbeat'],
  require => Package['heartbeat'],
}
```

This tells Heartbeat about the resource it should manage (that's a Heartbeat resource, such as an IP address or a service, not a Puppet resource). The resulting `haresources` file might look as follows:

```
cookbook.example.com IPaddr::192.168.122.200/24/eth0:1
```

The file is interpreted by Heartbeat as follows:

- `cookbook.example.com`: This is the name of the primary node, which should be the default owner of the resource
- `IPaddr`: This is the type of resource to manage; in this case, an IP address
- `192.168.122.200/24`: This is the value for the IP address
- `eth0:1`: This is the virtual interface to configure with the managed IP address

For more information on how heartbeat is configured, please visit the high-availability site at `http://linux-ha.org/wiki/Heartbeat`.

We will also build the `ha.cf` file that tells Heartbeat how to communicate between cluster nodes:

```
file { '/etc/ha.d/ha.cf':
  content => template('heartbeat/vip.ha.cf.erb'),
  notify  => Service['heartbeat'],
  require => Package['heartbeat'],
}
```

To do this, we use the template file:

```
use_logd yes
udpport 694
autojoin none
```

```
ucast eth0 <%= @ip1 %>
ucast eth0 <%= @ip2 %>
keepalive 1
deadtime 10
warntime 5
auto_failback off
node <%= @node1 %>
node <%= @node2 %>
```

The interesting values here are the IP addresses of the two nodes (ip1 and ip2), and the names of the two nodes (node1 and node2).

Finally, we create an instance of heartbeat::vip on both machines and pass it an identical set of parameters as follows:

```
class { 'heartbeat::vip':
  ip1   => '192.168.122.132',
  ip2   => '192.168.122.133',
  node1 => 'cookbook.example.com',
  node2 => 'cookbook2.example.com',
  vip   => '192.168.122.200/24',
}
```

There's more...

With Heartbeat set up as described in the example, the virtual IP address will be configured on cookbook by default. If something happens to interfere with this (for example, if you halt or reboot cookbook, or stop the heartbeat service, or the machine loses network connectivity), cookbook2 will immediately take over the virtual IP.

The auto_failback setting in ha.cf governs what happens next. If auto_failback is set to on, when cookbook becomes available once more, it will automatically take over the IP address. Without auto_failback, the IP will stay where it is until you manually fail it again (by stopping heartbeart on cookbook2, for example).

One common use for a Heartbeat-managed virtual IP is to provide a highly available website or service. To do this, you need to set the DNS name for the service (for example, cat-pictures.com) to point to the virtual IP. Requests for the service will be routed to whichever of the two servers currently has the virtual IP. If this server should go down, requests will go to the other, with no visible interruption in service to users.

Heartbeat works great for the previous example but is not in widespread use in this form. Heartbeat only works in two node clusters; for n-node clusters, the newer pacemaker project should be used. More information on Heartbeat, pacemaker, corosync, and other clustering packages can be found at http://www.linux-ha.org/wiki/Main_Page.

Managing cluster configuration is one area where exported resources are useful. Each node in a cluster would export information about itself, which could then be collected by the other members of the cluster. Using the puppetlabs-concat module, you can build up a configuration file using exported concat fragments from all the nodes in the cluster.

Remember to look at the Forge before starting your own module. If nothing else, you'll get some ideas that you can use in your own module. Corosync can be managed with the Puppet labs module at `https://forge.puppetlabs.com/puppetlabs/corosync`.

Managing NFS servers and file shares

NFS (**Network File System**) is a protocol to mount a shared directory from a remote server. For example, a pool of web servers might all mount the same NFS share to serve static assets such as images and stylesheets. Although NFS is generally slower and less secure than local storage or a clustered filesystem, the ease with which it can be used makes it a common choice in the datacenter. We'll use our `myfw` module from before to ensure the local firewall permits `nfs` communication. We'll also use the Puppet labs-concat module to edit the list of exported filesystems on our `nfs` server.

How to do it...

In this example, we'll configure an `nfs` server to share (export) some filesystem via NFS.

1. Create an `nfs` module with the following `nfs::exports` class, which defines a concat resource:

```
class nfs::exports {
  exec {'nfs::exportfs':
    command     => 'exportfs -a',
    refreshonly => true,
    path        => '/usr/bin:/bin:/sbin:/usr/sbin',
  }
  concat {'/etc/exports':
    notify => Exec['nfs::exportfs'],
  }
}
```

2. Create the `nfs::export` defined type, we'll use this definition for any `nfs` exports we create:

```
define nfs::export (
  $where = $title,
  $who = '*',
  $options = 'async,ro',
```

```
      $mount_options = 'defaults',
      $tag          = 'nfs'
   ) {
     # make sure the directory exists
     # export the entry locally, then export a resource to be picked
   up later.
      file {"$where":
        ensure => 'directory',
      }
      include nfs::exports
      concat::fragment { "nfs::export::$where":
        content => "${where} ${who}(${options})\n",
        target  => '/etc/exports'
      }
      @@mount { "nfs::export::${where}::${::ipaddress}":
        name    => "$where",
        ensure  => 'mounted',
        fstype  => 'nfs',
        options => "$mount_options",
        device  => "${::ipaddress}:${where}",
        tag     => "$tag",
      }
   }
```

3. Now create the `nfs::server` class, which will include the OS-specific configuration for the server:

```
class nfs::server {
  # ensure nfs server is running
  # firewall should allow nfs communication
  include nfs::exports
  case $::osfamily {
    'RedHat': { include nfs::server::redhat }
    'Debian': { include nfs::server::debian }
  }
  include myfw
  firewall {'2049 NFS TCP communication':
    proto  => 'tcp',
    port   => '2049',
    action => 'accept',
  }
  firewall {'2049 UDP NFS communication':
    proto  => 'udp',
    port   => '2049',
    action => 'accept',
```

```
  }
  firewall {'0111 TCP PORTMAP':
    proto  => 'tcp',
    port   => '111',
    action => 'accept',
  }
  firewall {'0111 UDP PORTMAP':
    proto  => 'udp',
    port   => '111',
    action => 'accept',
  }
  firewall {'4000 TCP STAT':
    proto  => 'tcp',
    port   => '4000-4010',
    action => 'accept',
  }
  firewall {'4000 UDP STAT':
    proto  => 'udp',
    port   => '4000-4010',
    action => 'accept',
  }
}
```

4. Next, create the `nfs::server::redhat` class:

```
class nfs::server::redhat {
  package {'nfs-utils':
    ensure => 'installed',
  }
  service {'nfs':
    ensure => 'running',
    enable => true
  }
  file {'/etc/sysconfig/nfs':
    source => 'puppet:///modules/nfs/nfs',
    mode   => 0644,
    notify => Service['nfs'],
  }
}
```

5. Create the `/etc/sysconfig/nfs` support file for RedHat systems in the files directory of our `nfs` repo (`modules/nfs/files/nfs`):

```
STATD_PORT=4000
STATD_OUTGOING_PORT=4001
RQUOTAD_PORT=4002
```

```
LOCKD_TCPPORT=4003
LOCKD_UDPPORT=4003
MOUNTD_PORT=4004
```

6. Now create the support class for Debian systems, `nfs::server::debian`:

```
class nfs::server::debian {
  # install the package
  package {'nfs':
    name   => 'nfs-kernel-server',
    ensure => 'installed',
  }
  # config
  file {'/etc/default/nfs-common':
    source => 'puppet:///modules/nfs/nfs-common',
    mode   => 0644,
    notify => Service['nfs-common']
  }
  # services
  service {'nfs-common':
    ensure => 'running',
    enable => true,
  }
  service {'nfs':
    name   => 'nfs-kernel-server',
    ensure => 'running',
    enable => true,
    require => Package['nfs-kernel-server']
  }
}
```

7. Create the nfs-common configuration for Debian (which will be placed in `modules/nfs/files/nfs-common`):

```
STATDOPTS="--port 4000 --outgoing-port 4001"
```

8. Apply the `nfs::server` class to a node and then create an export on that node:

```
node debian {
  include nfs::server
  nfs::export {'/srv/home':
    tag => "srv_home" }
}
```

9. Create a collector for the exported resource created by the `nfs::server` class in the preceding code snippet:

```
node cookbook {
  Mount <<| tag == "srv_home" |>> {
    name    => '/mnt',
  }
}
```

10. Finally, run Puppet on the node Debian to create the exported resource. Then, run Puppet on the cookbook node to mount that resource:

```
root@debian:~# puppet agent -t

Info: Caching catalog for debian.example.com

Info: Applying configuration version '1415602532'

Notice: Finished catalog run in 0.78 seconds

[root@cookbook ~]# puppet agent -t

Info: Caching catalog for cookbook.example.com

Info: Applying configuration version '1415603580'

Notice: /Stage[main]/Main/Node[cookbook]/Mount[nfs::export::/srv/
home::192.168.122.148]/ensure: ensure changed 'ghost' to 'mounted'

Info: Computing checksum on file /etc/fstab

Info: /Stage[main]/Main/Node[cookbook]/Mount[nfs::export::/srv/
home::192.168.122.148]: Scheduling refresh of Mount[nfs::export::/
srv/home::192.168.122.148]

Info: Mount[nfs::export::/srv/home::192.168.122.148]
(provider=parsed): Remounting

Notice: /Stage[main]/Main/Node[cookbook]/Mount[nfs::export::/srv/
home::192.168.122.148]: Triggered 'refresh' from 1 events

Info: /Stage[main]/Main/Node[cookbook]/Mount[nfs::export::/srv/
home::192.168.122.148]: Scheduling refresh of Mount[nfs::export::/
srv/home::192.168.122.148]

Notice: Finished catalog run in 0.34 seconds
```

11. Verify the mount with `mount`:

```
[root@cookbook ~]# mount -t nfs
192.168.122.148:/srv/home on /mnt type nfs (rw)
```

How it works...

The `nfs::exports` class defines an exec, which runs `'exportfs -a'`, to export all filesystems defined in `/etc/exports`. Next, we define a concat resource to contain `concat::fragments`, which we will define next in our `nfs::export` class. Concat resources specify the file that the fragments are to be placed into; `/etc/exports` in this case. Our `concat` resource has a notify for the previous exec. This has the effect that whenever `/etc/exports` is updated, we run `'exportfs -a'` again to export the new entries:

```
class nfs::exports {
  exec {'nfs::exportfs':
    command     => 'exportfs -a',
    refreshonly => true,
    path        => '/usr/bin:/bin:/sbin:/usr/sbin',
  }
  concat {'/etc/exports':
    notify => Exec['nfs::exportfs'],
  }
}
```

We then created an `nfs::export` defined type, which does all the work. The defined type adds an entry to `/etc/exports` via a `concat::fragment` resource:

```
define nfs::export (
  $where = $title,
  $who = '*',
  $options = 'async,ro',
  $mount_options = 'defaults',
  $tag       = 'nfs'
) {
  # make sure the directory exists
  # export the entry locally, then export a resource to be picked up
later.
  file {"$where":
    ensure => 'directory',
  }
  include nfs::exports
  concat::fragment { "nfs::export::$where":
    content => "${where} ${who}(${options})\n",
    target  => '/etc/exports'
  }
```

In the definition, we use the attribute `$where` to define what filesystem we are exporting. We use `$who` to specify who can mount the filesystem. The attribute `$options` contains the exporting options such as **rw (read-write)**, **ro (read-only)**. Next, we have the options that will be placed in `/etc/fstab` on the client machine, the mount options, stored in `$mount_options`. The `nfs::exports` class is included here so that `concat::fragment` has a concat target defined.

Next, the exported mount resource is created; this is done on the server, so the ${::ipaddress} variable holds the IP address of the server. We use this to define the device for the mount. The device is the IP address of the server, a colon, and then the filesystem being exported. In this example, it is '192.168.122.148:/srv/home':

```
@@mount { "nfs::export::${where}::${::ipaddress}":
    name     => "$where",
    ensure   => 'mounted',
    fstype   => 'nfs',
    options  => "$mount_options",
    device   => "${::ipaddress}:${where}",
    tag      => "$tag",
  }
```

We reuse our myfw module and include it in the nfs::server class. This class illustrates one of the things to consider when writing your modules. Not all Linux distributions are created equal. Debian and RedHat deal with NFS server configuration quite differently. The nfs::server module deals with this by including OS-specific subclasses:

```
class nfs::server {
  # ensure nfs server is running
  # firewall should allow nfs communication
  include nfs::exports
  case $::osfamily {
    'RedHat': { include nfs::server::redhat }
    'Debian': { include nfs::server::debian }
  }
  include myfw
  firewall {'2049 NFS TCP communication':
    proto  => 'tcp',
    port   => '2049',
    action => 'accept',
  }
  firewall {'2049 UDP NFS communication':
    proto  => 'udp',
    port   => '2049',
    action => 'accept',
  }
  firewall {'0111 TCP PORTMAP':
    proto  => 'tcp',
    port   => '111',
    action => 'accept',
  }
```

```
      firewall {'0111 UDP PORTMAP':
        proto  => 'udp',
        port   => '111',
        action => 'accept',
      }
      firewall {'4000 TCP STAT':
        proto  => 'tcp',
        port   => '4000-4010',
        action => 'accept',
      }
      firewall {'4000 UDP STAT':
        proto  => 'udp',
        port   => '4000-4010',
        action => 'accept',
      }
    }
```

The `nfs::server` module opens several firewall ports for NFS communication. NFS traffic is always carried over port 2049 but ancillary systems, such as locking, quota, and file status daemons, use ephemeral ports chosen by the portmapper, by default. The portmapper itself uses port 111. So our module needs to allow 2049, 111, and a few other ports. We attempt to configure the ancillary services to use ports 4000 through 4010.

In the `nfs::server::redhat` class, we modify `/etc/sysconfig/nfs` to use the ports specified. Also, we install the nfs-utils package and start the nfs service:

```
    class nfs::server::redhat {
      package {'nfs-utils':
        ensure => 'installed',
      }
      service {'nfs':
        ensure => 'running',
        enable => true
      }
      file {'/etc/sysconfig/nfs':
        source => 'puppet:///modules/nfs/nfs',
        mode   => 0644,
        notify => Service['nfs'],
      }
    }
```

We do the same for Debian-based systems in the `nfs::server::debian` class. The packages and services have different names but overall the process is similar:

```
    class nfs::server::debian {
      # install the package
```

```
package {'nfs':
  name   => 'nfs-kernel-server',
  ensure => 'installed',
}
# config
file {'/etc/default/nfs-common':
  source => 'puppet:///modules/nfs/nfs-common',
  mode   => 0644,
  notify => Service['nfs-common']
}
# services
service {'nfs-common':
  ensure => 'running',
  enable => true,
}
service {'nfs':
  name   => 'nfs-kernel-server',
  ensure => 'running',
  enable => true,
}
}
```

With everything in place, we include the server class to configure the NFS server and then define an export:

```
include nfs::server
nfs::export {'/srv/home':
  tag => "srv_home" }
```

What's important here is that we defined the `tag` attribute, which will be used in the exported resource we collect in the following code snippet:

```
Mount <<| tag == "srv_home" |>> {
  name   => '/mnt',
}
```

We use the spaceship syntax (`<< |   | >>`) to collect all the exported mount resources that have the tag we defined earlier (`srv_home`). We then use a syntax called "override on collect" to modify the name attribute of the mount to specify where to mount the filesystem.

Using this design pattern with exported resources, we can change the server exporting the filesystem and have any nodes that mount the resource updated automatically. We can have many different nodes collecting the exported mount resource.

Using HAProxy to load-balance multiple web servers

Load balancers are used to spread a load among a number of servers. Hardware load balancers are still somewhat expensive, whereas software balancers can achieve most of the benefits of a hardware solution.

HAProxy is the software load balancer of choice for most people: fast, powerful, and highly configurable.

How to do it...

In this recipe, I'll show you how to build an HAProxy server to load-balance web requests across web servers. We'll use exported resources to build the haproxy configuration file just like we did for the NFS example.

1. Create the file modules/haproxy/manifests/master.pp with the following contents:

```
class haproxy::master ($app = 'myapp') {
  # The HAProxy master server
  # will collect haproxy::slave resources and add to its balancer
  package { 'haproxy': ensure => installed }
  service { 'haproxy':
    ensure  => running,
    enable  => true,
    require => Package['haproxy'],
  }

  include haproxy::config

  concat::fragment { 'haproxy.cfg header':
    target  => 'haproxy.cfg',
    source  => 'puppet:///modules/haproxy/haproxy.cfg',
    order   => '001',
    require => Package['haproxy'],
    notify  => Service['haproxy'],
  }

  # pull in the exported entries
  Concat::Fragment <<| tag == "$app" |>> {
    target => 'haproxy.cfg',
    notify => Service['haproxy'],
  }
}
```

2. Create the file `modules/haproxy/files/haproxy.cfg` with the following contents:

```
global
        daemon
        user haproxy
        group haproxy
        pidfile /var/run/haproxy.pid

defaults
        log     global
        stats   enable
        mode    http
        option  httplog
        option  dontlognull
        option  dontlog-normal
        retries 3
        option  redispatch
        timeout connect 4000
        timeout client 60000
        timeout server 30000

listen  stats :8080
        mode http
        stats uri /
        stats auth haproxy:topsecret

listen  myapp 0.0.0.0:80
        balance leastconn
```

3. Modify your `manifests/nodes.pp` file as follows:

```
node 'cookbook' {
  include haproxy
}
```

4. Create the slave server configuration in the `haproxy::slave` class:

```
class haproxy::slave ($app = "myapp", $localport = 8000) {
  # haproxy slave, export haproxy.cfg fragment
  # configure simple web server on different port
  @@concat::fragment { "haproxy.cfg $::fqdn":
    content => "\t\tserver ${::hostname}
${::ipaddress}:${localport}   check maxconn 100\n",
    order   => '0010',
```

```
      tag      => "$app",
    }
    include myfw
    firewall {"${localport} Allow HTTP to haproxy::slave":
      proto  => 'tcp',
      port   => $localport,
      action => 'accept',
    }

    class {'apache': }
    apache::vhost { 'haproxy.example.com':
      port        => '8000',
      docroot => '/var/www/haproxy',
    }
    file {'/var/www/haproxy':
      ensure  => 'directory',
      mode    => 0755,
      require => Class['apache'],
    }
    file {'/var/www/haproxy/index.html':
      mode    => '0644',
      content => "<html><body><h1>${::fqdn} haproxy::slave\n</
body></html>\n",
      require => File['/var/www/haproxy'],
    }
  }
```

5. Create the `concat` container resource in the `haproxy::config` class as follows:

```
class haproxy::config {
  concat {'haproxy.cfg':
    path  => '/etc/haproxy/haproxy.cfg',
    order => 'numeric',
    mode  => '0644',
  }
}
```

6. Modify `site.pp` to define the master and slave nodes:

```
node master {
  class {'haproxy::master':
    app => 'cookbook'
  }
}
node slave1,slave2 {
  class {'haproxy::slave':
```

```
        app => 'cookbook'
    }
}
```

7. Run Puppet on each of the slave servers:

```
root@slave1:~# puppet agent -t

Info: Caching catalog for slave1

Info: Applying configuration version '1415646194'

Notice: /Stage[main]/Haproxy::Slave/Apache::Vhost[haproxy.example.
com]/File[25-haproxy.example.com.conf]/ensure: created

Info: /Stage[main]/Haproxy::Slave/Apache::Vhost[haproxy.example.
com]/File[25-haproxy.example.com.conf]: Scheduling refresh of
Service[httpd]

Notice: /Stage[main]/Haproxy::Slave/Apache::Vhost[haproxy.example.
com]/File[25-haproxy.example.com.conf symlink]/ensure: created

Info: /Stage[main]/Haproxy::Slave/Apache::Vhost[haproxy.example.
com]/File[25-haproxy.example.com.conf symlink]: Scheduling refresh
of Service[httpd]

Notice: /Stage[main]/Apache::Service/Service[httpd]/ensure: ensure
changed 'stopped' to 'running'

Info: /Stage[main]/Apache::Service/Service[httpd]: Unscheduling
refresh on Service[httpd]

Notice: Finished catalog run in 1.71 seconds
```

8. Run Puppet on the master node to configure and run `haproxy`:

```
[root@master ~]# puppet agent -t

Info: Caching catalog for master.example.com

Info: Applying configuration version '1415647075'

Notice: /Stage[main]/Haproxy::Master/Package[haproxy]/ensure:
created

Notice: /Stage[main]/Myfw::Pre/Firewall[0000 Allow all traffic on
loopback]/ensure: created

Notice: /Stage[main]/Myfw::Pre/Firewall[0001 Allow all ICMP]/
ensure: created

Notice: /Stage[main]/Haproxy::Master/Firewall[8080 haproxy
statistics]/ensure: created

Notice: /File[/etc/sysconfig/iptables]/seluser: seluser changed
'unconfined_u' to 'system_u'

Notice: /Stage[main]/Myfw::Pre/Firewall[0022 Allow all TCP on port
22 (ssh)]/ensure: created

Notice: /Stage[main]/Haproxy::Master/Firewall[0080 http haproxy]/
ensure: created
```

```
Notice: /Stage[main]/Myfw::Pre/Firewall[0002 Allow all established
traffic]/ensure: created

Notice: /Stage[main]/Myfw::Post/Firewall[9999 Drop all other
traffic]/ensure: created

Notice: /Stage[main]/Haproxy::Config/Concat[haproxy.cfg]/
File[haproxy.cfg]/content:

...

+listen  myapp 0.0.0.0:80

+        balance leastconn

+    server slave1 192.168.122.148:8000    check maxconn 100

+    server slave2 192.168.122.133:8000    check maxconn 100


Info: Computing checksum on file /etc/haproxy/haproxy.cfg

Info: /Stage[main]/Haproxy::Config/Concat[haproxy.cfg]/
File[haproxy.cfg]: Filebucketed /etc/haproxy/haproxy.cfg to puppet
with sum 1f337186b0e1ba5ee82760cb437fb810

Notice: /Stage[main]/Haproxy::Config/Concat[haproxy.cfg]/
File[haproxy.cfg]/content: content changed '{md5}1f337186b0e1ba5ee
82760cb437fb810' to '{md5}b070f076e1e691e053d6853f7d966394'

Notice: /Stage[main]/Haproxy::Master/Service[haproxy]/ensure:
ensure changed 'stopped' to 'running'

Info: /Stage[main]/Haproxy::Master/Service[haproxy]: Unscheduling
refresh on Service[haproxy]

Notice: Finished catalog run in 33.48 seconds
```

9. Check the HAProxy stats interface on master port 8080 in your web browser (http://
    master.example.com:8080) to make sure everything is okay (The username
    and password are in haproxy.cfg, haproxy, and topsecret). Try going to the
    proxied service as well. Notice that the page changes on each reload as the service is
    redirected from slave1 to slave2 (http://master.example.com).

How it works...

We built a complex configuration from various components of the previous sections. This type
of deployment becomes easier the more you do it. At a top level, we configured the master to
collect exported resources from slaves. The slaves exported their configuration information to
allow haproxy to use them in the load balancer. As slaves are added to the system, they can
export their resources and be added to the balancer automatically.

We used our myfw module to configure the firewall on the slaves and the master to
allow communication.

We used the Forge Apache module to configure the listening web server on the slaves. We were able to generate a fully functioning website with five lines of code (10 more to place index.html on the website).

There are several things going on here. We have the firewall configuration and the Apache configuration in addition to the haproxy configuration. We'll focus on how the exported resources and the haproxy configuration fit together.

In the haproxy::config class, we created the concat container for the haproxy configuration:

```
class haproxy::config {
  concat {'haproxy.cfg':
    path  => '/etc/haproxy/haproxy.cfg',
    order => 'numeric',
    mode  => 0644,
  }
}
```

We reference this in haproxy::slave:

```
class haproxy::slave ($app = "myapp", $localport = 8000) {
  # haproxy slave, export haproxy.cfg fragment
  # configure simple web server on different port
  @@concat::fragment { "haproxy.cfg $::fqdn":
    content => "\t\tserver ${::hostname} ${::ipaddress}:${localport}
check maxconn 100\n",
    order   => '0010',
    tag     => "$app",
  }
}
```

We are doing a little trick here with concat; we don't define the target in the exported resource. If we did, the slaves would try and create a /etc/haproxy/haproxy.cfg file, but the slaves do not have haproxy installed so we would get catalog failures. What we do is modify the resource when we collect it in haproxy::master:

```
# pull in the exported entries
  Concat::Fragment <<| tag == "$app" |>> {
    target => 'haproxy.cfg',
    notify => Service['haproxy'],
  }
```

In addition to adding the target when we collect the resource, we also add a notify so that the haproxy service is restarted when we add a new host to the configuration. Another important point here is that we set the order attribute of the slave configurations to 0010, when we define the header for the haproxy.cfg file; we use an order value of 0001 to ensure that the header is placed at the beginning of the file:

```
concat::fragment { 'haproxy.cfg header':
    target  => 'haproxy.cfg',
    source  => 'puppet:///modules/haproxy/haproxy.cfg',
    order   => '001',
    require => Package['haproxy'],
    notify  => Service['haproxy'],
}
```

The rest of the `haproxy::master` class is concerned with configuring the firewall as we did in previous examples.

There's more...

HAProxy has a vast range of configuration parameters, which you can explore; see the HAProxy website at `http://haproxy.1wt.eu/#docs`.

Although it's most often used as a web server, HAProxy can proxy a lot more than just HTTP. It can handle any kind of TCP traffic, so you can use it to balance the load of MySQL servers, SMTP, video servers, or anything you like.

You can use the design we showed to attack many problems of coordination of services between multiple servers. This type of interaction is very common; you can apply it to many configurations for load balancing or distributed systems. You can use the same workflow described previously to have nodes export firewall resources (`@@firewall`) to permit their own access.

Managing Docker with Puppet

Docker is a platform for rapid deployment of containers. Containers are like a lightweight virtual machine that might only run a single process. The containers in Docker are called docks and are configured with files called Dockerfiles. Puppet can be used to configure a node to not only run Docker but also configure and start several docks. You can then use Puppet to ensure that your docks are running and are consistently configured.

Getting ready

Download and install the Puppet Docker module from the Forge (`https://forge.puppetlabs.com/garethr/docker`):

```
t@mylaptop ~ $ cd puppet
t@mylaptop ~/puppet $ puppet module install -i modules garethr-docker
Notice: Preparing to install into /home/thomas/puppet/modules ...
Notice: Downloading from https://forgeapi.puppetlabs.com ...
```

```
Notice: Installing -- do not interrupt ...
/home/thomas/puppet/modules
└─┬ garethr-docker (v3.3.0)
  ├── puppetlabs-apt (v1.7.0)
  ├── puppetlabs-stdlib (v4.3.2)
  └── stahnma-epel (v1.0.2)
```

Add these modules to your Puppet repository. The `stahnma-epel` module is required for Enterprise Linux-based distributions; it contains the Extra Packages for Enterprise Linux YUM repository.

How to do it...

Perform the following steps to manage Docker with Puppet:

1. To install Docker on a node, we just need to include the `docker` class. We'll do more than install Docker; we'll also download an image and start an application on our test node. In this example, we'll create a new machine called `shipyard`. Add the following node definition to `site.pp`:

   ```
   node shipyard {
   class {'docker': }
   docker::image {'phusion/baseimage': }
   docker::run {'cookbook':
     image   => 'phusion/baseimage',
     expose  => '8080',
     ports   => '8080',
     command => 'nc -k -l 8080',
   }
   }
   ```

2. Run Puppet on your shipyard node to install Docker. This will also download the `phusion/baseimage docker` image:

   ```
   [root@shipyard ~]# puppet agent -t
   Info: Retrieving pluginfacts
   Info: Retrieving plugin
   Info: Loading facts
   Info: Caching catalog for shipyard
   Info: Applying configuration version '1421049252'
   ```

```
Notice: /Stage[main]/Epel/File[/etc/pki/rpm-gpg/RPM
-GPG-KEY-EPEL-6]/ensure: defined content as '{md5}
d865e6b948a74cb03bc3401c0b01b785'

Notice: /Stage[main]/Epel/Epel::Rpm_gpg_key[EPEL-6]/Exec[import
-EPEL-6]/returns: executed successfully

...

Notice: /Stage[main]/Docker::Install/Package[docker]/
ensure: created

...

Notice: /Stage[main]/Main/Node[shipyard]/Docker::Run[cookbook]/
File[/etc/init.d/docker-cookbook]/ensure: created

Info: /Stage[main]/Main/Node[shipyard]/Docker::Run[cookbook]/
File[/etc/init.d/docker-cookbook]: Scheduling refresh of
Service[docker-cookbook]

Notice: /Stage[main]/Main/Node[shipyard]/Docker::Run[cookbook]/
Service[docker-cookbook]: Triggered 'refresh' from 1 events
```

3. Verify that your container is running on shipyard using `docker ps`:

```
[root@shipyard ~]# docker ps
CONTAINER ID          IMAGE                     COMMAND
CREATED               STATUS              PORTS
NAMES
f6f5b799a598          phusion/baseimage:0.9.15    "/bin/nc -l 8080"
About a minute ago    Up About a minute   0.0.0.0:49157->8080/tcp
suspicious_hawking
```

4. Verify that the dock is running netcat on port 8080 by connecting to the port listed previously (`49157`):

```
[root@shipyard ~]# nc -v localhost 49157
Connection to localhost 49157 port [tcp/*] succeeded!
```

How it works...

We began by installing the docker module from the Forge. This module installs the `docker-io` package on our node, along with any required dependencies.

We then defined a `docker::image` resource. This instructs Puppet to ensure that the named image is downloaded and available to docker. On our first run, Puppet will make docker download the image. We used `phusion/baseimage` as our example because it is quite small, well-known, and includes the netcat daemon we used in the example. More information on `baseimage` can be found at `http://phusion.github.io/baseimage-docker/`.

We then went on to define a `docker::run` resource. This example isn't terribly useful; it simply starts netcat in listen mode on port 8080. We need to expose that port to our machine, so we define the expose attribute of our `docker::run` resource. There are many other options available for the `docker::run` resource. Refer to the source code for more details.

We then used docker ps to list the running docks on our shipyard machine. We parsed out the listening port on our local machine and verified that netcat was listening.

There's more...

Docker is a great tool for rapid deployment and development. You can spin as many docks as you need on even the most modest hardware. One great use for docker is having docks act as test nodes for your modules. You can create a docker image, which includes Puppet, and then have Puppet run within the dock. For more information on docker, visit `http://www.docker.com/`.

9
External Tools and the Puppet Ecosystem

"By all means leave the road when you wish. That is precisely the use of a road: to reach individually chosen points of departure."

– Robert Bringhurst, The Elements of Typographic Style

In this chapter, we will cover the following recipes:

- ▸ Creating custom facts
- ▸ Adding external facts
- ▸ Setting facts as environment variables
- ▸ Generating manifests with the Puppet resource command
- ▸ Generating manifests with other tools
- ▸ Using an external node classifier
- ▸ Creating your own resource types
- ▸ Creating your own providers
- ▸ Creating custom functions
- ▸ Testing your Puppet manifests with rspec-puppet
- ▸ Using librarian-puppet
- ▸ Using r10k

Introduction

Puppet is a useful tool by itself, but you can get much greater benefits by using Puppet in combination with other tools and frameworks. We'll look at some ways of getting data into Puppet, including custom Facter facts, external facts, and tools to generate Puppet manifests automatically from the existing configuration.

You'll also learn how to extend Puppet by creating your own custom functions, resource types, and providers; how to use an external node classifier script to integrate Puppet with other parts of your infrastructure; and how to test your code with rspec-puppet.

Creating custom facts

While Facter's built-in facts are useful, it's actually quite easy to add your own facts. For example, if you have machines in different data centers or hosting providers, you could add a custom fact for this so that Puppet can determine whether any local settings need to be applied (for example, local DNS servers or network routes).

How to do it...

Here's an example of a simple custom fact:

1. Create the directory `modules/facts/lib/facter` and then create the file `modules/facts/lib/facter/hello.rb` with the following contents:

```
Facter.add(:hello) do
  setcode do
    "Hello, world"
  end
end
```

2. Modify your `site.pp` file as follows:

```
node 'cookbook' {
  notify { $::hello: }
}
```

3. Run Puppet:

```
[root@cookbook ~]# puppet agent -t
Notice: /File[/var/lib/puppet/lib/facter/hello.rb]/ensure: defined
content as '{md5}f66d5e290459388c5ffb3694dd22388b'
Info: Loading facts
Info: Caching catalog for cookbook.example.com
Info: Applying configuration version '1416205745'
```

```
Notice: Hello, world
Notice: /Stage[main]/Main/Node[cookbook]/Notify[Hello, world]/
message: defined 'message' as 'Hello, world'
Notice: Finished catalog run in 0.53 seconds
```

How it works...

Facter facts are defined in Ruby files that are distributed with facter. Puppet can add additional facts to facter by creating files within the `lib/facter` subdirectory of a module. These files are then transferred to client nodes as we saw earlier with the `puppetlabs-stdlib` module. To have the command-line facter use these `puppet` facts, append the `-p` option to facter as shown in the following command line:

```
[root@cookbook ~]# facter hello


[root@cookbook ~]# facter -p hello
Hello, world
```

 If you are using an older version of Puppet (older than 3.0), you will need to enable `pluginsync` in your `puppet.conf` file as shown in the following command line:

```
[main]
pluginsync = true
```

Facts can contain any Ruby code, and the last value evaluated inside the `setcode do ...` `end` block will be the value returned by the fact. For example, you could make a more useful fact that returns the number of users currently logged in to the system:

```
Facter.add(:users) do
  setcode do
    %x{/usr/bin/who |wc -l}.chomp
  end
end
```

To reference the fact in your manifests, just use its name like a built-in fact:

```
notify { "${::users} users logged in": }
Notice:  2 users logged in
```

You can add custom facts to any Puppet module. When creating facts that will be used by multiple modules, it may make sense to place them in a facts module. In most cases, the custom fact is related to a specific module and should be placed in that module.

There's more...

The name of the Ruby file that holds the fact definition is irrelevant. You can name this file whatever you wish; the name of the fact comes from the `Facter.add()` function call. You may also call this function several times within a single Ruby file to define multiple facts as necessary. For instance, you could `grep` the `/proc/meminfo` file and return several facts based on memory information as shown in the `meminfo.rb` file in the following code snippet:

```
File.open('/proc/meminfo') do |f|
  f.each_line { |line|
  if (line[/^Active:/])
    Facter.add(:memory_active) do
      setcode do line.split(':')[1].to_i
      end
    end
  end
  if (line[/^Inactive:/])
    Facter.add(:memory_inactive) do
      setcode do line.split(':')[1].to_i
      end
    end
  end
  }
end
```

After synchronizing this file to a node, the `memory_active` and `memory_inactive` facts would be available as follows:

```
[root@cookbook ~]# facter -p |grep memory_
memory_active => 63780
memory_inactive => 58188
```

You can extend the use of facts to build a completely nodeless Puppet configuration; in other words, Puppet can decide what resources to apply to a machine, based solely on the results of facts. Jordan Sissel has written about this approach at `http://www.semicomplete.com/blog/geekery/puppet-nodeless-configuration.html`.

You can find out more about custom facts, including how to make sure that OS-specific facts work only on the relevant systems, and how to weigh facts so that they're evaluated in a specific order at the puppetlabs website:

`http://docs.puppetlabs.com/guides/custom_facts.html`

- ▶ The *Importing dynamic information* recipe in *Chapter 3, Writing Better Manifests*
- ▶ The *Configuring Hiera* recipe in *Chapter 2, Puppet Infrastructure*

Adding external facts

The *Creating custom facts* recipe describes how to add extra facts written in Ruby. You can also create facts from simple text files or scripts with external facts instead.

External facts live in the `/etc/facter/facts.d` directory and have a simple `key=value` format like this:

```
message="Hello, world"
```

Getting ready

Here's what you need to do to prepare your system to add external facts:

1. You'll need Facter Version 1.7 or higher to use external facts, so look up the value of `facterversion` or use `facter -v`:

   ```
   [root@cookbook ~]# facter facterversion
   2.3.0
   [root@cookbook ~]# facter -v
   2.3.0
   ```

2. You'll also need to create the external facts directory, using the following command:

   ```
   [root@cookbook ~]# mkdir -p /etc/facter/facts.d
   ```

How to do it...

In this example, we'll create a simple external fact that returns a message, as shown in the *Creating custom facts* recipe:

1. Create the file `/etc/facter/facts.d/local.txt` with the following contents:

   ```
   model=ED-209
   ```

2. Run the following command:

   ```
   [root@cookbook ~]# facter model
   ED-209
   ```

Well, that was easy! You can add more facts to the same file, or other files, of course, as follows:

```
model=ED-209
builder=OCP
directives=4
```

However, what if you need to compute a fact in some way, for example, the number of logged-in users? You can create executable facts to do this.

3.   Create the file `/etc/facter/facts.d/users.sh` with the following contents:

```
#!/bin/sh
echo users=`who |wc -l`
```

4.   Make this file executable with the following command:

```
[root@cookbook ~]# chmod a+x /etc/facter/facts.d/users.sh
```

5.   Now check the `users` value with the following command:

```
[root@cookbook ~]# facter users
2
```

How it works...

In this example, we'll create an external fact by creating files on the node. We'll also show how to override a previously defined fact.

1.   Current versions of Facter will look into `/etc/facter/facts.d` for files of type `.txt`, `.json`, or `.yaml`. If facter finds a text file, it will parse the file for `key=value` pairs and add the key as a new fact:

```
[root@cookbook ~]# facter model
ED-209
```

2.   If the file is a YAML or JSON file, then facter will parse the file for `key=value` pairs in the respective format. For YAML, for instance:

```
---
registry: NCC-68814
class: Andromeda
shipname: USS Prokofiev
```

3.   The resulting output will be as follows:

```
[root@cookbook ~]# facter registry class shipname
class => Andromeda
registry => NCC-68814
shipname => USS Prokofiev
```

4. In the case of executable files, Facter will assume that their output is a list of `key=value` pairs. It will execute all the files in the `facts.d` directory and add their output to the internal fact hash.

 In Windows, batch files or PowerShell scripts may be used in the same way that executable scripts are used in Linux.

5. In the `users` example, Facter will execute the `users.sh` script, which results in the following output:

   users=2

6. It will then search this output for `users` and return the matching value:

   ```
   [root@cookbook ~]# facter users
   2
   ```

7. If there are multiple matches for the key you specified, Facter determines which fact to return based on a weight property. In my version of facter, the weight of external facts is 10,000 (defined in `facter/util/directory_loader.rb` as `EXTERNAL_FACT_WEIGHT`). This high value is to ensure that the facts you define can override the supplied facts. For example:

   ```
   [root@cookbook ~]# facter architecture
   x86_64
   [root@cookbook ~]# echo "architecture=ppc64">>/etc/facter/facts.d/myfacts.txt
   [root@cookbook ~]# facter architecture
   ppc64
   ```

There's more...

Since all external facts have a weight of 10,000, the order in which they are parsed within the `/etc/facter/facts.d` directory sets their precedence (with the last one encountered having the highest precedence). To create a fact that will be favored over another, you'll need to have it created in a file that comes last alphabetically:

```
[root@cookbook ~]# facter architecture
ppc64
[root@cookbook ~]# echo "architecture=r10000" >>/etc/facter/facts.d/z-architecture.txt
[root@cookbook ~]# facter architecture
r10000
```

Debugging external facts

If you're having trouble getting Facter to recognize your external facts, run Facter in debug mode to see what's happening:

```
ubuntu@cookbook:~/puppet$ facter -d robin
Fact file /etc/facter/facts.d/myfacts.json was parsed but returned an
empty data set
```

The X JSON file was parsed but returned an empty data set error, which means Facter didn't find any `key=value` pairs in the file or (in the case of an executable fact) in its output.

> Note that if you have external facts present, Facter parses or runs all the facts in the `/etc/facter/facts.d` directory every time you query Facter. If some of these scripts take a long time to run, that can significantly slow down anything that uses Facter (run Facter with the `--iming` switch to troubleshoot this). Unless a particular fact needs to be recomputed every time it's queried, consider replacing it with a cron job that computes it every so often and writes the result to a text file in the Facter directory.

Using external facts in Puppet

Any external facts you create will be available to both Facter and Puppet. To reference external facts in your Puppet manifests, just use the fact name in the same way you would for a built-in or custom fact:

```
notify { "There are $::users people logged in right now.": }
```

Unless you are specifically attempting to override a defined fact, you should avoid using the name of a predefined fact.

See also

- ▶ The *Importing dynamic information* recipe in *Chapter 3, Writing Better Manifests*
- ▶ The *Configuring Hiera* recipe in *Chapter 2, Puppet Infrastructure*
- ▶ The *Creating custom facts* recipe in this chapter

Setting facts as environment variables

Another handy way to get information into Puppet and Facter is to pass it using environment variables. Any environment variable whose name starts with FACTER_ will be interpreted as a fact. For example, ask facter the value of hello using the following command:

```
[root@cookbook ~]# facter -p hello
Hello, world
```

Now override the value with an environment variable and ask again:

```
[root@cookbook ~]# FACTER_hello='Howdy!' facter -p hello
Howdy!
```

It works just as well with Puppet, so let's run through an example.

How to do it...

In this example we'll set a fact using an environment variable:

1. Keep the node definition for cookbook the same as our last example:

    ```
    node cookbook {
      notify {"$::hello": }
    }
    ```

2. Run the following command:

    ```
    [root@cookbook ~]# FACTER_hello="Hallo Welt" puppet agent -t
    Info: Caching catalog for cookbook.example.com
    Info: Applying configuration version '1416212026'
    Notice: Hallo Welt
    Notice: /Stage[main]/Main/Node[cookbook]/Notify[Hallo Welt]/
    message: defined 'message' as 'Hallo Welt'
    Notice: Finished catalog run in 0.27 seconds
    ```

Generating manifests with the Puppet resource command

If you have a server that is already configured as it needs to be, or nearly so, you can capture that configuration as a Puppet manifest. The Puppet resource command generates Puppet manifests from the existing configuration of a system. For example, you can have `puppet resource` generate a manifest that creates all the users found on the system. This is very useful to take a snapshot of a working system and get its configuration quickly into Puppet.

How to do it...

Here are some examples of using `puppet resource` to get data from a running system:

1. To generate the manifest for a particular user, run the following command:

    ```
    [root@cookbook ~]# puppet resource user thomas
    user { 'thomas':
    ```

```
        ensure                => 'present',
        comment               => 'thomas Admin User',
        gid                   => '1001',
        groups                => ['bin', 'wheel'],
        home                  => '/home/thomas',
        password              => '!!',
        password_max_age => '99999',
        password_min_age => '0',
        shell                 => '/bin/bash',
        uid                   => '1001',
}
```

2. For a particular service, run the following command:

```
[root@cookbook ~]# puppet resource service sshd
service { 'sshd':
  ensure => 'running',
  enable => 'true',
}
```

3. For a package, run the following command:

```
[root@cookbook ~]# puppet resource package kernel
package { 'kernel':
  ensure => '2.6.32-431.23.3.el6',
}
```

There's more...

You can use `puppet resource` to examine each of the resource types available in Puppet. In the preceding examples, we generated a manifest for a specific instance of the resource type, but you can also use `puppet resource` to dump all instances of the resource:

```
[root@cookbook ~]# puppet resource service
service { 'abrt-ccpp':
  ensure => 'running',
  enable => 'true',
}
service { 'abrt-oops':
  ensure => 'running',
  enable => 'true',
}
```

```
service { 'abrtd':
  ensure => 'running',
  enable => 'true',
}
service { 'acpid':
  ensure => 'running',
  enable => 'true',
}
service { 'atd':
  ensure => 'running',
  enable => 'true',
}
service { 'auditd':
  ensure => 'running',
  enable => 'true',
}
```

This will output the state of each service on the system; this is because each service is an enumerable resource. When you try the same command with a resource that is not enumerable, you get an error message:

```
[root@cookbook ~]# puppet resource file
Error: Could not run: Listing all file instances is not supported.
Please specify a file or directory, e.g. puppet resource file /etc
```

Asking Puppet to describe each file on the system will not work; that's something best left to an audit tool such as `tripwire` (a system designed to look for changes on every file on the system, `http://www.tripwire.com`).

Generating manifests with other tools

If you want to quickly capture the complete configuration of a running system as a Puppet manifest, there are a couple of tools available to help. In this example, we'll look at Blueprint, which is designed to examine a machine and dump its state as Puppet code.

Getting ready

Here's what you need to do to prepare your system to use Blueprint.

Run the following command to install Blueprint; we'll use `puppet resource` here to change the state of the `python-pip` package:

```
[root@cookbook ~]# puppet resource package python-pip ensure=installed
Notice: /Package[python-pip]/ensure: created
```

```
package { 'python-pip':
  ensure => '1.3.1-4.el6',
}
[root@cookbook ~]# pip install blueprint
Downloading/unpacking blueprint
  Downloading blueprint-3.4.2.tar.gz (59kB): 59kB downloaded
  Running setup.py egg_info for package blueprint
Installing collected packages: blueprint
  Running setup.py install for blueprint
    changing mode of build/scripts-2.6/blueprint from 644 to 755
...
Successfully installed blueprint
Cleaning up...
```

> You may need to install Git on your cookbook node if it is not already installed.

How to do it...

These steps will show you how to run Blueprint:

1. Run the following commands:

```
[root@cookbook ~]# mkdir blueprint && cd blueprint
[root@cookbook blueprint]# blueprint create -P blueprint_test
# [blueprint] searching for APT packages to exclude
# [blueprint] searching for Yum packages to exclude
# [blueprint] caching excluded Yum packages
# [blueprint] parsing blueprintignore(5) rules
# [blueprint] searching for npm packages
# [blueprint] searching for configuration files
# [blueprint] searching for APT packages
# [blueprint] searching for PEAR/PECL packages
# [blueprint] searching for Python packages
# [blueprint] searching for Ruby gems
# [blueprint] searching for software built from source
# [blueprint] searching for Yum packages
# [blueprint] searching for service dependencies
blueprint_test/manifests/init.pp
```

2. Read the `blueprint_test/manifests/init.pp` file to see the generated code:

```
#
# Automatically generated by blueprint(7).  Edit at your own risk.
#
class blueprint_test {
  Exec {
    path => '/usr/lib64/qt-3.3/bin:/usr/local/sbin:/usr/local/
bin:/sbin:/bin:/usr/sbin:/usr/bin:/root/bin',
  }
  Class['sources'] -> Class['files'] -> Class['packages']
    class files {
      file {
        '/etc':
          ensure => directory;
        '/etc/aliases.db':
content => template('blueprint_test/etc/aliases.db'),
          ensure  => file,
group     => root,
          mode    => 0644,
          owner   => root;
'/etc/audit':
          ensure => directory;
'/etc/audit/audit.rules':
          content => template('blueprint_test/etc/audit/audit.
rules'),
          ensure  => file,
          group   => root,
          mode    => 0640,
          owner   => root;
        '/etc/blkid':
          ensure => directory;
'/etc/cron.hourly':
          ensure => directory;
'/etc/cron.hourly/run-backup':
          content => template('blueprint_test/etc/cron.hourly/run-
backup'),
          ensure  => file,
          group   => root,
          mode    => 0755,
owner     => root;
'/etc/crypttab':
          content => template('blueprint_test/etc/crypttab'),
          ensure  => file,
          group   => root,
          mode    => 0644,
          owner   => root;
```

There's more...

Blueprint just takes a snapshot of the system as it stands; it makes no intelligent decisions, and Blueprint captures all the files on the system and all the packages. It will generate a configuration much larger than you may actually require. For instance, when configuring a server, you may specify that you want the Apache package installed. The dependencies for the Apache package will be installed automatically and you need to specify them. When generating the configuration with a tool such as Blueprint, you will capture all those dependencies and lock the versions that are installed on your system currently. Looking at our generated Blueprint code, we can see that this is the case:

```
class yum {
  package {
    'GeoIP':
      ensure => '1.5.1-5.el6.x86_64';
    'PyXML':
      ensure => '0.8.4-19.el6.x86_64';
    'SDL':
      ensure => '1.2.14-3.el6.x86_64';
    'apr':
      ensure => '1.3.9-5.el6_2.x86_64';
    'apr-util':
      ensure => '1.3.9-3.el6_0.1.x86_64';
```

If you were creating this manifest yourself, you would likely specify `ensure => installed` instead of a specific version.

Packages install default versions of files. Blueprint has no notion of this and will add all the files to the manifest, even those that have not changed. By default, Blueprint will indiscriminately capture all the files in `/etc` as file resources.

Blueprint and similar tools have a very small use case generally, but may help you to get familiar with the Puppet syntax and give you some ideas on how to specify your own manifests. I would not recommend blindly using this tool to create a system, however.

There's no shortcut to good configuration management, those who hope to save time and effort by cutting and pasting someone else's code as a whole (as with public modules) are likely to find that it saves neither.

Using an external node classifier

When Puppet runs on a node, it needs to know which classes should be applied to that node. For example, if it is a web server node, it might need to include an `apache` class. The normal way to map nodes to classes is in the Puppet manifest itself, for example, in your `site.pp` file:

```
node 'web1' {
    include apache
}
```

Alternatively, you can use an **External Node Classifier (ENC)** to do this job. An ENC is any executable program that can accept the fully-qualified domain name (FQDN) as the first command-line argument (`$1`). The script is expected to return a list of classes, parameters, and an optional environment to apply to the node. The output is expected to be in the standard YAML format. When using an ENC, you should keep in mind that the classes applied through the standard `site.pp` manifest are merged with those provided by the ENC.

 Parameters returned by the ENC are available as top-scope variables to the node.

An ENC could be a simple shell script, for example, or a wrapper around a more complicated program or API that can decide how to map nodes to classes. The ENC provided by Puppet enterprise and The Foreman (`http://theforeman.org/`) are both simple scripts, which connect to the web API of their respective systems.

In this example, we'll build the most simple of ENCs, a shell script that simply prints a list of classes to include. We'll start by including an `enc` class, which defines `notify` that will print a top-scope variable `$enc`.

Getting ready

We'll start by creating our `enc` class to include with the `enc` script:

1. Run the following command:

   ```
   t@mylaptop ~/puppet $ mkdir -p modules/enc/manifests
   ```

2. Create the file `modules/enc/manifests/init.pp` with the following contents:

   ```
   class enc {
     notify {"We defined this from $enc": }
   }
   ```

How to do it...

Here's how to build a simple external node classifier. We'll perform all these steps on our Puppet master server. If you are running masterless, then do these steps on a node:

1. Create the file `/etc/puppet/cookbook.sh` with the following contents:

   ```
   #!/bin/bash
   cat <<EOF
   ---
   classes:
   enc:
   parameters:
     enc: $0
   EOF
   ```

2. Run the following command:

   root@puppet:/etc/puppet# chmod a+x cookbook.sh

3. Modify your `/etc/puppet/puppet.conf` file as follows:

   ```
   [main]
     node_terminus = exec
     external_nodes = /etc/puppet/cookbook.sh
   ```

4. Restart Apache (restart the master) to make the change effective.

5. Ensure your `site.pp` file has the following empty definition for the default node:

   ```
   node default {}
   ```

6. Run Puppet:

   [root@cookbook ~]# puppet agent -t
   Info: Caching catalog for cookbook.example.com
   Info: Applying configuration version '1416376937'
   Notice: We defined this from /etc/puppet/cookbook.sh
   Notice: /Stage[main]/Enc/Notify[We defined this from /etc/puppet/
   cookbook.sh]/message: defined 'message' as 'We defined this from /
   etc/puppet/cookbook.sh'
   Notice: Finished catalog run in 0.17 seconds

How it works...

When an ENC is set in `puppet.conf`, Puppet will call the specified program with the node's fqdn (technically, the certname variable) as the first command-line argument. In our example script, this argument is ignored, and it just outputs a fixed list of classes (actually, just one class).

Obviously this script is not terribly useful; a more sophisticated script might check a database to find the class list, or look up the node in a hash, or an external text file or database (often an organization's configuration management database, **CMDB**). Hopefully, this example is enough to get you started with writing your own external node classifier. Remember that you can write your script in any language you prefer.

There's more...

An ENC can supply a whole list of classes to be included in the node, in the following (YAML) format:

```
---
classes:
  CLASS1:
  CLASS2:
  CLASS3:
```

For classes that take parameters, you can use this format:

```
---
classes:
  mysql:
    package: percona-server-server-5.5
    socket:  /var/run/mysqld/mysqld.sock
    port:    3306
```

You can also produce top-scope variables using an ENC with this format:

```
---
parameters:
  message: 'Anyone home MyFly?'
```

Variables that you set in this way will be available in your manifest using the normal syntax for a top-scope variable, for example `$::message`.

See also

▶ See the puppetlabs ENC page for more information on writing and using ENCs:
  `http://docs.puppetlabs.com/guides/external_nodes.html`

Creating your own resource types

As you know, Puppet has a bunch of useful built-in resource types: packages, files, users, and so on. Usually, you can do everything you need to do by using either combinations of these built-in resources, or `define`, which you can use more or less in the same way as a resource (see *Chapter 3, Writing Better Manifests* for information on definitions).

In the early days of Puppet, creating your own resource type was more common as the list of core resources was shorter than it is today. Before you consider creating your own resource type, I suggest searching the Forge for alternative solutions. Even if you can find a project that only partially solves your problem, you will be better served by extending and helping out that project, rather than trying to create your own. However, if you need to create your own resource type, Puppet makes it quite easy. The native types are written in Ruby, and you will need a basic familiarity with Ruby in order to create your own.

Let's refresh our memory on the distinction between types and providers. A type describes a resource and the parameters it can have (for example, the `package` type). A provider tells Puppet how to implement a resource type for a particular platform or situation (for example, the `apt/dpkg` providers implement the `package` type for Debian-like systems).

A single type (`package`) can have many providers (APT, YUM, Fink, and so on). If you don't specify a provider when declaring a resource, Puppet will choose the most appropriate one given the environment.

We'll use Ruby in this section; if you are not familiar with Ruby try visiting `http://www.ruby-doc.org/docs/Tutorial/` or `http://www.codecademy.com/tracks/ruby/`.

How to do it...

In this section, we'll see how to create a custom type that we can use to manage Git repositories, and in the next section, we'll write a provider to implement this type.

Create the file `modules/cookbook/lib/puppet/type/gitrepo.rb` with the following contents:

```
Puppet::Type.newtype(:gitrepo) do
  ensurable

  newparam(:source) do
    isnamevar
  end

  newparam(:path)
end
```

How it works...

Custom types can live in any module, in a `lib/puppet/type` subdirectory and in a file named for the type (in our example, that's `modules/cookbook/lib/puppet/type/gitrepo.rb`).

The first line of `gitrepo.rb` tells Puppet to register a new type named `gitrepo`:

```
Puppet::Type.newtype(:gitrepo) do
```

The `ensurable` line automatically gives the type an `ensure` property, such as Puppet's built-in resources:

```
ensurable
```

We'll now give the type some parameters. For the moment, all we need is a `source` parameter for the Git source URL, and a `path` parameter to tell Puppet where the repo should be created in the filesystem:

```
newparam(:source) do
  isnamevar
end
```

The `isnamevar` declaration tells Puppet that the `source` parameter is the type's namevar. So when you declare an instance of this resource, whatever name you give, it will be the value of `source`, for example:

```
gitrepo { 'git://github.com/puppetlabs/puppet.git':
  path => '/home/ubuntu/dev/puppet',
}
```

Finally, we tell Puppet that the type accepts the `path` parameter:

```
newparam(:path)
```

There's more...

When deciding whether or not you should create a custom type, you should ask a few questions about the resource you are trying to describe such as:

- ▶ Is the resource enumerable? Can you easily obtain a list of all the instances of the resource on the system?

- ▶ Is the resource atomic? Can you ensure that only one copy of the resource exists on the system (this is particularly important when you want to use `ensure=>absent` on the resource)?

- ▶ Is there any other resource that describes this resource? In such a case, a defined type based on the existing resource would, in most cases, be a simpler solution.

Documentation

Our example is deliberately simple, but when you move on to developing real custom types for your production environment, you should add documentation strings to describe what the type and its parameters do, for example:

```
Puppet::Type.newtype(:gitrepo) do
  @doc = "Manages Git repos"

  ensurable

  newparam(:source) do
    desc "Git source URL for the repo"
    isnamevar
  end

  newparam(:path) do
    desc "Path where the repo should be created"
  end
end
```

Validation

You can use parameter validation to generate useful error messages when someone tries to pass bad values to the resource. For example, you could validate that the directory where the repo is to be created actually exists:

```
newparam(:path) do
  validate do |value|
    basepath = File.dirname(value)
    unless File.directory?(basepath)
      raise ArgumentError , "The path %s doesn't exist" % basepath
    end
  end
end
```

You can also specify the list of allowed values that the parameter can take:

```
newparam(:breakfast) do
  newvalues(:bacon, :eggs, :sausages)
end
```

Creating your own providers

In the previous section, we created a new custom type called `gitrepo` and told Puppet that it takes two parameters, `source` and `path`. However, so far, we haven't told Puppet how to actually check out the repo; in other words, how to create a specific instance of this type. That's where the provider comes in.

We saw that a type will often have several possible providers. In our example, there is only one sensible way to instantiate a Git repo, so we'll only supply one provider: `git`. If you were to generalize this type—to just repo, say—it's not hard to imagine creating several different providers depending on the type of repo, for example, `git`, `svn`, `cvs`, and so on.

How to do it...

We'll add the `git` provider, and create an instance of a `gitrepo` resource to check that it all works. You'll need Git installed for this to work, but if you're using the Git-based manifest management setup described in *Chapter 2, Puppet Infrastructure*, we can safely assume that Git is available.

1. Create the file `modules/cookbook/lib/puppet/provider/gitrepo/git.rb` with the following contents:

    ```ruby
    require 'fileutils'

    Puppet::Type.type(:gitrepo).provide(:git) do
      commands :git => "git"

      def create
        git "clone", resource[:source], resource[:path]
      end

      def exists?
        File.directory? resource[:path]
      end
    end
    ```

2. Modify your `site.pp` file as follows:

    ```puppet
    node 'cookbook' {
      gitrepo { 'https://github.com/puppetlabs/puppetlabs-git':
        ensure => present,
        path   => '/tmp/puppet',
      }
    }
    ```

3. Run Puppet:

```
[root@cookbook ~]# puppet agent -t
Notice: /File[/var/lib/puppet/lib/puppet/type/gitrepo.rb]/ensure:
defined content as '{md5}6471793fe2b4372d40289ad4b614fe0b'
Notice: /File[/var/lib/puppet/lib/puppet/provider/gitrepo]/ensure:
created
Notice: /File[/var/lib/puppet/lib/puppet/provider/gitrepo/git.rb]/
ensure: defined content as '{md5}f860388234d3d0bdb3b3ec98bbf5115b'
Info: Caching catalog for cookbook.example.com
Info: Applying configuration version '1416378876'
Notice: /Stage[main]/Main/Node[cookbook]/Gitrepo[https://github.
com/puppetlabs/puppetlabs-git]/ensure: created
Notice: Finished catalog run in 2.59 seconds
```

How it works...

Custom providers can live in any module, in a `lib/puppet/provider/TYPE_NAME` subdirectory in a file named after the provider. (The provider is the actual program that is run on the system; in our example, the program is Git and the provider is in `modules/cookbook/lib/puppet/provider/gitrepo/git.rb`. Note that the name of the module is irrelevant.)

After an ntitial require line in `git.rb`, we tell Puppet to register a new provider for the `gitrepo` type with the following line:

```
Puppet::Type.type(:gitrepo).provide(:git) do
```

When you declare an instance of the `gitrepo` type in your manifest, Puppet will first of all check whether the instance already exists, by calling the `exists?` method on the provider. So we need to supply this method, complete with code to check whether an instance of the `gitrepo` type already exists:

```
def exists?
  File.directory? resource[:path]
end
```

This is not the most sophisticated implementation; it simply returns `true` if a directory exists matching the `path` parameter of the instance. A better implementation of `exists?` might check, for example, whether there is a `.git` subdirectory and that it contains valid Git metadata. But this will do for now.

If `exists?` returns `true`, then Puppet will take no further action because the specified resource exists (as far as Puppet knows). If it returns `false`, Puppet assumes the resource doesn't yet exist, and will try to create it by calling the provider's `create` method.

Accordingly, we supply some code for the `create` method that calls the `git clone` command to create the repo:

```
def create
  git "clone", resource[:source], resource[:path]
end
```

The method has access to the instance's parameters, which we need to know where to check out the repo from, and which directory to create it in. We get this by looking at `resource[:source]` and `resource[:path]`.

There's more...

You can see that custom types and providers in Puppet are very powerful. In fact, they can do anything—at least, anything that Ruby can do. If you are managing some parts of your infrastructure with complicated `define` statements and `exec` resources, you may want to consider replacing these with a custom type. However, as stated previously, it's worth looking around to see if someone else has already done this before implementing your own.

Our example was very simple, and there is much more to learn about writing your own types. If you're going to distribute your code for others to use, or even if you aren't, it's a good idea to include tests with it. puppetlabs has a useful page on the interface between custom types and providers:

```
http://docs.puppetlabs.com/guides/custom_types.html
```

on implementing providers:

```
http://docs.puppetlabs.com/guides/provider_development.html
```

and a complete worked example of developing a custom type and provider, a little more advanced than that presented in this book:

```
http://docs.puppetlabs.com/guides/complete_resource_example.html
```

Creating custom functions

If you've read the recipe *Using GnuPG to encrypt secrets* in *Chapter 4, Working with Files and Packages*, then you've already seen an example of a custom function (in that example, we created a `secret` function, which shelled out to GnuPG). Let's look at `custom` functions in a little more detail now and build an example.

How to do it...

If you've read the recipe *Distributing cron jobs efficiently* in *Chapter 6, Managing Resources and Files*, you might remember that we used the `inline_template` function to set a random time for cron jobs to run, based on the hostname of the node. In this example, we'll take that idea and turn it into a custom function called `random_minute`:

1. Create the file `modules/cookbook/lib/puppet/parser/functions/random_minute.rb` with the following contents:

```
module Puppet::Parser::Functions
  newfunction(:random_minute, :type => :rvalue) do |args|
    lookupvar('hostname').sum % 60
  end
end
```

2. Modify your `site.pp` file as follows:

```
node 'cookbook' {
  cron { 'randomised cron job':
    command => '/bin/echo Hello, world >>/tmp/hello.txt',
    hour    => '*',
    minute  => random_minute(),
  }
}
```

3. Run Puppet:

```
[root@cookbook ~]# puppet agent -t
Info: Retrieving pluginfacts
Info: Retrieving plugin
Notice: /File[/var/lib/puppet/lib/puppet/parser/functions/
random_minute.rb]/ensure: defined content as '{md5}
e6ff40165e74677e5837027bb5610744'
Info: Loading facts
Info: Caching catalog for cookbook.example.com
Info: Applying configuration version '1416379652'
Notice: /Stage[main]/Main/Node[cookbook]/Cron[custom fuction
example job]/ensure: created
Notice: Finished catalog run in 0.41 seconds
```

4. Check `crontab` with the following command:

```
[root@cookbook ~]# crontab -l
# HEADER: This file was autogenerated at Wed Nov 19 01:48:11 -0500
2014 by puppet.
# HEADER: While it can still be managed manually, it is definitely
not recommended.
# HEADER: Note particularly that the comments starting with
'Puppet Name' should
# HEADER: not be deleted, as doing so could cause duplicate cron
jobs.
# Puppet Name: run-backup
0 15 * * * /usr/local/bin/backup
# Puppet Name: custom fuction example job
15 * * * * /bin/echo Hallo, welt >>/tmp/hallo.txt
```

How it works...

Custom functions can live in any module, in the `lib/puppet/parser/functions` subdirectory in a file named after the function (in our example, `random_minute.rb`).

The function code goes inside a `module ... end` block like this:

```
module Puppet::Parser::Functions
  ...
end
```

We then call `newfunction` to declare our new function, passing the name (`:random_minute`) and the type of function (`:rvalue`):

```
newfunction(:random_minute, :type => :rvalue) do |args|
```

The `:rvalue` bit simply means that this function returns a value.

Finally, the function code itself is as follows:

```
lookupvar('hostname').sum % 60
```

The `lookupvar` function lets you access facts and variables by name; in this case, `hostname` to get the name of the node we're running on. We use the Ruby `sum` method to get the numeric sum of the characters in this string, and then perform integer division modulo 60 to make sure the result is in the range `0..59`.

There's more...

You can, of course, do a lot more with custom functions. In fact, anything you can do in Ruby, you can do in a custom function. You also have access to all the facts and variables that are in scope at the point in the Puppet manifest where the function is called, by calling `lookupvar` as shown in the example. You can also work on arguments, for example, a general purpose hashing function that takes two arguments: the size of the hash table and optionally the thing to hash. Create `modules/cookbook/lib/puppet/parser/functions/hashtable.rb` with the following contents:

```
module Puppet::Parser::Functions
  newfunction(:hashtable, :type => :rvalue) do |args|
    if args.length == 2
      hashtable=lookupvar(args[1]).sum
    else
      hashtable=lookupvar('hostname').sum
    end

    if args.length > 0
      size = args[0].to_i
    else
      size = 60
    end
    unless size == 0
      hashtable % size
    else
      0
    end
  end
end
```

Now we'll create a test for our `hashtable` function and alter `site.pp` as follows:

```
node cookbook {
  $hours = hashtable(24)
  $minutes = hashtable()
  $days = hashtable(30)
  $days_fqdn = hashtable(30,'fqdn')
  $days_ipaddress = hashtable(30,'ipaddress')
  notify {"\n hours=${hours}\n minutes=${minutes}\n days=${days}\n
    days_fqdn=${days_fqdn}\n days_ipaddress=${days_ipaddress}\n":}
}
```

Now, run Puppet and observe the values that are returned:

```
Notice:   hours=15
 minutes=15
 days=15
 days_fqdn=4
 days_ipaddress=2
```

Our simple definition quickly grew when we added the ability to add arguments. As with all programming, care should be taken when working with arguments to ensure that you do not have any error conditions. In the preceding code, we specifically looked for the situation where the size variable was 0, to avoid a divide by zero error.

To find out more about what you can do with custom functions, see the puppetlabs website:

```
http://docs.puppetlabs.com/guides/custom_functions.html
```

Testing your puppet manifests with rspec-puppet

It would be great if we could verify that our Puppet manifests satisfy certain expectations without even having to run Puppet. The `rspec-puppet` tool is a nifty tool to do this. Based on RSpec, a testing framework for Ruby programs, `rspec-puppet` lets you write test cases for your Puppet manifests that are especially useful to catch regressions (bugs introduced when fixing another bug), and refactoring problems (bugs introduced when reorganizing your code).

Getting ready

Here's what you'll need to do to install `rspec-puppet`.

Run the following commands:

```
t@mylaptop~ $ sudo puppet resource package rspec-puppet ensure=installed
provider=gem
Notice: /Package[rspec-puppet]/ensure: created
package { 'rspec-puppet':
  ensure => ['1.0.1'],
}
t@mylaptop ~ $ sudo puppet resource package puppetlabs_spec_helper
ensure=installed provider=gem
Notice: /Package[puppetlabs_spec_helper]/ensure: created
package { 'puppetlabs_spec_helper':
  ensure => ['0.8.2'],
}
```

How to do it...

Let's create an example class, `thing`, and write some tests for it.

1. Define the `thing` class:

```
class thing {
  service {'thing':
    ensure  => 'running',
    enable  => true,
    require => Package['thing'],
  }
  package {'thing':
    ensure => 'installed'
  }
  file {'/etc/thing.conf':
    content => 'fubar\n',
    mode    => 0644,
    require => Package['thing'],
    notify  => Service['thing'],
  }
}
```

2. Run the following commands:

```
t@mylaptop ~/puppet]$cd modules/thing

t@mylaptop~/puppet/modules/thing $ rspec-puppet-init
  + spec/
  + spec/classes/
  + spec/defines/
  + spec/functions/
  + spec/hosts/
  + spec/fixtures/
  + spec/fixtures/manifests/
  + spec/fixtures/modules/
  + spec/fixtures/modules/heartbeat/
  + spec/fixtures/manifests/site.pp
  + spec/fixtures/modules/heartbeat/manifests
  + spec/fixtures/modules/heartbeat/templates
  + spec/spec_helper.rb
  + Rakefile
```

3. Create the file `spec/classes/thing_spec.rb` with the following contents:

```
require 'spec_helper'

describe 'thing' do
  it { should create_class('thing') }
  it { should contain_package('thing') }
  it { should contain_service('thing').with(
    'ensure' => 'running'
  ) }
  it { should contain_file('/etc/things.conf') }
end
```

4. Run the following commands:

```
t@mylaptop ~/.puppet/modules/thing $ rspec
...F

Failures:

  1) thing should contain File[/etc/things.conf]
     Failure/Error: it { should contain_file('/etc/things.conf') }
       expected that the catalogue would contain File[/etc/things.
conf]
       # ./spec/classes/thing_spec.rb:9:in `block (2 levels) in <top
(required)>'

Finished in 1.66 seconds
4 examples, 1 failure

Failed examples:

rspec ./spec/classes/thing_spec.rb:9 # thing should contain File[/
etc/things.conf]
```

How it works...

The `rspec-puppet-init` command creates a framework of directories for you to put your specs (test programs) in. At the moment, we're just interested in the `spec/classes` directory. This is where you'll put your class specs, one per class, named after the class it tests, for example, `thing_spec.rb`.

The `spec` code itself begins with the following statement, which sets up the RSpec environment to run the specs:

```
require 'spec_helper'
```

Then, a `describe` block follows:

```
describe 'thing' do
  ..
end
```

The `describe` identifies the class we're going to test (`thing`) and wraps the list of assertions about the class inside a `do .. end` block.

Assertions are our stated expectations of the `thing` class. For example, the first assertion is the following:

```
it { should create_class('thing') }
```

The `create_class` assertion is used to ensure that the named class is actually created. The next line:

```
it { should contain_package('thing') }
```

The `contain_package` assertion means what it says: the class should contain a package resource named `thing`.

Next, we test for the existence of the `thing` service:

```
it { should contain_service('thing').with(
  'ensure' => 'running'
) }
```

The preceding code actually contains two assertions. First, that the class contains a `thing` service:

```
contain_service('thing')
```

Second, that the service has an `ensure` attribute with the value `running`:

```
with(
  'ensure' => 'running'
)
```

You can specify any attributes and values you want using the `with` method, as a comma-separated list. For example, the following code asserts several attributes of a `file` resource:

```
it { should contain_file('/tmp/hello.txt').with(
  'content' => "Hello, world\n",
  'owner'   => 'ubuntu',
  'group'   => 'ubuntu',
  'mode'    => '0644'
) }
```

In our `thing` example, we need to only test that the file `thing.conf` is present, using the following code:

```
it { should contain_file('/etc/thing.conf') }
```

When you run the `rake spec` command, `rspec-puppet` will compile the relevant Puppet classes, run all the specs it finds, and display the results:

```
...F
Failures:
  1) thing should contain File[/etc/things.conf]
     Failure/Error: it { should contain_file('/etc/things.conf') }
        expected that the catalogue would contain File[/etc/things.conf]
     # ./spec/classes/thing_spec.rb:9:in `block (2 levels) in <top
(required)>'
Finished in 1.66 seconds
4 examples, 1 failure
```

As you can see, we defined the file in our test as `/etc/things.conf` but the file in the manifests is `/etc/thing.conf`, so the test fails. Edit `thing_spec.rb` and change `/etc/things.conf` to `/etc/thing.conf`:

```
it { should contain_file('/etc/thing.conf') }
```

Now run rspec again:

```
t@mylaptop ~/.puppet/modules/thing $ rspec
....
Finished in 1.6 seconds
4 examples, 0 failures
```

There's more...

There are many conditions you can verify with rspec. Any resource type can be verified with `contain_<resource type>`(title). In addition to verifying your classes will apply correctly, you can also test functions and definitions by using the appropriate subdirectories within the spec directory (classes, defines, or functions).

You can find more information about `rspec-puppet`, including complete documentation for the assertions available and a tutorial, at `http://rspec-puppet.com/`.

When you want to start testing how your code applies to nodes, you'll need to look at another tool, beaker. Beaker works with various virtualization platforms to create temporary virtual machines to which Puppet code is applied. The results are then used for acceptance testing of the Puppet code. This method of testing and developing at the same time is known as **Test-driven development** (**TDD**). More information about beaker is available on the GitHub site at `https://github.com/puppetlabs/beaker`.

See also

> ▶ The *Checking your manifests with puppet-lint* recipe in *Chapter 1, Puppet Language and Style*

Using librarian-puppet

When you begin to include modules from the forge in your Puppet infrastructure, keeping track of which versions you installed and ensuring consistency between all your testing areas can become a bit of a problem. Luckily, the tools we will discuss in the next two sections can bring order to your system. We will first begin with librarian-puppet, which uses a special configuration file named Puppetfile to specify the source location of your various modules.

Getting ready

We'll install librarian-puppet to work through the example.

Install `librarian-puppet` on your Puppet master, using Puppet of course:

```
root@puppet:~# puppet resource package librarian-puppet ensure=installed
provider=gem
Notice: /Package[librarian-puppet]/ensure: created
package { 'librarian-puppet':
  ensure => ['2.0.0'],
}
```

 If you are working in a masterless environment, install `librarian-puppet` on the machine from which you will be managing your code. Your gem install may fail if the Ruby development packages are not available on your master; install the `ruby-dev` package to fix this issue (use Puppet to do it).

How to do it...

We'll use librarian-puppet to download and install a module in this example:

1. Create a working directory for yourself; librarian-puppet will overwrite your modules directory by default, so we'll work in a temporary location for now:

   ```
   root@puppet:~# mkdir librarian
   root@puppet:~# cd librarian
   ```

2. Create a new Puppetfile with the following contents:

```
#!/usr/bin/env ruby
#^syntax detection

forge "https://forgeapi.puppetlabs.com"

# A module from the Puppet Forge
mod 'puppetlabs-stdlib'
```

 Alternatively, you can use `librarian-puppet init` to create an example Puppetfile and edit it to match our example:

root@puppet:~/librarian# librarian-puppet init
create   Puppetfile

3. Now, run librarian-puppet to download and install the `puppetlabs-stdlib` module in the `modules` directory:

```
root@puppet:~/librarian# librarian-puppet install

root@puppet:~/librarian # ls

modules  Puppetfile  Puppetfile.lock

root@puppet:~/librarian # ls modules

stdlib
```

How it works...

The first line of the `Puppetfile` makes the `Puppetfile` appear to be a Ruby source file. These are completely optional but coerces editors into treating the file as though it was written in Ruby (which it is):

```
#!/usr/bin/env ruby
```

We next define where the Puppet Forge is located; you may specify an internal Forge here if you have a local mirror:

```
forge "https://forgeapi.puppetlabs.com"
```

Now, we added a line to include the `puppetlabs-stdlib` module:

```
mod 'puppetlabs-stdlib'
```

With the `Puppetfile` in place, we ran `librarian-puppet` and it downloaded the module from the URL given in the Forge line. As the module was downloaded, `librarian-puppet` created a `Puppetfile.lock` file, which includes the location used as source and the version number for the downloaded module:

```
FORGE
  remote: https://forgeapi.puppetlabs.com
  specs:
    puppetlabs-stdlib (4.4.0)

DEPENDENCIES
  puppetlabs-stdlib (>= 0)
```

There's more...

The `Puppetfile` allows you to pull in modules from sources other than the forge. You may use a local Git url or even a GitHub url to download modules that are not on the Forge. More information on librarian-puppet can be found on the GitHub website at `https://github.com/rodjek/librarian-puppet`.

Note that librarian-puppet will create the modules directory and remove any modules you placed in there by default. Most installations using librarian-puppet opt to place their local modules in a `/local` subdirectory (`/dist` or `/companyname` are also used).

In the next section, we'll talk about r10k, which goes one step further than librarian and manages your entire environment directory.

Using r10k

The `Puppetfile` is a very good format to describe which modules you wish to include in your environment. Building upon the `Puppetfile` is another tool, **r10k**. r10k is a total environment management tool. You can use r10k to clone a local Git repository into your `environmentpath` and then place the modules specified in your `Puppetfile` into that directory. The local Git repository is known as the master repository; it is where r10k expects to find your `Puppetfile`. r10k also understands Puppet environments and will clone Git branches into subdirectories of your `environmentpath`, simplifying the deployment of multiple environments. What makes r10k particularly useful is its use of a local cache directory to speed up deployments. Using a configuration file, `r10k.yaml`, you can specify where to store this cache and also where your master repository is held.

Getting ready

We'll install r10k on our controlling machine (usually the master). This is where we will control all the modules downloaded and installed.

1. Install r10k on your puppet master, or on whichever machine you wish to manage your `environmentpath` directory:

```
root@puppet:~# puppet resource package r10k ensure=installed
provider=gem
Notice: /Package[r10k]/ensure: created
package { 'r10k':
  ensure => ['1.3.5'],
}
```

2. Make a new copy of your Git repository (optional, do this on your Git server):

```
[git@git repos]$ git clone --bare puppet.git puppet-r10k.git
Initialized empty Git repository in /home/git/repos/puppet-r10k.
git/
```

3. Check out the new Git repository (on your local machine) and move the existing modules directory to a new location. We'll use `/local` in this example:

```
t@mylaptop ~ $ git clone git@git.example.com:repos/puppet-r10k.git
Cloning into 'puppet-r10k'...
remote: Counting objects: 2660, done.
remote: Compressing objects: 100% (2136/2136), done.
remote: Total 2660 (delta 913), reused 1049 (delta 238)
Receiving objects: 100% (2660/2660), 738.20 KiB | 0 bytes/s, done.
Resolving deltas: 100% (913/913), done.
Checking connectivity... done.
t@mylaptop ~ $ cd puppet-r10k/
t@mylaptop ~/puppet-r10k $ git checkout production
Branch production set up to track remote branch production from
origin.
Switched to a new branch 'production'
t@mylaptop ~/puppet-r10k $ git mv modules local
t@mylaptop ~/puppet-r10k $ git commit -m "moving modules in
preparation for r10k"
[master c96d0dc] moving modules in preparation for r10k
 9 files changed, 0 insertions(+), 0 deletions(-)
 rename {modules => local}/base (100%)
 rename {modules => local}/puppet/files/papply.sh (100%)
 rename {modules => local}/puppet/files/pull-updates.sh (100%)
 rename {modules => local}/puppet/manifests/init.pp (100%)
```

How to do it...

We'll create a Puppetfile to control r10k and install modules on our master.

1. Create a `Puppetfile` into the new Git repository with the following contents:

```
forge "http://forge.puppetlabs.com"
mod 'puppetlabs/puppetdb', '3.0.0'
mod 'puppetlabs/stdlib', '3.2.0'
mod 'puppetlabs/concat'
mod 'puppetlabs/firewall'
```

2. Add the `Puppetfile` to your new repository:

```
t@mylaptop ~/puppet-r10k $ git add Puppetfile
t@mylaptop ~/puppet-r10k $ git commit -m "adding Puppetfile"
[production d42481f] adding Puppetfile
 1 file changed, 7 insertions(+)
 create mode 100644 Puppetfile
t@mylaptop ~/puppet-r10k $ git push
Counting objects: 7, done.
Delta compression using up to 4 threads.
Compressing objects: 100% (5/5), done.
Writing objects: 100% (5/5), 589 bytes | 0 bytes/s, done.
Total 5 (delta 2), reused 0 (delta 0)
To git@git.example.com:repos/puppet-r10k.git
   cf8dfb9..d42481f  production -> production
```

3. Back to your master, create `/etc/r10k.yaml` with the following contents:

```
---
:cachedir: '/var/cache/r10k'
:sources:
 :plops:
   remote: 'git@git.example.com:repos/puppet-r10k.git'
   basedir: '/etc/puppet/environments'
```

4. Run r10k to have the `/etc/puppet/environments` directory populated (hint: create a backup of your `/etc/puppet/environments` directory first):

```
root@puppet:~# r10k deploy environment -p
```

5. Verify that your `/etc/puppet/environments` directory has a production subdirectory. Within that directory, the `/local` directory will exist and the modules directory will have all the modules listed in the `Puppetfile`:

```
root@puppet:/etc/puppet/environments# tree -L 2
.
├── master
│   ├── manifests
│   ├── modules
│   └── README
└── production
    ├── environment.conf
    ├── local
    ├── manifests
    ├── modules
    ├── Puppetfile
    └── README
```

How it works...

We started by creating a copy of our Git repository; this was only done to preserve the earlier work and is not required. The important thing to remember with r10k and librarian-puppet is that they both assume they are in control of the `/modules` subdirectory. We need to move our modules out of the way and create a new location for the modules.

In the `r10k.yaml` file, we specified the location of our new repository. When we ran r10k, it first downloaded this repository into its local cache. Once the Git repository is downloaded locally, r10k will go through each branch and look for a `Puppetfile` within the branch. For each `branch/Puppetfile` combination, the modules specified within are downloaded first to the local cache directory (`cachedir`) and then into the `basedir`, which was given in `r10k.yaml`.

There's more...

You can automate the deployment of your environments using `r10k`. The command we used to run `r10k` and populate our environments directory can be easily placed inside a Git hook to automatically update your environment. There is also a **marionette collective** (**mcollective**) plugin (`https://github.com/acidprime/r10k`), which can be used to have `r10k` run on an arbitrary set of servers.

Using either of these tools will help keep your site consistent, even if you are not taking advantage of the various modules available on the Forge.

10
Monitoring, Reporting, and Troubleshooting

"Show me a completely smooth operation and I'll show you someone who's covering mistakes. Real boats rock."

—*Frank Herbert, Chapterhouse: Dune*

In this chapter, we will cover the following recipes:

- ▶ Noop: the don't change anything option
- ▶ Logging command output
- ▶ Logging debug messages
- ▶ Generating reports
- ▶ Producing automatic HTML documentation
- ▶ Drawing dependency graphs
- ▶ Understanding Puppet errors
- ▶ Inspecting configuration settings

Introduction

We've all had the experience of sitting in an exciting presentation about some new technology and rushing home to play with it. Of course, once you start experimenting with it, you immediately run into problems. What's going wrong? Why doesn't it work? How can I see what's happening under the hood? This chapter will help you answer some of these questions, and give you the tools to solve common Puppet problems.

We'll also see how to generate useful reports on your Puppet infrastructure and how Puppet can help you monitor and troubleshoot your network as a whole.

Noop – the don't change anything option

Sometimes your Puppet manifest doesn't do exactly what you expected, or perhaps someone else has checked in changes you didn't know about. Either way, it's good to know exactly what Puppet is going to do before it does it.

When you are retrofitting Puppet into an existing infrastructure you might not know whether Puppet is going to update a `config` file or restart a production service. Any such change could result in unplanned downtime. Also, sometimes manual configuration changes are made on a server that Puppet would overwrite.

To avoid these problems, you can use Puppet's noop mode, which means no operation or do nothing. When run with the noop option, Puppet only reports what it would do but doesn't actually do anything. One caveat here is that even during a noop run, pluginsync still runs and any `lib` directories in modules will be synced to nodes. This will update external fact definitions and possibly Puppet's types and providers.

How to do it...

You may run noop mode when running `puppet agent` or `puppet apply` by appending the `--noop` switch to the command. You may also create a `noop=true` line in your `puppet.conf` file within the `[agent]` or `[main]` sections.

1. Create a `noop.pp` manifest that creates a file as follows:

    ```
    file {'/tmp/noop':
      content => 'nothing',
      mode    => 0644,
    }
    ```

2. Now run puppet agent with the `noop` switch:

    ```
    t@mylaptop ~/puppet/manifests $ puppet apply noop.pp --noop
    Notice: Compiled catalog for mylaptop in environment production in
    0.41 seconds
    Notice: /Stage[main]/Main/File[/tmp/noop]/ensure: current_value
    absent, should be file (noop)
    Notice: Class[Main]: Would have triggered 'refresh' from 1 events
    Notice: Stage[main]: Would have triggered 'refresh' from 1 events
    Notice: Finished catalog run in 0.02 seconds
    ```

3. Now run without the `noop` option to see that the file is created:

   ```
   t@mylaptop ~/puppet/manifests $ puppet apply noop.pp
   Notice: Compiled catalog for mylaptop in environment production in
   0.37 seconds
   Notice: /Stage[main]/Main/File[/tmp/noop]/ensure: defined content
   as '{md5}3e47b75000b0924b6c9ba5759a7cf15d'
   ```

How it works...

In the `noop` mode, Puppet does everything it would normally, with the exception of actually making any changes to the machine (the `exec` resources, for example, won't run). It tells you what it would have done, and you can compare this with what you expected to happen. If there are any differences, double-check the manifest or the current state of the machine.

 Note that when we ran with `--noop`, Puppet warned us that it would have created the `/tmp/noop` file. This may or may not be what we want, but it's useful to know in advance. If you are making changes to the code applied to your production servers, it's useful to run puppet agent with the `--noop` option to ensure that your changes will not affect the production services.

There's more...

You can also use noop mode as a simple auditing tool. It will tell you whether any changes have been made to the machine since Puppet last applied its manifest. Some organizations require all config changes to be made with Puppet, which is one way of implementing a change control process. Unauthorized changes to the resources managed by Puppet can be detected using Puppet in noop mode and you can then decide whether to merge the changes back into the Puppet manifest or undo them.

You can also use the `--debug` switch when running puppet agent to see the details of every change Puppet makes during an agent run. This can be helpful when trying to figure out how Puppet is applying certain exec resources or to see in what order things are happening.

If you are running a master, you can compile the catalog for a node on the master with the `--trace` option in addition to `--debug`. If the catalog is failing to compile, this method will also fail to compile the catalog (if you have an old definition for the cookbook node that is failing, try commenting it out before running this test). This produces a lot of debugging output. For example, to compile the catalog for our cookbook host on our master and place the results into `/tmp/cookbook.log`:

```
root@puppet: ~#puppet master --compile cookbook.example.com --debug
--trace --logdest /tmp/cookbook.log
Debug: Executing '/etc/puppet/cookbook.sh cookbook.example.com'
Debug: Using cached facts for cookbook.example.com
Info: Caching node for cookbook.example.com
Debug: importing '/etc/puppet/environments/production/modules/enc/
manifests/init.pp' in environment production
Debug: Automatically imported enc from enc into production
Notice: Compiled catalog for cookbook.example.com in environment
production in 0.09 seconds
Info: Caching catalog for cookbook.example.com
Debug: Configuring PuppetDB terminuses with config file /etc/puppet/
puppetdb.conf
Debug: Using cached certificate for ca
Debug: Using cached certificate for puppet
Debug: Using cached certificate_revocation_list for ca
Info: 'replace catalog' command for cookbook.example.com submitted to
PuppetDB with UUIDe2a655ca-bd81-4428-b70a-a3a76c5f15d1
{
  "metadata": {
    "api_version": 1
  },
  "data": {
    "edges": [
      {
        "target": "Class[main]",
        "source": "Stage[main]"

  ...
```

 After compiling the catalog, Puppet will print out the catalog to the command line. The log file (`/tmp/cookbook.log`) will have a lot of information on how the catalog was compiled.

- ▸ The *Auditing resources* recipe in *Chapter 6, Managing Resources and Files*
- ▸ The *Automatic syntax checking with Git hooks* recipe in *Chapter 2, Puppet Infrastructure*
- ▸ The *Generating reports* recipe in this chapter
- ▸ The *Testing your Puppet manifests with rspec-puppet* recipe in *Chapter 9, External Tools and the Puppet Ecosystem*

Logging command output

When you use the `exec` resources to run commands on the node, Puppet will give you an error message such as the following if a command returns a non-zero exit status:

```
Notice: /Stage[main]/Main/Exec[/bin/cat /tmp/missing]/returns: /bin/cat:
/tmp/missing: No such file or directory

Error: /bin/cat /tmp/missing returned 1 instead of one of [0]

Error: /Stage[main]/Main/Exec[/bin/cat /tmp/missing]/returns: change from
notrun to 0 failed: /bin/cat /tmp/missing returned 1 instead of one of
[0]
```

As you can see, Puppet not only reports that the command failed, but shows its output:

```
/bin/cat: /tmp/missing: No such file or directory
```

This is useful to figure out why the command didn't work, but sometimes the command actually succeeds (in that it returns a zero exit status) but still doesn't do what we wanted. In that case, how can you see the command output? You can use the `logoutput` attribute.

How to do it...

Follow these steps in order to log command output:

1. Define an `exec` resource with the `logoutput` parameter as shown in the following code snippet:

```
exec { 'exec with output':
  command   => '/bin/cat /etc/hostname',
logoutput => true,
}
```

2. Run Puppet:

```
t@mylaptop ~/puppet/manifests $ puppet apply exec.pp
Notice: Compiled catalog for mylaptop in environment production in
0.46 seconds
Notice: /Stage[main]/Main/Exec[exec with outout]/returns: mylaptop
Notice: /Stage[main]/Main/Exec[exec with outout]/returns: executed
successfully
Notice: Finished catalog run in 0.06 seconds
```

3. As you can see, even though the command succeeds, Puppet prints the output:

```
mylaptop
```

How it works...

The `logoutput` attribute has three possible settings:

▶ `false`: This never prints the command output

▶ `on_failure`: This only prints the output if the command fails (the default setting)

▶ `true`: This always prints the output, whether the command succeeds or fails

There's more...

You can set the default value of `logoutput` to always display command output for all `exec` resources by defining the following in your `site.pp` file:

```
Exec {
logoutput => true,
```

 Resource defaults: What's this Exec syntax? It looks like an `exec` resource, but it's not. When you use `Exec` with a capital E, you're setting the resource default for exec. You may set the resource default for any resource by capitalizing the first letter of the resource type. Anywhere that Puppet see's that resource within the current scope or a nested subscope, it will apply the defaults you define.

If you never want to see the command output, whether it succeeds or fails, use:

```
logoutput => false,
```

More information is available at `https://docs.puppetlabs.com/references/latest/type.html#exec`.

Logging debug messages

It can be very helpful when debugging problems if you can print out information at a certain point in the manifest. This is a good way to tell, for example, if a variable isn't defined or has an unexpected value. Sometimes it's useful just to know that a particular piece of code has been run. Puppet's `notify` resource lets you print out such messages.

How to do it...

Define a `notify` resource in your manifest at the point you want to investigate:

```
notify { 'Got this far!': }
```

How it works...

When this resource is applied, Puppet will print out the message:

```
notice: Got this far!
```

There's more...

In addition to simple messages, we can output variables within our `notify` statements. Additionally, we can treat the `notify` calls the same as other resources, having them require or be required by other resources.

Printing out variable values

You can refer to variables in the message:

```
notify { "operatingsystem is ${::operatingsystem}": }
```

Puppet will interpolate the values in the printout:

```
Notice: operatingsystem is Fedora
```

The double colon (`::`) before the fact name tells Puppet that this is a variable in top scope (accessible to all classes) and not local to the class. For more about how Puppet handles variable scope, see the Puppet Labs article:

```
http://docs.puppetlabs.com/guides/scope_and_puppet.html
```

Resource ordering

Puppet compiles your manifests into a catalog; the order in which resources are executed on the client (node) may not be the same as the order of the resources within your source files. When you are using a `notify` resource for debugging, you should use resource chaining to ensure that the `notify resource` is executed before or after your failing resource.

For example, if the exec `failing exec` is failing, you can chain a `notify resource` to run directly before the failed exec resource as shown here:

```
notify{"failed exec on ${hostname}": }->
exec {'failing exec':
  command  => "/bin/grep ${hostname} /etc/hosts",
logoutput => true,
  }
```

If you don't chain the resource or use a metaparameter such as `before` or `require`, there is no guarantee your `notify` statement will be executed near the other resources you are interested in debugging. More information on resource ordering can be found at `https://docs.puppetlabs.com/puppet/latest/reference/lang_relationships.html`.

For example, to have your `notify resource` run after `'failing exec'` in the preceding code snippet, use:

```
notify { 'Resource X has been applied':
  require => Exec['failing exec'],
  }
```

Note, however, that in this case the `notify resource` will fail to execute since the exec failed. When a resource fails, all the resources that depended on that resource are skipped:

```
notify {'failed exec failed':
  require => Exec['failing exec']
  }
```

When we run Puppet, we see that the `notify resource` is skipped:

t@mylaptop ~/puppet/manifests $ puppet apply fail.pp

...

Error: /bin/grepmylaptop /etc/hosts returned 1 instead of one of [0]

Error: /Stage[main]/Main/Exec[failing exec]/returns: change from notrun to 0 failed: /bin/grepmylaptop /etc/hosts returned 1 instead of one of [0]

Notice: /Stage[main]/Main/Notify[failed exec failed]: Dependency Exec[failing exec] has failures: true

Warning: /Stage[main]/Main/Notify[failed exec failed]: Skipping because of failed dependencies

Notice: Finished catalog run in 0.06 seconds

Generating reports

If you're managing a lot of machines, Puppet's reporting facility can give you some valuable information on what's actually happening out there.

How to do it...

To enable reports, just add this to a client's `puppet.conf:` within the `[main]` or `[agent]` sections:

```
report = true
```

 In recent versions (greater than 3.0) of Puppet, `report = true` is the default setting.

How it works...

With reporting enabled, Puppet will generate a report file, containing data such as:

- ▸ Date and time of the run
- ▸ Total time for the run
- ▸ Log messages output during the run
- ▸ List of all the resources in the client's manifest
- ▸ Whether Puppet changed any resources, and how many
- ▸ Whether the run succeeded or failed

By default, these reports are stored on the node at `/var/lib/puppet/reports` in a directory named after the hostname, but you can specify a different destination using the `reportdir` option. You can create your own scripts to process these reports (which are in the standard YAML format). When we run puppet agent on `cookbook.example.com`, the following file is created on the master:

```
/var/lib/puppet/reports/cookbook.example.com/201411230717.yaml
```

There's more...

If you have more than one master server, you can have all your reports sent to the same server by specifying `report_server` in the `[agent]` section of `puppet.conf`.

If you just want one report, or you don't want to enable reporting all the time, you can add the `--report` switch to the command line when you run Puppet agent manually:

```
[root@cookbook ~]# puppet agent -t --report
Notice: Finished catalog run in 0.34 seconds
```

You won't see any additional output, but a report file will be generated in the `report` directory.

You can also see some overall statistics about a Puppet run by supplying the `--summarize` switch:

```
[root@cookbook ~]# puppet agent -t --report --summarize
Notice: Finished catalog run in 0.35 seconds
Changes:
            Total: 2
Events:
            Total: 2
          Success: 2
Resources:
            Total: 10
          Changed: 2
      Out of sync: 2
Time:
Filebucket: 0.00
         Schedule: 0.00
           Notify: 0.00
Config retrieval: 0.94
            Total: 0.95
         Last run: 1416727357
Version:
Config: 1416727291
           Puppet: 3.7.3
```

Other report types

Puppet can generate different types of reports with the reports option in the `[main]` or `[master]` section of `puppet.conf` on your Puppet master servers. There are several built-in report types listed at `https://docs.puppetlabs.com/references/latest/report.html`. In addition to the built-in report types, there are some community developed reports that are quite useful. The Foreman (`http://theforeman.org`), for example, provides a Foreman report type that you can enable to forward your node reports to the Foreman.

See also

▶ The *Auditing resources* recipe in *Chapter 6, Managing Resources and Files*

Producing automatic HTML documentation

As your manifests get bigger and more complex, it can be helpful to create HTML documentation for your nodes and classes using Puppet's automatic documentation tool, `puppet doc`.

How to do it...

Follow these steps to generate HTML documentation for your manifest:

1. Run the following command:

   ```
   t@mylaptop ~/puppet $ puppet doc --all --outputdir=/tmp/puppet
   --mode rdoc --modulepath=modules/
   ```

2. This will generate a set of HTML files at `/tmp/puppet`. Open the top-level `index.html` file with your web browser (`file:///tmp/puppet/index.html`), and you'll see something like the following screenshot:

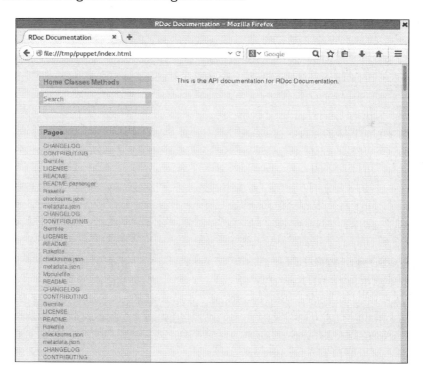

3. Click the classes link on the left and select the Apache module, something similar to the following will be displayed:

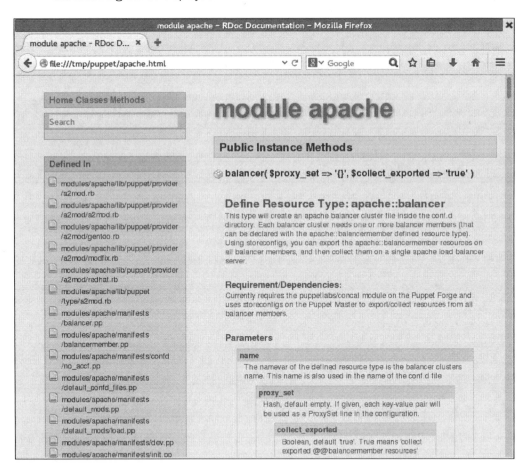

How it works...

The `puppet doc` command creates a structured HTML documentation tree similar to that produced by **RDoc**, the popular Ruby documentation generator. This makes it easier to understand how different parts of the manifest relate to one another.

There's more...

The `puppet doc` command will generate basic documentation of your manifests as they stand, but you can include more useful information by adding comments to your manifest files, using the standard RDoc syntax. When we created our base class using puppet module generate, these comments were created for us:

```
# == Class: base
#
# Full description of class base here.
#
# === Parameters
#
# Document parameters here.
#
# [*sample_parameter*]
#   Explanation of what this parameter affects and what it defaults to.
#   e.g. "Specify one or more upstream ntp servers as an array."
#
# === Variables
#
# Here you should define a list of variables that this module
would require.
#
# [*sample_variable*]
#   Explanation of how this variable affects the funtion of this class
and if
#   it has a default. e.g. "The parameter enc_ntp_servers must be set
by the
#   External Node Classifier as a comma separated list of hostnames."
(Note,
#   global variables should be avoided in favor of class parameters as
#   of Puppet 2.6.)
#
# === Examples
#
#  class { base:
#    servers => [ 'pool.ntp.org', 'ntp.local.company.com' ],
#  }
#
# === Authors
#
# Author Name <author@domain.com>
#
# === Copyright
#
# Copyright 2014 Your name here, unless otherwise noted.
#
class base {
```

After generating the HTML documentation, we can see the result for the base module as shown in the following screenshot:

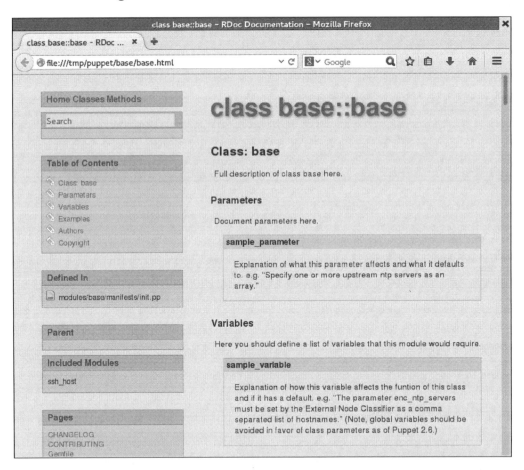

Drawing dependency graphs

Dependencies can get complicated quickly, and it's easy to end up with a circular dependency (where A depends on B, which depends on A) that will cause Puppet to complain and stop working. Fortunately, Puppet's --graph option makes it easy to generate a diagram of your resources and the dependencies between them, which can be a big help in fixing such problems.

Getting ready

Install the `graphviz` package to view the diagram files:

```
t@mylaptop ~ $ sudo puppet resource package graphviz ensure=installed
Notice: /Package[graphviz]/ensure: created
package { 'graphviz':
  ensure => '2.34.0-9.fc20',
}
```

How to do it...

Follow these steps to generate a dependency graph for your manifest:

1. Create the directories for a new `trifecta` module:

   ```
   ubuntu@cookbook:~/puppet$ mkdir modules/trifecta
   ubuntu@cookbook:~/puppet$ mkdir modules/trifecta/manifests
   ubuntu@cookbook:~/puppet$ mkdir modules/trifecta/files
   ```

2. Create the file `modules/trifecta/manifests/init.pp` with the following code containing a deliberate circular dependency (can you spot it?):

   ```
   class trifecta {
     package { 'ntp':
       ensure  => installed,
       require => File['/etc/ntp.conf'],
     }

     service { 'ntp':
       ensure  => running,
       require => Package['ntp'],
     }

     file { '/etc/ntp.conf':
       source  => 'puppet:///modules/trifecta/ntp.conf',
       notify  => Service['ntp'],
       require => Package['ntp'],
     }
   }
   ```

3. Create a simple `ntp.conf` file:

    `t@mylaptop~/puppet $ cd modules/trifecta/files`

    `t@mylaptop~/puppet/modules/trifecta/files $ echo "server 127.0.0.1" >ntp.conf`

4. Since we'll be working locally on this problem, create a `trifecta.pp` manifest that includes the broken trifecta class:

    ```
    include trifecta
    ```

5. Run Puppet:

    `t@mylaptop ~/puppet/manifests $ puppet apply trifecta.pp`

    `Notice: Compiled catalog for mylaptop in environment production in 1.32 seconds`

    `Error: Could not apply complete catalog: Found 1 dependency cycle:`

    `(File[/etc/ntp.conf] => Package[ntp] => File[/etc/ntp.conf])`

    `Try the '--graph' option and opening the resulting '.dot' file in OmniGraffle or GraphViz`

6. Run Puppet with the `--graph` option as suggested:

    `t@mylaptop ~/puppet/manifests $ puppet apply trifecta.pp --graph`

    `Notice: Compiled catalog for mylaptop in environment production in 1.26 seconds`

    `Error: Could not apply complete catalog: Found 1 dependency cycle:`

    `(File[/etc/ntp.conf] => Package[ntp] => File[/etc/ntp.conf])`

    `Cycle graph written to /home/tuphill/.puppet/var/state/graphs/cycles.dot.`

    `Notice: Finished catalog run in 0.03 seconds`

7. Check whether the graph files have been created:

    `t@mylaptop ~/puppet/manifests $ cd ~/.puppet/var/state/graphs`

    `t@mylaptop ~/.puppet/var/state/graphs $ ls -1`

    `total 16`

    `-rw-rw-r--. 1 thomasthomas  121 Nov 23 23:11 cycles.dot`

    `-rw-rw-r--. 1 thomasthomas 2885 Nov 23 23:11 expanded_relationships.dot`

    `-rw-rw-r--. 1 thomasthomas 1557 Nov 23 23:11 relationships.dot`

    `-rw-rw-r--. 1 thomasthomas 1680 Nov 23 23:11 resources.dot`

8. Create a graphic using the `dot` command as follows:

   ```
   ubuntu@cookbook:~/puppet$ dot -Tpng -o relationships.png /var/lib/
   puppet/state/graphs/relationships.dot
   ```

9. The graphic will look something like the this:

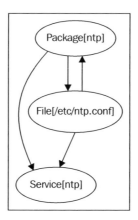

When you run `puppet agent --graph` (or enable the `graph` option in `puppet.conf`), Puppet will generate three graphs in the DOT format (a graphics language):

  ▸ `resources.dot`: This shows the hierarchical structure of your classes and resources, but without dependencies

  ▸ `relationships.dot`: This shows the dependencies between resources as arrows, as shown in the preceding image

  ▸ `expanded_relationships.dot`: This is a more detailed version of the relationships graph

The `dot` tool (part of the `graphviz` package) will convert these to an image format such as PNG for viewing.

In the relationships graph, each resource in your manifest is shown as a balloon (known as a vertex), with arrowed lines connecting them to indicate the dependencies. You can see that in our example, the dependencies between `File['/etc/ntp.conf']` and `Package['ntp']` are bidirectional. When Puppet tries to decide where to begin applying these resources, it can start at `File['/etc/ntp.conf']` and look for what depends on `File['/etc/ntp.conf']` and end up at `Package['ntp']`. When Puppet looks for the dependencies of `Package['ntp']`, it will end up back at `File['/etc/ntp.conf']`, forming a circular path. This type of problem is known as a circular dependency problem; Puppet can't decide where to start because the two resources depend on each other.

To fix the circular dependency problem, all you need to do is remove one of the dependency lines and break the circle. The following code fixes the problem:

```
class trifecta {
  package { 'ntp':
    ensure  => installed,
  }

  service { 'ntp':
    ensure  => running,
    require => Package['ntp'],
  }

  file { '/etc/ntp.conf':
    source  => 'puppet:///modules/trifecta/ntp.conf',
    notify  => Service['ntp'],
    require => Package['ntp'],
  }
}
```

Now when we run `puppet apply` or `agent` with the `--graph` option, the resulting graph does not have any circular paths (cycles):

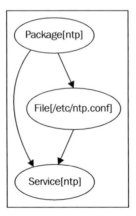

In this graph it is easy to see that **Package[ntp]** is the first resource to be applied, then **File[/etc/ntp.conf]**, and finally **Service[ntp]**.

A graph such as that shown previously is known as a Directed Acyclic Graph (DAG). Reducing the resources to a DAG ensures that Puppet can calculate the shortest path of all the vertices (resources) in linear time. For more information on DAGs, look at `http://en.wikipedia.org/wiki/Directed_acyclic_graph`.

There's more...

Resource and relationship graphs can be useful even when you don't have a bug to find. If you have a very complex network of classes and resources, for example, studying the resources graph can help you see where to simplify things. Similarly, when dependencies become too complicated to understand from reading the manifest, the graphs can be a useful form of documentation. For instance, a graph will make it readily apparent which resources have the most dependencies and which resources are required by the most other resources. Resources that are required by a large number of other resources will have numerous arrows pointing at them.

See also

▶   The *Using run stages* recipe in *Chapter 3, Writing Better Manifests*

Understanding Puppet errors

Puppet's error messages can sometimes be a little confusing. Updated and increasingly helpful error messages are one reason to upgrade your Puppet installation if you are running any version prior to Version 3.

Here are some of the most common errors you might encounter, and what to do about them.

How to do it...

Often the first step is simply to search the Web for the error message text and see what explanations you can find for the error, along with any helpful advice about fixing it. Here are some of the most common puzzling errors, with possible explanations:

`Could not retrieve file metadata for XXX: getaddrinfo: Name or service not known`

Where XXX is a file resource, you may have accidentally typed `puppet://modules...` in a file source instead of `puppet:///modules...` (note the triple slash):

`Could not evaluate: Could not retrieve information from environment production source(s) XXX`

The source file may not be present or may not be in the right location in the Puppet repo:

```
Error: Could not set 'file' on ensure: No such file or directory XXX
```

The file path may specify a parent directory (or directories) that doesn't exist. You can use separate file resources in Puppet to create these:

```
change from absent to file failed: Could not set 'file on ensure: No such file or directory
```

This is often caused by Puppet trying to write a file to a directory that doesn't exist. Check that the directory either exists already or is defined in Puppet, and that the file resource requires the directory (so that the directory is always created first):

```
undefined method 'closed?' for nil:NilClass
```

This unhelpful error message is roughly translated as *something went wrong*. It tends to be a catch-all error caused by many different problems, but you may be able to determine what is wrong from the name of the resource, the class, or the module. One trick is to add the `--debug` switch, to get more useful information:

```
[root@cookbook ~]# puppet agent -t --debug
```

If you check your Git history to see what was touched in the most recent change, this may be another way to identify what's upsetting Puppet:

```
Could not parse for environment --- "--- production": Syntax error at end
of file at line 1
```

This can be caused by mistyping command line options, for example, if you type `puppet -verbose` instead of `puppet --verbose`. This kind of error can be hard to see:

```
Duplicate definition: X is already defined in [file] at line Y; cannot
redefine at [file] line Y
```

This one has caused me a bit of puzzlement in the past. Puppet's complaining about a duplicate definition, and normally if you have two resources with the same name, Puppet will helpfully tell you where they are both defined. But in this case, it's indicating the same file and line number for both. How can one resource be a duplicate of itself?

The answer is, if it's a defined type (a resource created with the `define` keyword). If you create two instances of a defined type you'll also have two instances of all the resources contained within the definition, and they need to have distinct names. For example:

```
define check_process() {
    exec { 'is-process-running?':
```

```
    command => "/bin/ps ax |/bin/grep ${name} >/tmp/pslist.${name}.
txt",
  }
}

check_process { 'exim': }
check_process { 'nagios': }
```

When we run Puppet, the same error is printed twice:

```
t@mylaptop ~$ puppet apply duplicate.pp
Error: Duplicate declaration: Exec[is-process-running?] is already
declared in file duplicate.pp:4; cannot redeclare at duplicate.pp:4 on
node cookbook.example.com
Error: Duplicate declaration: Exec[is-process-running?] is already
declared in file duplicate.pp:4; cannot redeclare at duplicate.pp:4 on
node cookbook.example.com
```

Because the `exec` resource is named `is-process-running?`, if you try to create more than one instance of the definition, Puppet will refuse because the result would be two `exec` resources with the same name. The solution is to include the name of the instance (or some other unique value) in the title of each resource:

```
exec { "is-process-${name}-running?":
  command => "/bin/ps ax |/bin/grep ${name} >/tmp/pslist.${name}.txt",
}
```

Every resource must have a unique name, and a good way to ensure this with a definition is to interpolate the `${name}` variable in its title. Note that we switched from using single to double quotes in the resource title:

```
"is-process-${name}-running?"
```

The double quotes are required when you want Puppet to interpolate the value of a variable into a string.

See also

- ▶ The *Generating reports* recipe in this chapter
- ▶ The *Noop: the don't change anything option* recipe in this chapter
- ▶ The *Logging debug messages* recipe in this chapter

Inspecting configuration settings

You probably know that Puppet's configuration settings are stored in `puppet.conf`, but there are many parameters, and those that aren't listed in `puppet.conf` will take a default value. How can you see the value of any configuration parameter, regardless of whether or not it's explicitly set in `puppet.conf`? The answer is to use the `puppet config print` command.

How to do it...

Run the following command. This will produce a lot of output (it may be helpful to pipe it through `less` if you'd like to browse the available configuration settings):

```
[root@cookbook ~]# puppet config print |head -25
report_serialization_format = pson
hostcsr = /var/lib/puppet/ssl/csr_cookbook.example.com.pem
filetimeout = 15
masterhttplog = /var/log/puppet/masterhttp.log
pluginsignore = .svn CVS .git
ldapclassattrs = puppetclass
certdir = /var/lib/puppet/ssl/certs
ignoreschedules = false
disable_per_environment_manifest = false
archive_files = false
hiera_config = /etc/puppet/hiera.yaml
req_bits = 4096
clientyamldir = /var/lib/puppet/client_yaml
evaltrace = false
module_working_dir = /var/lib/puppet/puppet-module
tags =
cacrl = /var/lib/puppet/ssl/ca/ca_crl.pem
manifest = /etc/puppet/manifests/site.pp
inventory_port = 8140
ignoreimport = false
dbuser = puppet
postrun_command =
document_all = false
splaylimit = 1800
certificate_expire_warning = 5184000
```

How it works...

Running `puppet config print` will output every configuration parameter and its current value (and there are lots of them).

To see the value for a specific parameter, add it as an argument to `puppet config print` command:

```
[root@cookbook ~]# puppet config print modulepath
/etc/puppet/modules:/usr/share/puppet/modules
```

See also

▶ The *Generating reports* recipe in this chapter

Index

F

Facter
  about 9
  used, for describing node 9
facts
  setting, as environment variables 258, 259
  using, in ERB templates 117
file_line resource
  adding 125-127
file shares
  managing 231-239
filter function 44
firewalls
  managing, with iptables 218-222
fully qualified domain name (FQDN) 10
future parser
  using 42

G

Git
  environments, managing with 89-91
  hook, creating with 86-89
  Puppet manifests, managing with 49-54
Git hooks
  syntax check, automating with 84-86
GnuPG
  about 140
  used, for encrypting secrets 141-144
GnuPG backend, Hiera
  URL 145
graphs, DOT format
  expanded_relationships.dot 305
  relationships.dot 305
  resources.dot 305

H

HAProxy
  about 240
  URL 246
  used, for load balancing multiple
      web servers 240-246
hashes
  using 30

Heartbeat
  reference link 229
  used, for building high-availability
      services 224-230
Hiera
  configuring 77-79
  node-specific data, setting with 80, 81
  parameters, passing from 112, 113
hiera-eyaml
  URL 83
hiera-gpg
  secret data, storing with 81-83
high-availability services
  about 224
  building, Heartbeat used 224-230
hook
  creating, with Git 86-89
host resources
  using 181, 182
httpd package 9

I

idempotency 12
if statements
  regular expressions, using in 34, 35
INI style files
  editing, with puppetlabs-inifile 127, 128
ini_subsetting
  using 128, 129
INI syntax 127
inline_epp function 140
inline_template function 29, 174
inline templates
  using 28
in operator
  using 39
installation, service 13, 14
iptables
  about 218
  firewalls, managing with 218-222
  reference link 218

O

old files
cleaning up, tidy resource used 192, 193
oneline.pp file
modifying 125-127
ordering 11

P

package
installing, before starting service 10, 11
installing, from third-party repository 146-149
package versions
comparing 149, 150
papply script
writing 58-60
parameters
default values, specifying for 111
passing, from Hiera 112, 113
passing, to classes 110, 111
parameter validation
used, for generating error messages 270
passenger
about 70
Puppet, running from 70-73
patterns
capturing 35
Percona
about 146
URL 146
profiles
using 108, 109
providers
about 26
creating 271-273
reference link 273
public modules
using 200, 201
Puppet
about 252
bootstrapping, with bash 64-66
Docker, managing with 247-249
external facts, using in 258

installing 48, 49
running, from cron 61, 63
running, from passenger 70-73
Puppet community
URL, for best practice guidelines 28
Puppet Cookbook
URL 202
PuppetDB
configuring 76, 77
puppet doc file
about 300
basic documentation, of manifests 300-302
Puppet errors 307-309
Puppetfile 284
Puppet Labs
URL 14
URL, for APT-based systems 17
URL, for YUM-based systems 17
puppetlabs-Apache module
using 216
puppetlabs-inifile
used, for editing INI style files 127, 128
puppetlabs-Mysql
using 216
puppetlabs-mysql module 211
puppetlabs-mysql package 213
Puppet labs release package
URL 48
puppetlabs-stdlib module
installing 124
Puppet-lint tool
about 19
manifests, checking with 20
URL 20
Puppet manifests
managing, with Git 49-54
testing, with rspec-puppet tool 277-281
puppet module command 200
Puppet resource command
manifests, creating with 259, 260
used, for examining resource types 260, 261

Q

quick edits
making, for config files 124, 125

R

r10k
about 284
using 285-287
RDoc 300
reduce function 44
regsubst function 41
regular expressions
syntax 36
URL, for tutorials 36
using 38
using, in if statements 34, 35
regular expression substitutions
using 40, 41
relationship graphs 307
repeat parameter 180
reports
generating 297
require metaparameter 12
resource
about 8, 307
adding, to node 8, 9
arrays, using of 94, 95
auditing 194
disabling, temporarily 195
reference link 273
Resource Abstraction Layer (RAL) 9
resource collectors
about 104
URL 104
resource defaults
about 294
specifying, for resource type 98
using 95-97
resource ordering
about 295
reference link 296
resource type
creating 268, 269
resource defaults, specifying for 98

reusable manifests
writing 113-115
ripienaar-module_data module 211
roles
using 108, 109
ro (read-only) 236
rspec-puppet tool
Puppet manifests, testing with 277-281
URL, for tutorial 281
Ruby
references 268
run stages
using 104-107
rw (read-write) 236

S

schedule metaparameter
using 178-180
scope 10
secret data
storing, with hiera-gpg 81-83
secret function
using 145
secrets
encrypting, GnuPG used 141-144
selectors
using 36, 37
service
configuring 13, 14
installing 13, 14
starting 13, 14
shell commands
arguments, passing to 120, 121
shellquote function 120
slice function 44
snippets
used, for building config files 132-134
split function
arrays, creating with 31
SSH keys 49
stages, Puppet
URL, for examples 107
stahnma-epel module 247
standard naming conventions
using 26, 27

Thank you for buying
Puppet Cookbook
Third Edition

About Packt Publishing

Packt, pronounced 'packed', published its first book, *Mastering phpMyAdmin for Effective MySQL Management*, in April 2004, and subsequently continued to specialize in publishing highly focused books on specific technologies and solutions.

Our books and publications share the experiences of your fellow IT professionals in adapting and customizing today's systems, applications, and frameworks. Our solution-based books give you the knowledge and power to customize the software and technologies you're using to get the job done. Packt books are more specific and less general than the IT books you have seen in the past. Our unique business model allows us to bring you more focused information, giving you more of what you need to know, and less of what you don't.

Packt is a modern yet unique publishing company that focuses on producing quality, cutting-edge books for communities of developers, administrators, and newbies alike. For more information, please visit our website at `www.packtpub.com`.

About Packt Open Source

In 2010, Packt launched two new brands, Packt Open Source and Packt Enterprise, in order to continue its focus on specialization. This book is part of the Packt open source brand, home to books published on software built around open source licenses, and offering information to anybody from advanced developers to budding web designers. The Open Source brand also runs Packt's open source Royalty Scheme, by which Packt gives a royalty to each open source project about whose software a book is sold.

Writing for Packt

We welcome all inquiries from people who are interested in authoring. Book proposals should be sent to `author@packtpub.com`. If your book idea is still at an early stage and you would like to discuss it first before writing a formal book proposal, then please contact us; one of our commissioning editors will get in touch with you.

We're not just looking for published authors; if you have strong technical skills but no writing experience, our experienced editors can help you develop a writing career, or simply get some additional reward for your expertise.

Puppet 3 Cookbook

ISBN: 978-1-78216-976-5   Paperback: 274 pages

Build reliable, scalable, secure, and high-performance systems to fully utilize the power of cloud computing

1.   Use Puppet 3 to take control of your servers and desktops, with detailed step-by-step instructions.

2.   Covers all the popular tools and frameworks used with Puppet: Dashboard, Foreman, and more.

3.   Teaches you how to extend Puppet with custom functions, types, and providers.

4.   Packed with tips and inspiring ideas for using Puppet to automate server builds, deployments, and workflows.

Puppet 3: Beginner's Guide

ISBN: 978-1-78216-124-0   Paperback: 204 pages

Start from scratch with the Puppet configuration management system, and learn hot to fully utilize Puppet through simple, practical examples

1.   Shows you step-by-step how to install Puppet and start managing your systems with simple examples.

2.   Every aspect of Puppet is explained in detail so that you really understand what you're doing.

3.   Gets you up and running immediately, from installation to using Puppet for practical tasks in a matter of minutes.

Please check **www.PacktPub.com** for information on our titles

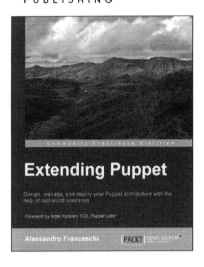
Extending Puppet

ISBN: 978-1-78398-144-1   Paperback: 328 pages

Design, manage, and deploy your Puppet architecture with the help of real-world scenarios

1. Plan, test, and execute your Puppet deployments.

2. Write reusable and maintainable Puppet code.

3. Handle challenges that might arise in upcoming versions of Puppet.

4. Explore the Puppet ecosystem in-depth, through a hands-on, example driven approach

Puppet 2.7 Cookbook

ISBN: 978-1-84951-538-2   Paperback: 300 pages

Build reliable, scalable, secure, high-performance systems to fully utilize the power of cloud computing

1. Shows you how to use 100 powerful advanced features of Puppet, with detailed step-by-step instructions.

2. Covers all the popular tools and frameworks used with Puppet: Dashboard, Foreman, MCollective, and more.

3. Includes the latest features and updates in Puppet 2.7.

Printed in Great Britain
by Amazon.co.uk, Ltd.,
Marston Gate.